CARRIERS
AT WAR

To all the good friends who were there
when I needed them.

CARRIERS
AT WAR

1939–1945

ADRIAN STEWART

Pen & Sword
MARITIME

First published in Great Britain in 2013 by
PEN & SWORD MARITIME
an imprint of
Pen & Sword Books Ltd
47 Church Street
Barnsley
South Yorkshire
S70 2AS

Copyright © Adrian Stewart, 2013

ISBN 978 1 78159 156 7

The right of Adrian Stewart to be identified as the
author of this work has been asserted by him in accordance
with the Copyright, Designs and Patents Act 1988.

A CIP catalogue record for this book is
available from the British Library.

Typeset in Ehrhardt by Chic Graphics

Printed and bound in England
by CPI Group (UK) Ltd, Croydon, CR0 4YY

Pen & Sword Books Ltd incorporates the imprints of
Pen & Sword Aviation, Pen & Sword Maritime,
Pen & Sword Military, Pen & Sword Family History,
Wharncliffe Local History, Wharncliffe True Crime,
Wharncliffe Transport, Pen & Sword Discovery, Pen & Sword Select,
Pen & Sword Military Classics, Leo Cooper, Remember When,
The Praetorian Press, Seaforth Publishing and Frontline Publishing.

For a complete list of Pen & Sword titles please contact
PEN & SWORD BOOKS LIMITED
47 Church Street, Barnsley, South Yorkshire, S70 2AS, England
E-mail: enquiries@pen-and-sword.co.uk
Website: www.pen-and-sword.co.uk

Contents

Acknowledgements

It has been my good fortune to have enjoyed the assistance of many people but in particular that of: Brigadier Henry Wilson and his team at my publishers, Pen & Sword Books Ltd.; Andrew Hewson and his team at my Agents, Johnson & Alcock Ltd.; the late Captain Donald MacIntyre and the late David Brown who – it seems many years ago now – helped to further my understanding of carrier warfare in the Pacific; Noel Bell and Mike Rossiter, both happily still with us, who performed a similar service with regard to British carrier operations; Karen Selley, my editor; Pamela Covey, my proofreader; Sylvia Menzies-Earl, who prepared the manuscript; Philip Fisher and the staff of the Birmingham Institute & Library, the Taylor Library and the Office of Information at the US Navy department, Washington, who between them provided the photographs. To all of these my sincere thanks.

Map I – Norway and the Arctic

ARCTIC OCEAN

N
W E
S

Alten Fjord

Petsamo

Kirkenes

Tromso

✗ Vaenga
Murmansk

Harstad

Narvik
✗

Bardufoss

RUSSIA

FINLAND

Vaernes
Namsos

SWEDEN

Aandalsnes
✗
Trondheim

NORWAY

✗ Lake Lesjaskog

Bergen

Oslo

Baltic Sea

Kristiansand

DENMARK

B A L T I C   S T A T E S

GERMANY

0   400 miles
0   400 km

Map II – The Mediterranean

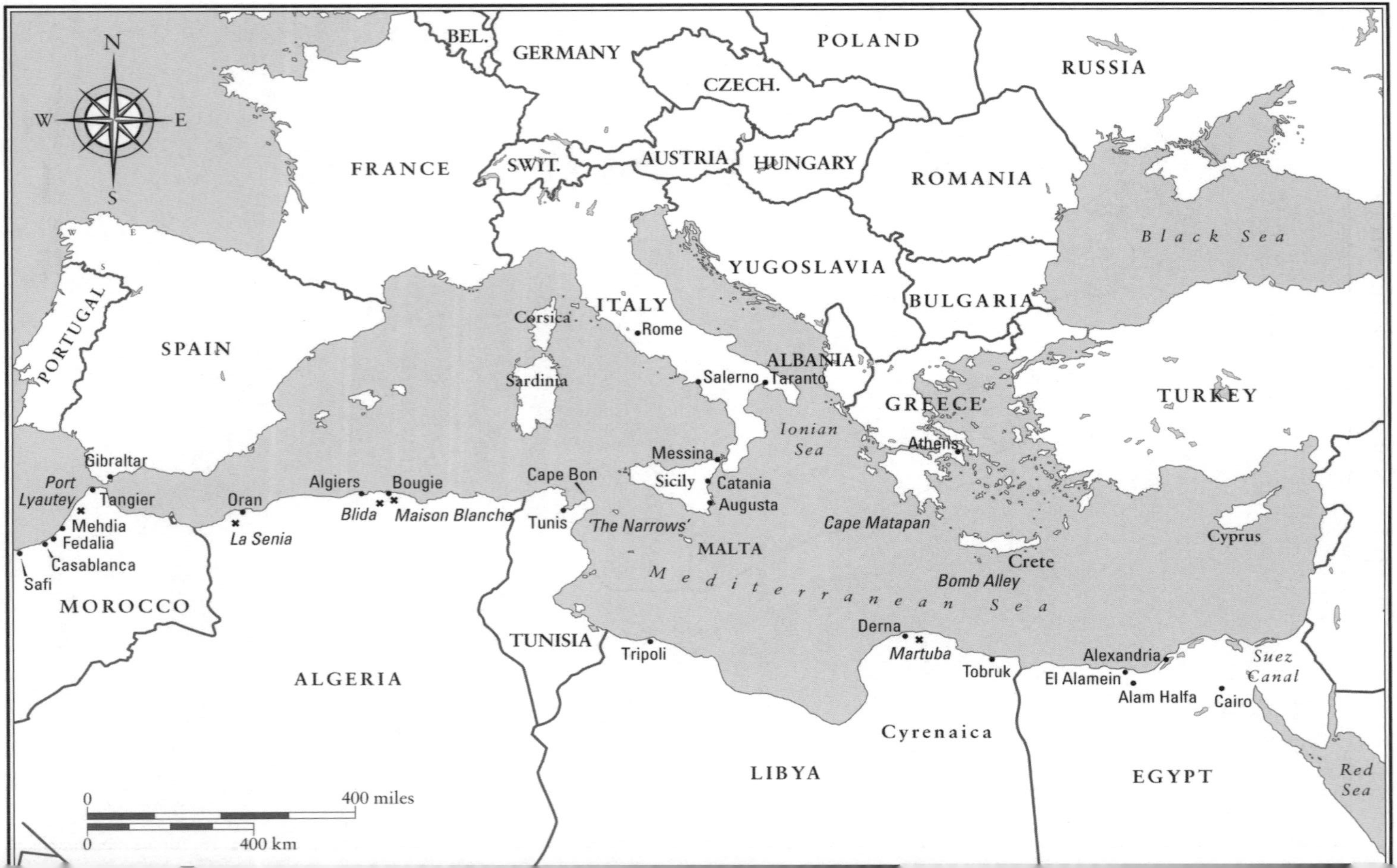

Map III – The Islands of the Pacific

Map IV – Guadalcanal

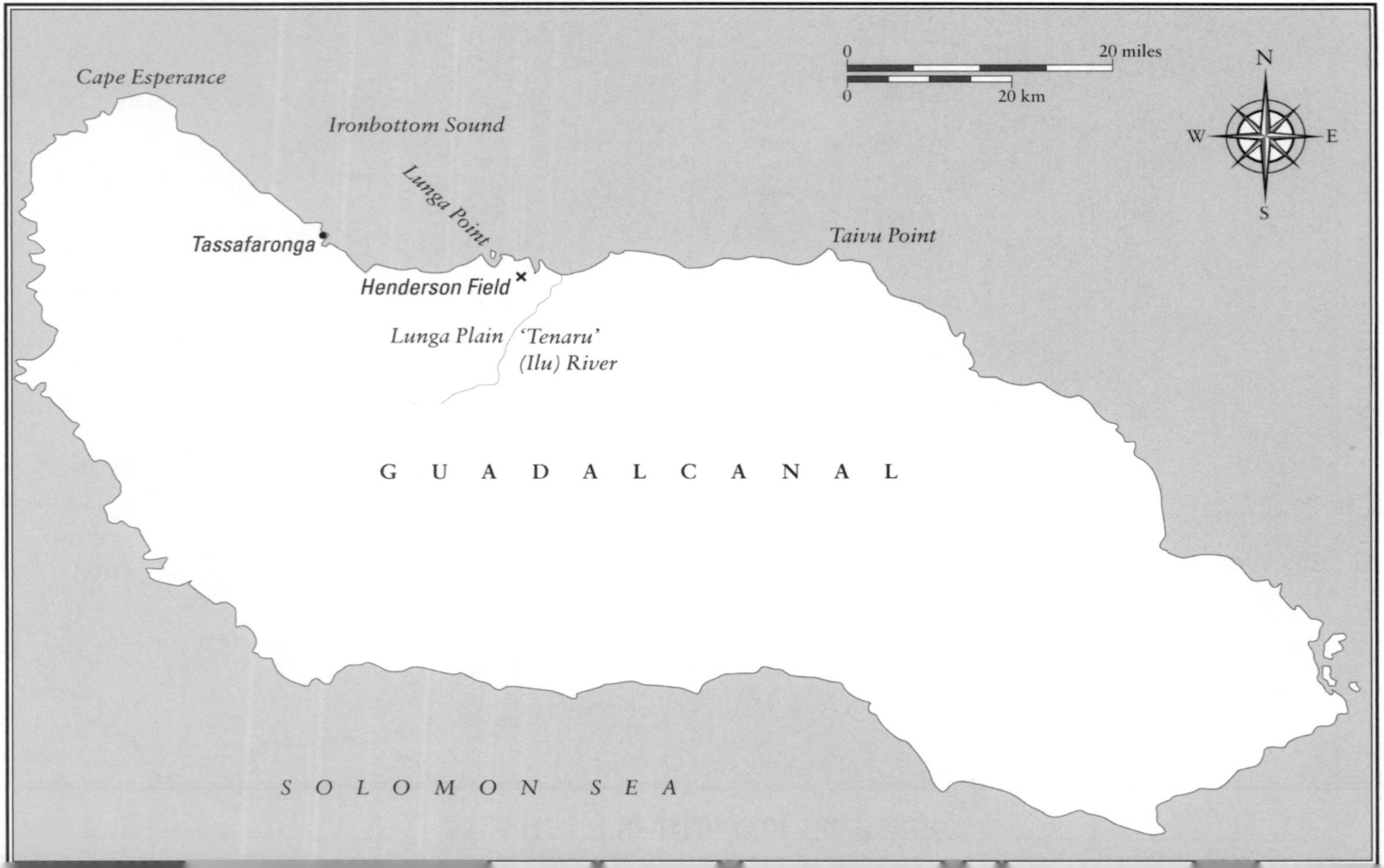

Cape Esperance

Ironbottom Sound

Tassafaronga

Lunga Point

Henderson Field ✕

Lunga Plain

'Tenaru'
(Ilu) River

Taivu Point

GUADALCANAL

SOLOMON SEA

N
W — E
S

0 ___ 20 km
0 ___ 20 miles

Map V – The Philippines

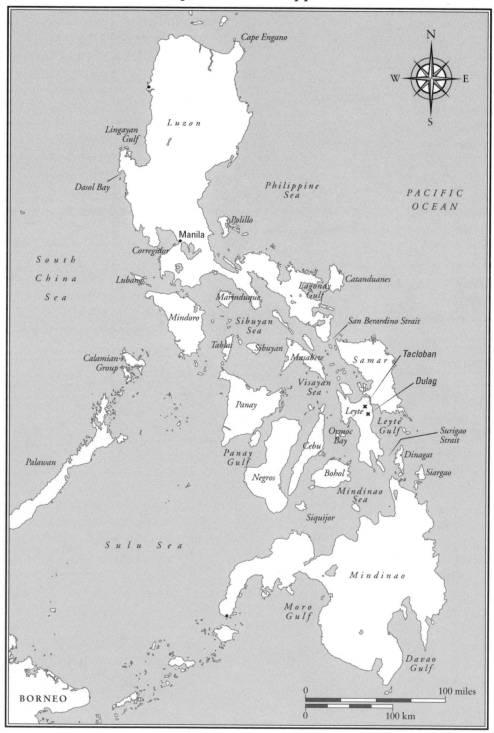

Cape Engano

Luzon

Lingayan
Gulf

Dasol Bay

Philippine
Sea

PACIFIC
OCEAN

Polillo

Manila

Corregidor

South
China
Sea

Lubang

Marinduque

Ilagonay
Gulf

Catanduanes

Mindoro

Sibuyan
Sea

San Berardino Strait

Tablas

Sibuyan

Samar

Tacloban

Calamian
Group

Masabete

Visayan
Sea

Dulag

Panay

Leyte

Leyte
Gulf

Surigao
Strait

Palawan

Ormoc
Bay

Cebu

Panay
Gulf

Negros

Bohol

Dinagat

Siargao

Mindinao
Sea

Siquijor

Mindinao

Sulu Sea

Moro
Gulf

Davao
Gulf

BORNEO

0   100 miles

0   100 km

Map VI – The Approaches to Japan

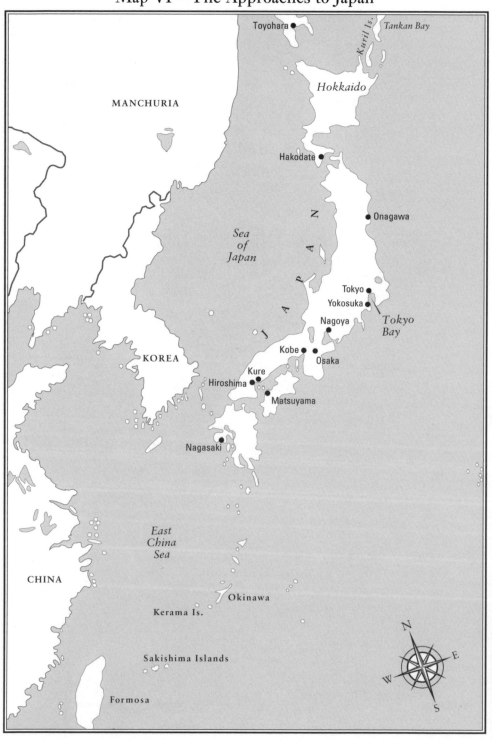

Toyohara ●

Tankan Bay

Kuril Is.

Hokkaido

MANCHURIA

Hakodate ●

Onagawa ●

Sea
of
Japan

J A P A N

Tokyo ●
Yokosuka ●

Tokyo
Bay

Nagoya ●

KOREA

Kobe ● ● Osaka

Kure ●
Hiroshima ●

Matsuyama ●

Nagasaki ●

East
China
Sea

CHINA

Okinawa

Kerama Is.

Sakishima Islands

Formosa

N
E
W
S

Chapter 1

The Coming of the Carrier

The date was 12 November 1921. Three years and one day had passed since the end of the war that, it had been promised, would end all wars. This assurance would soon become a hideous mockery; but now, as representatives of the victors assembled in Washington, it was still believed that permanent peace was possible, and one major way to attain it would be to limit the armaments of the great powers. The Washington Conference was concerned with naval limitations and when it concluded on 6 February 1922, with the signing of a number of treaties, it appeared to have achieved its aim and ended a ruinously expensive and potentially dangerous arms race.

First in importance of the agreements reached was the provision that in future the capital ships of the great powers would be maintained in the proportions: Britain: 5; United States: 5; Japan: 3; Italy: 1.75; France: 1.75. By 'capital ships', there seems little doubt that most of those present meant battleships and battle-cruisers. These were strictly limited by the ratio agreed and Britain, America and Japan all scrapped large numbers of them that were either already in service or in the course of construction; moreover the standard displacement of future vessels was limited to 35,000 tons and their main armament to guns of 16-inch calibre. In addition, though, probably to the surprise of the more conservative delegates, other detailed regulations were laid down regarding a type of capital ship that as yet scarcely existed: the aircraft carrier.

Of the three countries concerned with the future of the carrier – for the French showed little interest and the Italians even less – it was Britain that had hitherto led the way in its development. Admittedly the first take-off from a temporary wooden platform erected on a warship and the first landing by an aircraft fitted with hooks to catch arrester wires stretched across a similar platform had been made in the United States – at the astonishingly early dates of 14 November 1910 and 18 January 1911 respectively. Yet in both cases the vessels were at anchor and the pilot, Eugene Ely, was a civilian in the service of the pioneer aircraft designer Glenn Curtiss; he was killed nine months later, performing aerobatics at a State Fair. Thereafter, the Royal Navy had taken centre stage, inspired first by a growing tension between Britain and Germany and later by the outbreak of the First World War. Lieutenant Charles Samson of the Naval Wing of the Royal Flying Corps – soon to become the Royal Naval Air Service – had taken off from the heavy cruiser *Hibernia* when she was underway on 2 May 1912, while Squadron Commander Dunning had made the first deck-landing on 2 August 1917, only to be killed five days later when attempting to repeat this achievement.

The vessel on which Dunning had landed was HMS *Furious*, one of three warships of 22,500 tons intended to deliver shore bombardments and so fitted with a single heavy gun fore and aft but completely unarmoured and thus able to reach an impressive speed of 31 knots. In early 1917, her forward turret was replaced by a hangar, the roof of which was constructed as a deck, 228 feet long by 50 feet wide, to which the five Sopwith Pups that she carried could be hoisted through a hatchway and from which they could take off. It was always anticipated that they would be unable to land on it but would have to 'ditch' or make for the nearest airfield, and after Dunning's tragic death all attempts at landing were expressly forbidden.

Soon afterwards, *Furious* was withdrawn for a further conversion, receiving a new hangar with a deck above it in place of her after turret. This deck, 285 feet long by 70 feet wide, was fitted with arrester wires so that aircraft could land on it. *Furious* thus had two flight decks separated by her main superstructure, past which her aircraft had to be moved laboriously over gangways on each side. Worse still, the superstructure caused such turbulence that of the first thirteen Pups that tried to land on her, all but three were wrecked or went over the side. Once again, all deck landings were forbidden.

Though *Furious* had undoubtedly foreshadowed the emergence of the true aircraft carrier, this lack of a continuous flight deck, the essential requirement for naval aviation, must invalidate claims that she was herself the earliest of the type. In August 1916, however, the Admiralty had purchased the *Conte Rosso*, a liner in the course of being built for the Italians, and in September 1918, she joined the Fleet as HMS *Argus* of 14,000 tons displacement and with a single flush flight deck, 567 feet long, from stem to stern. Gone was her superstructure; her bridge replaced by a small chart-house that could be raised or lowered hydraulically as required; her funnel replaced by ducts running under the flight deck to discharge the gases over the stern. Her odd, ungainly appearance earned her the nickname of 'The Flat Iron', but it entitled her to be recognized as the first of that new class of capital ship that would play such a potent part in the Second World War.

By the time the delegates assembled at the Washington Conference, the Royal Navy possessed not only *Argus* but also *Eagle*, originally laid down as a Chilean battleship, the *Almirante Cochrane*, and converted to become the first large fleet carrier – 22,600 tons – and the first to have its bridge, funnel and mast offset on the starboard side of the flight deck to form a streamlined superstructure that would become known as the 'island'. Moreover, they would soon be joined by light carrier *Hermes*, the first vessel to be designed and built as a carrier, and *Furious*, now finally given a continuous flight deck. Both *Hermes* and *Furious* were also given starboard 'islands'.

By contrast, in no other country was a carrier yet in service and only two were even nearing completion. Of these, the American *Langley*, undergoing conversion from a collier, small with a short flight deck, and painfully slow, was perhaps best summarized by being exempted from the provisions of the Washington Treaty on the ground that she was 'experimental'.[1] And the Japanese *Hosho*, originally laid down as a tanker, was much the smallest carrier to appear in the years before the Second World War, though a speed of 25 knots did enable her, like *Argus* and unlike *Langley*, to take an active part in that conflict.

This situation, so advantageous to Britain, was ended by the Washington Conference. Total aircraft carrier tonnages were fixed, in accordance with the 5:5:3 ratio, at 185,000 for Britain and America and 81,000 for Japan. It was originally intended that individual vessels should not exceed 27,000 tons, but the Americans wished to convert battle-cruisers *Lexington* and *Saratoga*, already under construction, so it was agreed that any of the great powers might have two carriers of 33,000 tons each. America accordingly proceeded with the conversion of her two battle-cruisers, and Japan similarly changed two uncompleted capital ships, battle-cruiser *Akagi* and battleship *Kaga*, into carriers. Britain, however, converted only the much smaller *Courageous* and *Glorious*, sister-ships of *Furious*. It may be added that both America and, still more blatantly, Japan in fact exceeded both the total and the individual tonnages allowed by the Washington Treaty, while Britain observed them.

Worse still, 1922 as well as seeing the beginning of the end of Britain's supremacy in naval aviation, also marked the start of political developments that would make naval supremacy of crucial importance. In October of that year, Benito Mussolini organized the Fascist 'March on Rome' that would lead to his becoming Prime Minister and the subsequent creation of a totalitarian state with himself as dictator. In the First World War, Italy had been Britain's ally. She would not be so in a later, larger conflict.

Nor for that matter would Japan – a rupture brought about by this same Washington Conference. The imposition of the 5:5:3 ratio was itself resented by many in Japan but, as her more far-sighted statesmen realized, it in fact gave her a clear local superiority in the North Pacific, strengthened by guarantees from Britain and America that no bases would be constructed nearer to Japan than Singapore and Hawaii; this grievance therefore would probably not have mattered too much had it not been for another decision made at the Conference. As Sir Winston Churchill explains in *The Second World War*: 'The United States made it clear to Britain that the continuance of her alliance with Japan' – which had begun in 1902 – 'to which the Japanese had punctiliously conformed, would constitute a barrier in Anglo-American relations. Accordingly this alliance was brought to an end.'

It was a fatal error. The Japanese had regarded the alliance with pride as a symbol of their nation's acceptance by the countries of Europe. Its termination, declares Professor Richard Storry in *A History of Modern Japan*, 'inflicted a wound received in sorrow and remembered in wrath'. Later events, notably the American prohibition against immigration by Japanese nationals in 1924, and the erection of crippling tariff barriers following the world depression of 1929, increased Japan's festering anger, gravely weakened the authority of her moderate and pro-Western civilian ministers, and put political control into the hands of the more extreme factions of the Japanese Army.

In 1931, without the authority, approval or even knowledge of their government in Tokyo, these Japanese militants staged an incident that led to the conquest of the whole of Manchuria, re-named Manchukuo, and began that series of aggressions that would culminate at Pearl Harbour. On 29 December 1934, Japan also ended the pious hopes raised by the Washington Conference, by giving the necessary two years notice that she would no longer be bound by the naval limitation treaties. All the powers promptly began further construction – and not least that power which the participants at the Conference had once joined together to defeat.

Germany had sent no delegates to Washington because the 1919 Treaty of Versailles had already limited her navy to six capital ships of no more than 10,000 tons with guns no larger than 11-inch. In reality, the first three of these, the famous 'pocket battleships', exceeded the treaty restrictions, and the next two, *Scharnhorst* and *Gneisenau*, ordered after Adolf Hitler had become Chancellor in 1933, openly disregarded them, turning out to be battle-cruisers of over 31,000 tons. Not that this concerned Hitler, who on 16 March 1935 publicly repudiated the terms of the Versailles Treaty.

Against this background, British development of a naval air arm after 1922 fell short in both quantity and quality. Prior to the termination of the Washington Treaty limitations, only one new 23,000-ton carrier had been ordered. It was launched on 13 April 1937, joined the Fleet in the following year, and was given the inspired name of *Ark Royal* once carried by the flagship of Charles, Lord Howard of Effingham at the time of the defeat of the Spanish Armada. When the Second World War began on 3 September 1939, six new fleet carriers were under construction, but the only modern one in service was *Ark Royal*, supported by the elderly *Eagle*, *Hermes*, *Furious*, *Courageous* and *Glorious*, with the veteran *Argus* in reserve.

Furthermore, apart from *Ark Royal*, which could house sixty, the number of aircraft on British carriers was much restricted by their small hangar-space. Thus while Japan's little *Hosho* could carry twenty-one aeroplanes, the larger *Hermes* could take only fifteen and the much larger *Eagle* eighteen. Even *Ark Royal*, though built as a carrier, could operate no more aircraft than the conversions *Akagi* and *Kaga*, and only about two-thirds of those on *Lexington* and *Saratoga*.

The greatest weakness of Britain's naval air arm in 1939, however, was the singularly poor quality of most of its machines. The disappearance of the Royal Naval Air Service into a newly-formed Royal Air Force controlling all aspects of aerial warfare on 1 April 1918, had at first made little difference to anything more important than the uniforms worn and the ranks held by its personnel. It was a very different story when hostilities ended. Since the war had supposedly ended all wars, there seemed no need for large fighting services and all were drastically reduced, especially the young Royal Air Force. Its Fleet Air Arm was almost wholly neglected as it was strongly held in many quarters that carriers would be too vulnerable to have much practical effect, and all naval air needs would be supplied and dominated by shore-based aircraft.

This attitude led to a lack of interest in the provision of aircraft intended specifically for use on carriers, as was the standard practice in America and Japan. Instead, the Fleet Air Arm was compelled, on the grounds of expense, to make do with adaptations of machines designed to operate on land, lacking the performance and the reliability needed for service at sea. When the Admiralty resumed control of a revived Naval Air Service[2] in 1937, there was no time to correct the position before war broke out.

In 1939, the Royal Navy's carriers were equipped with three main types of aircraft, only one of which was a monoplane. This was the Blackburn Skua, originally intended as a two-seater fighter, armed with four 0.303-inch Browning machine guns in its wings and a Lewis machine gun in its rear cockpit.

Unfortunately, with a speed of 225 mph and a poor rate of climb, it was not really suitable in this role, and its subsequent development called the Roc, which had four machine guns in a power-operated turret was still less suitable, being slower both in level flight and when climbing. The Skua did, however, have a secondary role as a dive-bomber and on 10 April 1940, during the Norwegian campaign, Skuas from Hatston in the Orkney Islands attacked the German light cruiser *Königsberg* at Bergen, scored three hits with their 500 lb bombs, and sank her in only a few minutes.

It is perhaps a sufficient verdict on the Skua and Roc as fighters that the biplane Sea Gladiator also carried four machine guns, was some 20 mph faster and had a better rate of climb. The most famous of the original British carrier-aircraft, though, was the three-seater Swordfish dual-purpose reconnaissance/torpedo-plane, designed and built as a private venture by Fairey Aviation Company in 1936. Desperately old-fashioned – a biplane with a fixed undercarriage, its cockpits open to the elements and extremely slow – the 'Stringbag', as it was affectionately known, was also very reliable, easy to fly and to land on a carrier's deck and capable of carrying bombs, rockets, depth charges and mines as well as a torpedo. It was to prove one of the great successes of the war in Europe.

Fortunately also, if Britain had not handled her naval air arm well, her enemies in Europe had scarcely considered the matter at all. Italy, which entered the war at midnight on 10 June 1940, had made no plans whatever to add aircraft carriers to her Fleet; Germany had given them a very low priority. Work had commenced on two, named *Graf Zeppelin* after the airship designer and manufacturer, and *Peter Strasser* after the head of the German Naval Airship Division in the First World War, but it was significant that the latter should be cancelled in 1940, so that the shipyard could concentrate on more 'urgent' work.

Graf Zeppelin was launched on 8 December 1938, but she endured many delays resulting from German inexperience in carrier design and the conflicting interests of Grand Admiral Erich Raeder, Hitler's naval chief, and Reichsmarschall Hermann Göring whose insistence was that 'anything that flies belongs to me'. A number of Messerschmitt Bf³ 109s, modified for use on carriers and with folded wings, and a few modified Junkers Ju 87 Stuka dive-bombers were converted to serve on *Graf Zeppelin* but the vessel herself was never completed and, again in 1940, work on her was suspended by the orders of Raeder. Though Hitler – and for that matter Mussolini – later realized the advantages that carriers would have given them, they were not granted enough time to rectify their errors.

Inexperience was also sadly evident in Britain's early use of her carriers. A number of duties for their aircraft had been envisaged, all of them, it is worth noting, subsidiary to the needs of the surface navy: reconnaissance; attacking enemy vessels so as to reduce their speed and allow British warships to catch and engage them; reporting fall of shot in gunnery actions; and helping to guard the Fleet against air and submarine attacks, a role where a certain lack of confidence is apparent in the additional comment that they were 'in particular to defend the carriers themselves'. On 3 September 1939, however, *Ark Royal*,

Courageous and *Hermes*, each with a small destroyer screen, were sent out on a yet different type of mission: protecting the crucial mercantile shipping lanes.

In the Official History of *The War at Sea*, Captain S.W. Roskill relates how the carriers formed part of groups directed to hunt down U-boats – 'cavalry divisions' as Churchill, then First Lord of the Admiralty, fancifully described them – and adds that it was 'surprising that they should have been risked on that type of duty'. His comment was undoubtedly correct. Carriers would later prove extremely effective against U-boats when defending convoys or in locations where U-boats had been specifically reported, but searches of 'large areas over a wide front' as Churchill wished, were very wasteful, particularly in these early days when naval aircraft were not equipped with radar. Moreover the later successes would be those of smaller escort carriers; the large fleet carriers were unsuitable and themselves made tempting targets for any submarines that they might encounter.

Tragically, this was soon to be proved. On the evening of 17 September, *Courageous* was preparing to recover her aircraft. She had detached two of her escorting destroyers to rescue the crew of a sunken freighter and neither the remaining two nor the Swordfish patrolling overhead had detected a U-boat that for two hours had been manoeuvring into a position to attack her. When *Courageous* turned into the wind to enable her aircraft to land on her, she unluckily provided *U-29* with the whole of her port side as a target. Hardly had the last Swordfish landed than two tremendous explosions, barely a second apart, shook *Courageous* from bow to stern. She immediately heeled over to port and sank by the bow in less than 20 minutes, taking down with her over 500 of her crew, including Captain Makeig-Jones. She was not only the first carrier ever to be sunk, but also the first major British surface warship to be lost in the Second World War and the first British warship of any sort to be lost to enemy action.[4]

If the hunting groups had proved a disaster – they were now hastily withdrawn – at least the British had the melancholy consolation that they might have fared much worse. On 14 September, *U-39*, also undetected, had fired torpedoes at *Ark Royal*. Mercifully, they missed, and counter-attacks by the escorting destroyers resulted in the destruction of the U-boat and the capture of her crew. This was the first 'kill' of an enemy submarine, and on the 26th, one of *Ark Royal*'s

Skuas, flown by Lieutenant McEwen, shot down a Dornier Do 18 flying-boat that was shadowing the Fleet, to record the first British fighter victory of the war as well.

Unfortunately, the Dornier and two others that were damaged and driven away were first able to signal details of their sightings, and that afternoon, the Fleet was attacked by Heinkel He 111 and Junkers Ju 88 bombers. On their return to base, Sergeant Carl Francke correctly reported a very near miss on *Ark Royal* and wrongly, though in perfect good faith, estimated that she had suffered severe damage. He made no larger claims but German propaganda had heard enough and Francke, to his own acute embarrassment, was promoted to Lieutenant and awarded the Iron Cross, First and Second Class, for 'sinking' *Ark Royal*.

It was a particularly stupid action, because *Ark Royal* was destined to haunt her enemies for a long time to come. On 17 December, her very survival played a vital, if rarely stressed part in the destruction of the pocket battleship *Admiral Graf Spee*. Rumours spread by British Intelligence had convinced Captain Langsdorff that *Ark Royal* and battle-cruiser *Renown* had joined the vessels lying in wait for him outside Montevideo harbour – though in reality neither would have been able to reach the area until the 19th. He therefore notified his superiors in Berlin that an attempt to 'break out into the open sea' would be 'hopeless', leaving him with the alternatives of internment in Uruguay or scuttling. In reply, Grand Admiral Raeder ruled out the former but urged him instead to 'fight your way through to Buenos Aires if possible'. Langsdorff made no attempt to do so and condemned his fine ship to an inglorious and sordid end. When he later learned the true location of *Ark Royal* and *Renown*, he shot himself.

Some four months later, *Ark Royal* would see action many thousands of miles away from the River Plate. Hitler had determined on the seizure of Norway in order to open the North Atlantic to his warships, provide naval and air bases for attacks on Britain, secure supplies of Swedish iron ore that in winter had to pass through the ice-free harbour at Narvik, and block communications between Britain and Russia. Russia had been his ally and co-conspirator in the occupation of Poland but was marked down for destruction in the Führer's mind in order to achieve Germany's 'Lebensraum'. So on 9 April 1940, his forces swallowed up Denmark, his airborne troops took the Norwegian capital

Oslo from the rear, and his seaborne assaults captured Kristiansand, Bergen, Trondheim, and even Narvik, over 600 miles from Oslo as the crow flies.

Allied counter-attacks followed quickly but not very effectively. The Royal Navy in two brilliant actions on 10 and 13 April annihilated all ten German destroyers that had carried troops to Narvik, allowing an Allied landing at nearby Harstad on the 15th. Next day, another landing was made at Namsos some 125 miles by road north of Trondheim and on the 18th, a third at Aandalsnes some 200 miles by road south of Trondheim. Thereafter everything went wrong. The troops at Harstad made no move against the German garrison of Narvik for over a month, allowing it time to recover from the demoralization caused by the destruction of its naval force. A planned assault on Trondheim itself was cancelled, largely, it seems, because of the dangers this would face from enemy air raids, and this left the Allies without an adequate harbour or an airfield from which fighter protection could be provided. And meanwhile the main German army units were pushing up from the south to the aid of their isolated beachheads.

The British carriers' part in the campaign was not very successful either. *Furious* was the first to participate, and on 11 April, eighteen of her Swordfish made the first torpedo attack of the war on German destroyers at Trondheim. Sadly, it was a total failure because the fjord was so shallow that the torpedoes hit the bottom and exploded. Bombing attacks at Narvik on the 12th and 13th were equally ineffective, two Swordfish being shot down on the latter occasion. Then on the 25th, *Furious* was herself bombed, damaged by near misses and forced to withdraw from the battle area.

Meanwhile on 24 April, *Ark Royal* and *Glorious* had arrived off central Norway, where their Skuas and Sea Gladiators, though much inferior to the Luftwaffe's machines, provided some protection to the troops in Namsos and Aandalsnes and to naval vessels in the vicinity. *Glorious* had also brought with her eighteen Gladiators of 263 Squadron RAF, which flew off her deck to frozen Lake Lesjaskog near Aandalsnes – the first example of a carrier ferrying land-based aircraft to within flying distance of the airfields from which they would operate. In practice, the Gladiators were all destroyed on the ground within 72 hours, compelling the Allies to evacuate both Namsos and Aandalsnes on 2 May. Nonetheless, the incident is worthy of especial notice for the precedent it had set. The future would see aircraft similarly supplied to Norway, Russia, Ceylon, the East Indies and West Africa whence they would travel over the continent to the Middle East and above all, as will be seen, to Malta, thereby preserving that vital island-fortress for the Allied cause.

Now the only Allied bridgehead left was the one near Narvik and on 6 May, *Ark Royal* moved to northern Norwegian waters where her Skuas continued to engage enemy aircraft in their fighter role, both inflicting and suffering losses. Later that month, *Ark Royal* would be joined by first *Furious*, then by *Glorious*, but they were operating as aircraft transporters, supplying fighters to cover the capture of Narvik, long delayed but by this time intended only as a preliminary to evacuation. On 10 May, the German assault on the Low Countries had begun and the British Chiefs of Staff had rightly concluded that: 'The security of France and the United Kingdom is essential; the retention of northern Norway is not.'

On *Furious*, 263 Squadron was back with a fresh batch of Gladiators, but its ill fortune continued, for when they took off on 21 May, the Swordfish guiding them to their base at Bardufoss lost its way in a fog and crashed into a mountainside, followed by two of the Gladiators. On 28 May, the eighteen Hurricanes of 46 Squadron flew off the decks of *Glorious* but they too met with trouble since their intended landing-ground at Skaanland proved quite unsuitable. The first three machines to touch down were wrecked – luckily without injury to the pilots – after which the rest were diverted to join 263 Squadron at Bardufoss. Both squadrons duly protected the ground troops who took Narvik on 28 May. Its port installations and industrial plants were then wrecked – though, ironically enough, less thoroughly than the Germans had done before they retired – and the Allies prepared for a further evacuation.

It was carried out over a period of five days ending on the morning of 8 June. *Ark Royal* covered the troop convoys, while *Glorious* was sent to rescue the remaining eight Gladiators. These lacked the hooks needed to catch the carrier's arrester wires but their low speed meant that if she steamed at maximum power, she could provide enough headwind to reduce their landing run sufficiently. So it proved and 263's pilots all landed without too many problems.

For the ten remaining Hurricanes of 46 Squadron, the situation was quite different. Their faster landing speed and longer landing run meant that should they attempt to come down on *Glorious*, the pilots would have to brake so hard that the aircrafts' tails would come up. This would cause them either to nose over completely or just keep going until they ran off the flight deck. It had therefore been ordered that they should be destroyed on their airfield.

The orders were not obeyed. Squadron Leader Kenneth Cross, knowing that every available Hurricane was needed, persuaded the senior RAF officer in Norway, Group Captain Moore, to allow him to take the risk. 'Extra weight', in the form of bags of sand was added to the rear of the Hurricanes' fuselages, and Cross called for volunteers to fly these unbalanced machines to *Glorious*. Every pilot stepped forward and every Hurricane landed safely. *Glorious*, which her captain reported was low on fuel, then headed for home, accompanied by destroyers *Ardent* and *Acasta*. The men of the Royal Air Force, declares Captain Roskill, had shown 'the qualities which, a few weeks later, saved their country and made the free world ring with their fame'. It is horrible to have to relate that their valour was shortly to cost most of them their lives.

Captain Guy D'Oyly-Hughes VC, skipper of HMS *Glorious*, was an officer with a brilliant record in the First World War – but in submarines. He had little knowledge of naval aviation and earlier in the campaign the fighter defence provided by his carrier's Sea Gladiators had not proved very effective. On two occasions, in fact, enemy bombers had broken past them to attack *Glorious* herself, happily scoring only near misses. Nonetheless, D'Oyly-Hughes, who had what has been politely called a 'mercurial temperament', was not normally willing to accept the advice of those who did have more experience of aerial operations; indeed, before returning to Norwegian waters with 46 Squadron aboard, he had ordered Commander Heath, his senior air officer, ashore to await a court martial. On 8 June 1940, he believed that his only danger would come from submarines, against which his escorts and his ship's speed would be a sufficient defence. He had not sent out any reconnaissance patrols and all his Swordfish were down in the hangar when, at about 1600, a formidable enemy appeared on the horizon.

As ill luck would have it, the Germans, though ignorant of the Narvik evacuation, had dispatched battle-cruisers *Scharnhorst* and *Gneisenau* to raid Allied shipping in the vicinity. They caught *Glorious* completely by surprise, opened fire at about 1630 and almost immediately scored a hit in her forward upper hangar, setting on fire the RAF aircraft stowed there. The fire thwarted desperate attempts to get the Swordfish up on deck and arm them with torpedoes, and at 1700, a hit on the bridge, quickly followed by further hits aft, sealed the carrier's fate. By 1720, she had come to a halt in a sinking condition and 20 minutes later, she rolled over to starboard and went down. *Ardent* and *Acasta*, nobly attempting to protect her, were sunk as well, though not before the latter had put a torpedo into *Scharnhorst*, forcing her to retire to Trondheim for repairs. In all, more than 1,500 officers and men were lost, including all the pilots of 263 Squadron and all but two of those of 46 Squadron. Only Cross and Flight Lieutenant Jameson survived, to become an Air Chief Marshal and an Air Commodore respectively.

In the early hours of 13 June – daylight in the land of the midnight sun – fifteen Skuas from 800 and 803 Squadrons left *Ark Royal* in an attempt to gain some revenge for *Glorious* by attacking the wounded *Scharnhorst*. It was not an advisable or a well-organized operation for it was known that *Ark Royal* had been sighted by enemy reconnaissance aircraft, that the AA defences at Trondheim were considerable and would be supported by the guns of warships present in the harbour, that there was a Luftwaffe fighter base at nearby Vaernes airfield and that the Skuas would have to fly over enemy-occupied territory for some 40 miles, giving ample warning of their approach. To make matters worse, a raid on Vaernes by RAF bombers proved ill timed and merely put the enemy on full alert.

It is not surprising then that some of *Ark Royal's* most experienced pilots would later state that they were tempted to refuse to take part in this mission. Needless to say, they all in fact did participate, but their doubts proved justified. Eight of the Skuas were shot down, their crews being killed or captured. One bomb hit the *Scharnhorst* but failed to explode.

So ended the Norwegian campaign. For the British aircraft carriers, it had proved almost totally discouraging. No one could fault the courage, adaptability and resilience of the naval airmen but it had been only too clear that there was still much disagreement as to how carriers should be used. There is indeed a strong suggestion that there were doubts as to whether they could be used effectively at all. In this respect, the most depressing aspect of the loss of *Glorious* seems never to have been mentioned. She was sent into waters where she might be in danger of attack by U-boats or bombers or, as it proved, surface vessels, solely to take off a squadron of Gladiators; it was not even anticipated at first that she might rescue the Hurricanes as well. A carrier was considered worth risking for the sake of eight obsolescent biplanes. It was hardly a vote of confidence.

Notes

1 *Langley* was downgraded to the status of seaplane tender in 1937 but in the Second World War she reverted to being an aircraft carrier – or at least an aircraft transporter. On 27 February 1942, she was sunk by Japanese land-based bombers when making for the port of Tjilatjap in Java with thirty-two Kittyhawk fighters on board her.

2 Purists will require it to be noted that the term Fleet Air Arm was henceforward technically incorrect until it was reinstated in 1953. It was, nonetheless, almost invariably used in practice, not least by the Senior Service.

3 'Bf' was short for 'Bayerische Flugzeugwerke' - Bavarian Aircraft Company. The abbreviation 'Me', though widely used, was not officially correct until 1944.

4 A week earlier, HM Submarine *Oxley* had been sunk by HM Submarine *Triton*. At the time this horrifying mistake was made, both had been on patrol and both had strayed from their correct locations.

Chapter 2

The Carrier proves its Worth

Over the next six months, however, confidence in the aircraft carrier steadily increased and with it a realization of what the carrier might achieve. This train of events began on 10 June 1940, when the war was extended to the Mediterranean by Italy's declaration of war – an action that seemed at the time to present a terrible threat, especially since it was swiftly followed by the surrender of France.

Italy's Regia Navale in particular was not an opponent that the British Mediterranean Fleet could afford to ignore. It was superior in numbers and in many cases in quality, for Italy, like most other countries, had ignored the limitations imposed by the Washington Conference. Thus her *Littorio*-class battleships, nominally of 35,000 tons, were in fact over 41,000 tons, while her *Trieste*-class heavy cruisers exceeded by about 1,000 tons and her *Zara*-class heavy cruisers by about 1,500 tons their official 10,000-ton limit. The Italians also had the advantage of having their Fleet concentrated, whereas the Royal Navy was forced to divide its strength by stationing at Gibraltar Vice Admiral Sir James Somerville's Force H, including the ubiquitous *Ark Royal* (its first action was the tragic assault on French units at Mers-el-Kebir, near Oran to ensure they did not fall into Axis hands.) Mention of *Ark Royal* prompts the reflection that the Italians did suffer from one considerable disadvantage: they had no aircraft carriers – a handicap made worse because liaison between their Navy and the Regia Aeronautica, which like the RAF was a separate service, was clumsy and cumbersome. On the other hand, the only carrier then with Britain's main Mediterranean Fleet based at Alexandria was the elderly *Eagle*, scheduled for replacement, in urgent need of a refit and provided with just eighteen Swordfish and three Sea Gladiators.

Nonetheless, the Commander-in-Chief, Mediterranean, Admiral Sir Andrew Browne Cunningham, inevitably known throughout the Navy as 'ABC', while retaining the traditional view that the battleship was his key weapon, did accept the carrier as a useful auxiliary, able to provide fighter cover and to attack his enemy at long range. Accordingly, *Eagle* formed part of Cunningham's strength when, on 9 July, he encountered an Italian battle-fleet under Admiral Inigo Campioni, and her Swordfish made torpedo attacks on this, though without success in the face of fierce AA fire. This 'Action off Calabria' as the British called it – the Italians dignified it with the title of the Battle of Punta Stilo – was in any case of brief duration, for Campioni hastily withdrew after his flagship *Guilio Cesare* was struck by a 15-inch shell from Cunningham's flagship *Warspite*.

Cunningham, however, remained at sea and on the following day, *Eagle* sent nine Swordfish against Italian warships reported in the harbour of Augusta, Sicily, where they torpedoed and sank destroyer *Pancaldo*.[1] In return over the next three days, Italian high-level bombers made repeated attacks, described by Cunningham as 'most frightening'; but they achieved only some near misses on *Warspite* and *Eagle*, while five of them were shot down by the carrier's three Sea Gladiators.

Sadly, *Eagle*'s maintenance problems were such that even near misses had their adverse effect. Later in the year, her aviation fuel system broke down, and early in 1941, she left the Mediterranean for her long-overdue refit. Luckily, by that time, Cunningham had already received a replacement: HMS *Illustrious*, first of the new carriers that were being built at the time the Second World War began. *Illustrious*, of 23,000 tons displacement, differed from all previous British – or for that matter American and Japanese carriers – by having an armour-plated flight deck, resting on 100-ton girders. This deck formed the roof of the hangar, which also had heavily armoured sides, was isolated from all machinery and had its own ventilation system, preventing it from being penetrated by petrol vapour in the event of the ship being hit. It was a new and revolutionary concept, which would save the *Illustrious*-class carriers from destruction by more than one form of attack in the future.

It did, however, have one disadvantage, for it greatly reduced the number of aircraft that *Illustrious* and her sisters could operate. When she joined Cunningham on 1 September 1940 after a surprisingly uneventful passage through the Mediterranean, *Illustrious* carried only twenty-two Swordfish of 815 and 819 Squadrons, though she did also have 806 Squadron equipped with twelve of the Naval Air Service's latest monoplane fighter, the Fairey Fulmar.

Designed specifically for use on carriers, provided with full naval equipment such as folding wings and boasting a Merlin engine and an armament of eight Browning machine guns, the Fulmar might have been as successful as the RAF's famous Spitfire and Hurricane had it not been that naval practice demanded an observer as well as a pilot. He was really there as a navigator to ensure that the aircraft could return to its parent ship, but neither the Americans nor the Japanese accepted this requirement, arguing that carrier fighters would be employed protecting either their Fleet, in which case they were unlikely to stray far from home, or their own strike aircraft, in which case these could be responsible for the navigation. Their attitude was undoubtedly wise, for the Fulmar's second (and vast) cockpit greatly reduced its speed, its rate of climb and its ceiling.

Even so, the Fulmars of 806 Squadron, aided by the radar their ship carried – another new feature in the *Illustrious*-class – delighted Admiral Cunningham by the effectiveness with which they disposed of Italian shadowers. They increased his respect for carriers and finally confirmed his determination always to have at least one with him if at all possible.[2]

With *Illustrious* also came Rear Admiral Lumley Lyster, whose title was Rear Admiral, Carriers, Mediterranean Fleet, and who was a firm believer in the carrier's potential for offensive action. In particular, he wished to mount a raid on the main Italian naval base at Taranto, plans of which he had studied extensively. He therefore conveyed these ideas to Cunningham, who gave them ready and delighted support.

Taranto harbour, the finest in Italy, consisted of a wide semi-circular bay called the Mar Grande, enclosed by breakwaters through which was only a single narrow entrance. The main Fleet anchorage was in the north-east of the bay, protected by another breakwater, lines of anti-torpedo nets, barrage balloons on three sides and twenty-one batteries of 4-inch anti-aircraft guns ashore or on ships berthed in the harbour. Further to the north-east, a narrow canal ran through the town of Taranto to give access to an inner harbour, the Mar Piccolo.

In view of the extent of the defences, there could be no question of a raid during the hours of daylight, so Lyster gave his airmen intensive training for an attack after dark. This was originally planned for the night of 21 October, Trafalgar Day, with a total of thirty Swordfish from both *Illustrious* and *Eagle* taking part, but a series of somewhat ill omened incidents conspired both to delay and to reduce the strength of Operation JUDGEMENT, as the proposed assault was code-named.

As a preliminary to the raid, the Swordfish were fitted with new 60-gallon long-range fuel tanks. Those detailed to carry bombs had the tank attached under the fuselage but in those armed with torpedoes the tank went into the cockpit of the observer who was therefore compelled to move back into the aircraft's rear cockpit. The addition of the tanks was essential but both pilot and observer were uneasily conscious of the close proximity of highly inflammable and potentially explosive petrol, and of the fact that they would have no gunner if they ran into enemy fighters.

Then, while this work was being carried out in *Illustrious*, a spark in the petrol-laden atmosphere started a fire in her hangar. Several aircraft were destroyed, while those that escaped were damaged by the salt water poured over them by the ship's highly efficient fire-fighting sprays; they had to be stripped down, washed in fresh water and reassembled. Next, as was mentioned earlier, *Eagle* broke down and was rendered non-operational, though she did transfer a number of her aircraft to *Illustrious*. Finally, three Swordfish were forced to 'ditch' as the result of an aviation fuel tank on *Illustrious* having been contaminated with sea water, presumably at the time of the hangar fire; it proved necessary to drain down and refill the fuel systems of all the remaining Swordfish.

These various misfortunes meant that Operation JUDGEMENT had to be postponed until the night of 11 November. Yet, ironically, the delay was probably an advantage rather than otherwise, since Admiral Campioni had expected the Mediterranean Fleet would make a special effort on Trafalgar Day and had placed Taranto's defenders on a high state of readiness. Moreover, November storms aided the attackers by wrecking some sixty balloons, leaving only twenty-seven to hamper them.

Shortly before sunset on 11 November, while Somerville's Force H carried out diversions, including attacks by *Ark Royal*'s aircraft on aerodromes in Sardinia, *Illustrious*, escorted by four cruisers and four destroyers, headed towards her launching position in the Ionian Sea, west of Greece, some 180 miles from Taranto. A parting signal from Cunningham wished: 'Good luck then to your lads in their enterprise. Their success may well have a most important bearing on the course of the war in the Mediterranean.'

As photographs taken by Maryland reconnaissance aircraft based at Malta had revealed, the Swordfish would have no shortage of targets at Taranto. In the main Fleet anchorage lay all six of Italy's battleships, the new *Littorio* and *Vittorio Veneto* and the older but modernized *Guilio Cesare*, *Conte di Cavour*, *Caio Duilio* and *Andrea Doria*, plus heavy cruisers *Zara*, *Fiume* and *Gorizia* and four destroyers. Four other destroyers were in the northern part of the Mar Grande, while the remainder of the Fleet, including heavy cruisers *Trieste*, *Trento*, *Bolzano* and *Pola*, could be found in the inner harbour, the Mar Piccolo.

Of the twenty-one Swordfish left available to attack these vessels, eleven carried torpedoes, the warheads of which were detonated by a new device called a 'Duplex' pistol. It was realized that they had to be set to run deep so as to pass under the anti-torpedo nets; the new pistol ensured that they would explode not only if they hit their target but if they passed beneath it, in which case they would be detonated by its magnetic field. The remaining Swordfish carried bombs but their main task was to create a diversion. Four of them also had the task of dropping flares that would illuminate the enemy battleships for the benefit of the torpedo-planes.

At 2030, six Swordfish with torpedoes, four with bombs and two with bombs and flares left the deck of *Illustrious* under the leadership of Lieutenant Commander Kenneth Williamson, Commanding Officer of 815 Squadron. The CO of 819 Squadron, Lieutenant Commander Hale led off a second wave an hour later, but this was short of one of its four bombers, a wing of which had been damaged in a collision as the Swordfish prepared to take off. Then 10 minutes after leaving *Illustrious*, the long-range fuel tank on another bomber broke loose and fell into the sea, leaving the crew with no option but to return to the carrier, which they did safely. The second wave was thus reduced to five torpedo-planes and two bombers, both of which luckily carried flares. There was, though, to be a third wave – if a single aeroplane may be so described. Lieutenants Clifford and Going, the crew of the damaged Swordfish, pleaded with Lyster and Captain Denis Boyd to be allowed to continue on the raid, assuring them that their aircraft could be repaired in 10 minutes and they could catch up with their formation. Impressed by their spirit and conscious of the small numbers committed to the attack, the senior officers gave their consent, even though the promised 10 minutes had stretched to 30 before Clifford and Going were finally airborne.

At least the second (and third) wave had no problems with the weather. Williamson's group encountered thick clouds and by the time it emerged from these, three bombers and one torpedo-plane had lost touch with the formation. Since there was no radio contact between the Swordfish, Williamson could not reunite his men but he was confident that his missing machines would proceed to the target independently; as they did, indeed. The torpedo-plane, piloted by Lieutenant Ian Swayne, was the first aircraft to arrive, and he wisely circled until the main formation appeared.

As this approached the harbour at 2250, Williamson's observer, Lieutenant Norman Scarlett, ordered the flare-droppers, by means of a signal lamp, to illuminate the targets. They performed their task perfectly, creating, according to the Italians' own account, 'a zone of intense light to the eastward of the battleships whose hulls were clearly outlined'. They then joined the other four bombers in attacks on vessels in the inner harbour and nearby shore installations. Sub-Lieutenant Sarra hit a hangar at the seaplane base, destroying it and the two aircraft inside, but the bombing, as intended, was most beneficial in helping to divert attention from the torpedo-planes.

That admittedly was not apparent to the crews of these as they came in at low level through a storm of anti-aircraft fire. Williamson who attacked first found himself heading almost directly towards destroyer *Fulmine*, beyond which was his target, battleship *Cavour*. Shells from the destroyer were already hitting the Swordfish as Williamson directed his torpedo at *Cavour*, striking her just under her foremost turret. Immediately afterwards, a final burst of fire from *Fulmine* smashed into the Swordfish and it plunged into the sea, leaving its tail sticking out of the water. To this, Williamson and Scarlett clung for half-an-hour, before finding the strength to swim to a floating dock; they would spend the next four-and-a-half years in prisoner of war camps.

Sub-Lieutenants Sparke and Macauley followed Williamson into the attack. They also launched their torpedoes at *Cavour* but without success. Lieutenants Kemp and Maund approached the anchorage by a more northerly route and were joined by Swayne, who thus co-ordinated his strike with the rest of the first wave after all. Kemp's torpedo tore a hole in *Littorio*'s starboard bow and a few seconds later Swayne's torpedo blew another one in her port quarter. Maund directed his torpedo at Campioni's flagship *Vittorio Veneto*³ but it missed. Apart from Williamson and Scarlett, all the crews in this first assault returned safely to *Illustrious*.

To the crews of the second wave, fires and flak were clearly visible at a distance of some 60 miles, warning them that there was no chance of their achieving surprise. Shortly before midnight, the two flare-droppers lit up the harbour once more, then attacked an oil storage depot where they started a fire, while the five torpedo-planes, following the same path as the last three of the first wave, swept in to deliver their lethal 'fish'. Lieutenant Commander Hale and Lieutenant Michael Torrens-Spence aimed theirs at *Littorio*. Both struck her and one exploded on the battleship's starboard bow just forward of the earlier hit. The other left only a dent in her starboard quarter: a doubly unfortunate occurrence because not only did she escape further damage but the torpedo was later recovered from the bed of the harbour, revealing to the Italians the secrets of its 'Duplex' pistol.

As Torrens-Spence wheeled away, so low that his machine's wheels struck the water and he was fortunate to pull it up in time, he narrowly avoided a collision with the Swordfish piloted by Lieutenant Bayley, who was closing in to attack heavy cruiser *Gorizia*. Moments later, it was hit by AA fire and exploded, scattering blazing debris over the water. Bayley's body was discovered some years after the war and given a decent burial. The body of the observer, Lieutenant Slaughter, was never found.

Of the remaining aircraft of the second wave, Lieutenant Lea torpedoed battleship *Caio Duilio* on her starboard side between two magazines. Both were flooded but her crew could count themselves lucky that neither magazine had been struck directly in which case the ship could well have blown up. Lieutenant Wellham selected *Vittorio Veneto* as his target but the torpedo missed. The Swordfish was damaged by AA fire but got back safely to *Illustrious* where Wellham delighted Captain Boyd by announcing that he hadn't taken the flak personally until his own machine was hit. The straggler manned by Clifford and Going arrived just as the rest of the second wave were retiring. The Italians, desperately trying to save their crippled battleships, took no notice of it until the Swordfish began its dive. Then the AA guns opened fire – but too late. A bomb landed on heavy cruiser *Trento*; it failed to explode but went right through her and fractured her fuel tanks to spread oil all over the inner harbour.

Illustrious rejoined the Fleet and returned to Alexandria, her Fulmars completing her triumph by shooting down three Italian flying-boats on the way. Although the fatal casualties in the torpedoed battleships were astonishingly light – twenty-three in *Littorio*, sixteen in *Cavour*, just one in *Duilio* – all three were left in a sinking condition. Emergency repairs kept *Littorio* afloat but she was out of action for five months. The other two had to be beached; *Duilio*'s repairs lasted for six months and *Cavour* took no further part in the war at sea.

It was a spectacular success for just twenty aged biplanes and it is rather sad to have to report that it received much less appreciation than might have been expected. Even Cunningham, as he would later admit, had not realized the dangers his airmen had faced or the full extent of their achievement, and while it would be invidious to make comparisons, the decorations awarded at the time – others were to be announced some months later – were ungenerously sparse to say the least.

In fact, it seems that Taranto was initially regarded most highly by Britain's enemies, actual or potential. In Japan, where a carrier attack on another naval base was already contemplated, it provided example and encouragement. In Italy, it served as a dreadful warning. The undamaged warships hurriedly left Taranto for bases further north and when on 27 November, they emerged again to encounter Vice Admiral Somerville's Force H south of Sardinia protecting a convoy to Malta, the discovery that *Ark Royal* was among those present caused Admiral Campioni to retire from the vicinity at his maximum speed.

A more alarming response was that of the Regia Aeronautica that attacked *Ark Royal* persistently. Several times she disappeared behind the towering columns of water raised by very close misses and although she somehow escaped damage, it was clear that in future carriers would become a priority target. The Germans too had been greatly impressed by Taranto and by early January 1941, Fliegerkorps X, a unit that had been specially trained in anti-shipping assaults was based in Sicily. The first admirably precise objective given by Hitler to its commander, General Geisler, was: '*Illustrious* must be sunk.'

On 10 January, Fliegerkorps X made a most determined attempt to do just that. The Mediterranean Fleet was steaming to the north-west of

Malta covering a convoy bound for the island and *Illustrious* had also sent out Swordfish to look for Italian shipping making for North Africa; they sank three unlucky merchantmen that morning. Above the carrier, the Fulmars of her Combat Air Patrol (CAP) were engaged in driving away probing enemy aircraft, but by 1223, all except two of them were out of ammunition; these were now lured away in pursuit of a pair of Savoia Marchetti SM 79 torpedo-bombers. At 1230, radar gave warning of a large new formation closing from the north. Captain Boyd prepared to launch six more Fulmars but standing orders required *Illustrious* to obtain permission from flagship *Warspite* before she could turn into the wind. She received this four minutes later, but before the Fulmars could gain enough height to intercept, the enemy aircraft were already attacking.

They were Junkers Ju 87 Stuka dive-bombers. There were forty-three of them, and while ten engaged other warships, mainly as a diversion, the rest, splitting into three groups, hurtled down on *Illustrious*. They attacked from port and starboard bows and port quarter simultaneously, and so brilliantly were their strikes co-ordinated that there were never less than six of them diving on her at the same time.

The armoured deck of the *Illustrious*-class carriers had been built to withstand a 500-lb bomb but some of the Stukas were armed with bombs of twice that weight and even the 500-lb weapons they carried had a greater penetrative power than those in existence at the time *Illustrious* had been designed. General Geisler had been confident that four direct hits with these would sink *Illustrious*. His men in fact scored six hits as well as three very near misses; furthermore three of the hits were with 1,000-lb bombs. The only glimmer of good fortune that *Illustrious* enjoyed was that of the first two of these, one smashed through a pom-pom gun position and burst only when it hit the water, while the other struck close to her bow, exploding in her paint store.

Then the luck ran out. In quick succession three 500-lb bombs found their mark. The first hit the after lift on which a Fulmar was just being raised to the flight deck, destroying this, killing the young midshipman who was its pilot and sending the 300-ton lift platform crashing into the hangar. Moments later, another struck the same lift but this one plunged right into the hangar where it exploded, setting four Fulmars and nine Swordfish ablaze. A third found the forward lift, causing further heavy damage. And finally a 1,000-lb bomb landed on the flight deck near the forward lift, burst clean through it and turned the hangar into an inferno. Just four Stukas had been lost in the attack.

Illustrious suffered over 200 casualties; among the dead being Lieutenant Kemp, the first man to put a torpedo into *Littorio*, and Lieutenant Clifford, who had flown alone to Taranto and bombed *Trento*; among the wounded being Clifford's observer Lieutenant Going who lost a leg. The carrier could no longer operate her aircraft, her steering gear had been damaged and fire raged through almost her entire length. Yet her armoured flight deck and hangar deck enabled her to survive where any other carrier then in service would have perished. Her hull, her boiler rooms, her engines, her aviation fuel tanks and her magazines all remained intact and protected from the flames. With her damage control parties striving to repair her injuries, she made her slow, painful way towards Malta.

Fliegerkorps X attempted to finish its work at about 1600, but the carrier's Fulmars which had flown to Malta, refuelled, rearmed and returned, broke up the attack. Only one bomb hit *Illustrious*, near her stern. This stirred up the flames in the hangar that were gradually being mastered and at one time these threatened a magazine, despite which Captain Boyd refused permission to flood it, feeling certain that he would need all his ammunition. Once more the exhausted damage control parties met the challenge and by 2215, *Illustrious* was safely at anchor in Grand Harbour, Valletta.

Her ordeal was still not over. On 16 January, the Germans launched a massive raid by about eighty Stukas and Junkers Ju 88 bombers but these scored only a single hit on *Illustrious* aft that caused minor damage, though they did inflict terrible harm on the neighbouring dockyards and residential areas. They were met by a massive AA barrage and were so harried by Malta's gallant handful of RAF Hurricanes, backed by the carrier's own Fulmars, that when they returned two days later, they struck not at *Illustrious* but at the island's fighter airfields. Some damage was done, yet not enough to prevent the Hurricanes putting up a further spirited resistance when Fliegerkorps X made its last assault on *Illustrious* on 19 January. Two near misses caused underwater injuries but these were made good and there were no more raids before *Illustrious* slipped out of Grand Harbour after dark on the 23rd, to reach Alexandria two days later.

While *Illustrious* had miraculously survived, there was no question of her remaining in action, so she withdrew through the Suez Canal, ultimately to the United States for extensive repairs. *Eagle* soon followed her but, happily for Cunningham's peace of mind, on 10 March, another *Illustrious*-class carrier passed through the Canal in the opposite direction. This was HMS *Formidable*, on board which were 803 Squadron with Fulmars and 826 and 829 Squadrons with Swordfish and Albacores – the Albacore being really a later version of the Swordfish with closed cockpits and a more powerful though, as it transpired, less reliable engine. Next morning, she hoisted the flag of Denis Boyd, former captain of *Illustrious*, now promoted to Rear Admiral, Carriers, Mediterranean Fleet.

By March 1941, disasters on land had been added to Italy's problems at sea. In North Africa, the British had repulsed an invasion of Egypt; then overrun the whole of Cyrenaica, the eastern half of Italy's colony of Libya. In the Balkans, Mussolini had invaded Greece from Albania – which he had seized in early 1939 – but his regiments, although boasting such titles as the Wolves of Tuscany, the Hercules of Ferrara, the Demigods of Julia and the Red Devils of Piedmont, had been ejected and were now being driven back in Albania as well. Furthermore, the British, fearing that a German invasion of Greece was also imminent, had begun to ship military and air forces to her aid.

These convoys presented a tempting target to the Regia Navale's new and much more forceful Commander-in-Chief, Admiral Angelo Iachino, who had succeeded Campioni in the previous December; it now seemed that events were conspiring to assist him. On 16 March 1941, Fliegerkorps X honestly but mistakenly claimed to have crippled battleships *Warspite* and *Barham*, leaving only *Valiant* – on which was serving a nineteen-year-old midshipman named Prince Philip of Denmark and Greece – fit for action.

On the night of the 26th therefore, Italian warships slipped quietly out of harbour to sweep both north and south of Crete in search of British convoys. Iachino took personal command of the southern group, flying his flag in *Vittorio Veneto*. She had a close escort of four destroyers and in advance steamed Vice Admiral Luigi Sansonetti with heavy cruisers *Trieste*, *Trento* and *Bolzano* and three destroyers. The raid north of Crete was entrusted to Vice Admiral Carlo Cattaneo commanding three even heavier cruisers, *Zara*, *Pola* and *Fiume*, two light cruisers and six destroyers.

Iachino could not know that Britain's Code and Cypher School at Bletchley Park, source of the famous 'Ultra' Intelligence, had already revealed his plans to Cunningham. At 1225 on the 27th, his own cypher experts on *Vittorio Veneto* decoded signals from a Sunderland flying-boat based in Greece, reporting the sighting of Sansonetti's cruisers. Shortly after 1800, however, he was reassured to learn that the bulk of the British Fleet was still at Alexandria.

Such indeed was the case, for Cunningham intended to leave after dark in order to preserve secrecy. To further mask his intentions, he left his flagship that afternoon, carrying a large suitcase, as if intending to pass the night ashore. He spent some time on the golf course making certain he was seen by a man he considered to be 'a known transmitter of information about naval movements'. This was the Japanese consul, whom he describes unkindly as being 'of vast and elephantine proportions', nicknamed 'the blunt end of the Axis'. It is really a pity to have to record that we now know the consul was not in fact sending news to Britain's enemies after all.

Having returned unobtrusively to harbour, at 1900, Cunningham took *Warspite, Valiant, Barham, Formidable* and nine destroyers out to sea, bound for a rendezvous south of Crete with light cruisers *Orion, Gloucester, Ajax* (of River Plate fame) and the Australian *Perth*, and four more destroyers under Vice Admiral Henry Pridham-Wippell, whose title was Vice Admiral Light Forces or VALF. By coincidence, Iachino and Cattaneo had also arranged to combine their strength south of Crete early on 28 March. An encounter between the rival navies seemed inevitable.

In the complicated series of clashes that made up the Battle of Matapan, the most remarkable feature would be the part played by Cunningham's naval aircraft. *Formidable*'s complement scarcely lived up to her name. There were just twelve Fulmars in 803 Squadron; 826 and 829 Squadrons between them could muster ten Albacores and four Swordfish; 815 Squadron, once based on *Illustrious* and now at Maleme airfield in Crete, could add a further handful of Swordfish to the total. Yet the effect they had would be quite out of proportion to their scanty numbers.

Formidable's aerial activities began at 0555 on 28 March, when she sent off a number of reconnaissance missions. These located both Cattaneo's and Sansonetti's cruisers but when their reports came in,

Cunningham and Boyd considered that they had sighted rather Pridham-Wippell's force. The Vice Admiral Light Forces shared their opinion when the report was relayed to him, but he quickly realized his error when at 0745, he encountered Sansonetti's three cruisers. There was an inconclusive exchange of fire, after which the Italians broke off the action and turned north-westward. Pridham-Wippell followed, not realizing that he was being lured into a trap. At 1058, a battleship was sighted north of his flagship *Orion*. A challenge was made. The reply was a 15-inch salvo.

Pouring out a smokescreen to protect themselves, the VALF's ships headed towards their own battle fleet at maximum speed, but with *Vittorio Veneto* directing an accurate fire on them from their port side and Sansonetti's cruisers closing in from starboard, they were in considerable danger when, at 1127, their rescuers arrived. At 0956, Lieutenant Commander Gerald Saunt, CO of 826 Squadron, had led six Albacores armed with torpedoes and two Fulmars off *Formidable*'s deck. Their orders were to attack either the Italian cruisers engaged with Pridham-Wippell or three battleships reported by a *Formidable* scout further north – apparently really the three big *Zara*-class cruisers. They did not find these but they were able to take action against a very real battleship nonetheless.

As the Albacores manoeuvred to attack *Vittorio Veneto* through intense, though happily ineffective AA fire, a pair of Junkers Ju 88 fighter-bombers dived on them out of the sun. The two Fulmar pilots, Lieutenant Gibson and Petty Officer Theobald, shot down one in flames, whereupon the other fled. The Albacores then launched their torpedoes. All missed but their assault was sufficient to persuade Iachino to abandon his chase of Pridham-Wippell and order all his ships to steer for home.[4]

Having saved the VALF's cruisers, *Formidable*'s next duty was to slow down the retreating Italians so as to give Cunningham a chance to get within range. At 1222, Lieutenant Commander Dalyell-Stead took off at the head of three Albacores and two Swordfish from 829 Squadron, escorted by two Fulmars, to carry out this task. At about 1510, he led his torpedo-planes into the attack on *Vittorio Veneto*.

It was 'conducted' says Admiral Iachino, 'with particular ability and bravery'. Dalyell-Stead closed to a range of little more than 1,000 yards before dropping his weapon. Then a hail of machine gun fire struck the

Albacore. It reeled over *Vittorio Veneto*'s bow and crashed into the sea, killing the gallant pilot, his observer, Lieutenant Cooke, and his telegraphist/air gunner, Petty Officer Blenkhorn, the only fatal casualties suffered by the British in this battle. Moments afterwards, the torpedo hit *Vittorio Veneto*'s port side near her stern, about 15 feet below the water line, damaging engines and rudder and tearing a huge hole through which poured 4,000 tons of water.

Though none of the other torpedoes found its mark and a raid by Blenheim bombers from Greece scored only a very near miss close to the battleship's stern, *Formidable* had once more changed the situation dramatically. Damage control parties checked the battleship's flooding and restored her steering but her speed and manoeuvrability were greatly reduced, leaving her highly vulnerable to further attacks. Happily for Iachino's peace of mind, he had received information from radio direction-finding stations (information that incidentally was wildly inaccurate), as a result of which he believed that the main British force was 170 miles away to the south-east. It was an error destined to have fatal consequences.

Iachino was, in any case, greatly concerned that *Formidable* had not yet finished with him. At 1800, his anxieties became realities when his cryptanalysts decoded a message from Cunningham ordering the Swordfish at Maleme to join in an attack by *Formidable*'s aircraft at sunset. *Formidable*'s third strike had already taken off at 1735; it consisted of six Albacores from 826 Squadron and two Swordfish from 829, all led by Lieutenant Commander Saunt. They would be joined by two of 815's Swordfish from Maleme, flown by Lieutenant Torrens-Spence who had attacked *Littorio* at Taranto, and Lieutenant Kiggell who had been one of the flare-droppers on that occasion. They were kept well informed of Iachino's dispositions, for *Formidable* had earlier sent other Albacores to trail him and these had been joined by a float-plane from *Warspite* flown by Petty Officer Rice. With Rice was a highly experienced observer, Lieutenant Commander Bolt, whose accurate situation reports, when decoded, aroused Iachino's reluctant admiration.

Iachino had adopted a formation well calculated to protect *Vittorio Veneto*. He had detached his two light cruisers and two destroyers with orders to make for Brindisi but the remainder of his ships were stationed in five parallel columns. The battleship and her four destroyers made up the centre column, with the heavy cruisers forming those on either side,

Sansonetti's to port, Cattaneo's to starboard. The destroyers of each cruiser division provided the outer columns. It was further arranged that if an attack took place, smoke screens and searchlights would be used to hamper and confuse the enemy aircraft.

The sun sank at 1851. It was almost dark when at 1930, the torpedo-planes closed in. Confronted by a tremendous barrage of anti-aircraft fire, Saunt's men approached separately from different directions but all resolutely pressed home their assaults. Twenty minutes later, these were over and, in accordance with previous instructions, the old biplanes, unable to land on their carrier after dark, headed for Crete. *Vittorio Veneto* was unscathed and made good her escape but one torpedo had struck the starboard side of heavy cruiser *Pola*, flooding an engine room and a boiler room and wrecking her electrical power system. Slowly she fell out of formation, to lie dead in the water.

Since this hit was scored near the end of the raid it has usually been credited to 815 Squadron, the last to attack, and specifically to Torrens-Spence as Kiggell approached from the port side of the Italian formation. It is permissible, however, to question this attribution. Torrens-Spence's own account of his attack states that 'no results were observed', whereas Saunt reports that 'one hit on a cruiser was observed'. This suggests it was a *Formidable* aircraft that obtained the hit. Moreover, Torrens-Spence's target was, he says, 'a cruiser towards the rear of the starboard column'. But *Pola* was the middle ship in her column. If Torrens-Spence attacked the rearmost cruiser he would have attacked *Fiume*, and some confirmation that he did comes from the fact that his Swordfish was hit by AA fire; the destruction of one of the torpedo-planes was claimed, though wrongly, by destroyer *Bersagliere* in the centre column steering directly to port of *Fiume*.

It is therefore suggested that, as related in Captain S.W.C. Pack's *The Battle of Matapan*, the successful assault was probably made by the Albacore flown by Sub-Lieutenant Williams of 826 Squadron, the last of Saunt's group to attack. This was at 1945, and one minute later *Pola* stopped a torpedo. Not, though, that it matters greatly who scored the hit. Captain De Pisa reportedly said that the pilot who crippled his ship was either 'mad' or 'the bravest man in the world', but all the airmen in *Formidable*'s third strike were equally brave and determined if not equally fortunate. And they had brought about the doom of more than just the *Pola*.

On learning that *Pola* had been brought to a standstill, Vice Admiral Cattaneo suggested that he send two destroyers to look for her. Iachino, though, felt that the decision whether *Pola* should be sunk or saved must be taken by a senior officer, and in the latter case she would need a stronger escort than two destroyers. He therefore ordered the whole of Cattaneo's division to go to her aid. 'It never occurred to me,' said Iachino afterwards, 'that we were within a relatively short distance of the entire British force.'

Tragically for the Italians, that was the case and when Cattaneo's wretched ships were detected by Cunningham at about 2225, they were caught completely by surprise, hopelessly outnumbered and unable to defend themselves since, unlike the British, they were neither trained nor equipped to fight a night action. Devastatingly accurate salvoes from all three British battleships sank heavy cruiser *Fiume* and reduced Cattaneo's flagship, heavy cruiser *Zara*, and destroyer *Alfieri* to blazing wrecks. British destroyers finished these off with torpedoes, sank destroyer *Carducci*, and finally located and sank the hapless *Pola*. The British rescued over 900 survivors and when compelled to retire by the appearance of enemy aircraft, sent a signal via Malta giving the Italian Naval Staff the exact position of others still in the water. A hospital ship was dispatched and saved another 160 lives but this brief, ferocious encounter had cost the Italians 2,400 seamen, including Vice Admiral Cattaneo.

Next day, twelve Junkers Ju 88s attacked *Formidable* at about 1530, but they had no success and two were shot down by AA fire. It was the last flicker of action in the Battle of Matapan. Although Cunningham was disappointed that *Vittorio Veneto* had only been damaged, he was greatly satisfied by the destruction of the three *Zara*-class cruisers that 'had always been a source of anxiety as a threat to our own less well-armed cruisers'. More to the point, he had finally broken the confidence of the Regia Navale.

In May, the waters around Crete became the scene of what Cunningham called 'a trial of strength between the Mediterranean Fleet and the German Air Force'. He was forced to 'admit defeat' with three light cruisers and six destroyers sunk and numerous other vessels damaged, many too badly to be repaired locally. These included *Warspite* and also *Formidable* which on the 26th was attacked by twenty Stukas, hit twice and compelled, like *Illustrious* before her, to retire to the United States. Had Italian surface vessels joined in the assault, Cunningham's command might have been doomed – but they remained in harbour.

Worse was to follow as the year neared its end. On 25 November, *Barham* was sunk by *U-331* with the loss of 56 officers and 812 men. On the night of 18/19 December, Italian 'human torpedoes' crippled both *Valiant* and battleship *Queen Elizabeth* that had joined Cunningham in May. There was then no British capital ship in the eastern Mediterranean – yet still the Italians would not send their warships east of the fateful Cape Matapan.

No wonder that Cunningham was to state that subsequent operations in the Mediterranean were 'conducted under cover of the Battle of Matapan'. Its greatest effect, though, was its revelation of the significance of the aircraft carrier. A few days after the battle, Admiral Iachino was summoned to meet Mussolini. He did not relish the prospect, but to his relief the dictator proved far from hostile. Indeed, to Iachino's astonishment, Mussolini's main complaint was that the Regia Navale lacked its own naval air arm – though he personally had always opposed this. In future, he declared, it was vital 'for naval forces at sea to be always accompanied by at least one carrier'. To this end, he ordered that two large liners should be converted to carriers and renamed *Aquila* and *Sparviero*. In practice, when Italy signed an armistice in September 1943, only the former had been completed and she was useless because there were no suitable aircraft that could serve on her.

Mussolini had been convinced by Matapan that his ships must 'take their own air support' in order to ensure them satisfactory and co-ordinated aerial reconnaissance and adequate fighter cover. Yet the battle also taught another lesson that was, if anything, more important. Like Taranto, Matapan showed that even a pitifully small number of carrier aircraft, striking at ranges far beyond those of the most powerful guns, could cripple the mightiest of warships. Fate would provide one more spectacular example of this in the European theatre of the war, before all doubts were ended for ever, thousands of miles away in the warm blue waters of the Pacific Ocean.

Notes

1 She was later salvaged but was sunk by air-attack for a second and final time on 30 April 1943.

2 Cunningham's policy of treating carriers as fully integrated parts of his Fleet had a further unexpected benefit. They had previously been expected to fall out of formation when their aircraft were landing or taking off, thereby avoiding the need for the whole force to change course into the wind. Cunningham insisted that all ships should manoeuvre as one so that his carriers could always enjoy the protection of the Fleet's AA guns.

3 It was a rather sad irony that this should have been the name of the enemy flagship. It recorded Italy's greatest victory in the First World War. At that time, she had been an ally of Britain and three British divisions had fought alongside the Italians in the battle.

4 The Italians treat these preliminary rounds of the Battle of Matapan as a separate action, the Battle of Gavdo, so named after a rocky islet some 20 miles south-west of central Crete. Matapan itself, incidentally, is the most southerly cape in mainland Greece.

Chapter 3

End of an Era

I t seemed the most uneven conflict imaginable. On one side, the
finest battleship afloat; of 42,500 tons standard displacement, of
well over 50,000 tons fully laden, with armour 13 inches thick in
places yet able to steam at 30 knots, boasting eight 15-inch guns in four
massive turrets each weighing 1,000 tons, a secondary armament of
twelve 5.9-inch guns and numerous AA weapons, manned by a crew of
almost 2,400 – the pride of her Navy and her nation. On the other,
fifteen old, slow, flimsy, ungainly biplanes, with a crew of three,
carrying a single torpedo. But it was the men on the warship who had
most reason to be afraid.

The story of the chase and destruction of Germany's giant *Bismarck*
has been recounted so often that it need only be summarized apart from
the crucial clash referred to above. Suffice then to say that on the night
of 18/19 May 1941, the battleship, flying the flag of Vice Admiral
Günther Lütjens, accompanied by the 14,000-ton heavy cruiser *Prinz
Eugen*[1], left the port of Gdynia in Poland under instructions to break
into the Atlantic and fall on the convoys carrying vital war-supplies
from North America. On the evening of 23 May, the German warships
were sighted in the Denmark Strait by heavy cruisers *Norfolk* and
Suffolk. These were able to track them by means of long-range radar
equipment on *Suffolk* that was far superior to anything the Germans
possessed, and early on the 24th, to guide two of Britain's capital ships
to engage them in combat.

Catastrophe swiftly followed. The battle-cruiser *Hood*, the largest
vessel in the Royal Navy, was struck in one of her main magazines by a
15-inch shell from *Bismarck* and vanished in a colossal explosion that
took the lives of all except three of her company of 1,419 men. The
brand new battleship *Prince of Wales*, heavily damaged, retired under a
smoke-screen. Fortunately, she had herself made three hits on

Bismarck, one of which tore through the battleship's bows. Water poured in, contaminating or preventing access to more than 1,000 tons of irreplaceable fuel. Lütjens was urged to return to Germany but he determined to make for a port in north-western France so that, once repairs had been completed, he could resume his assault on the convoy routes, perhaps in company with *Scharnhorst* and *Gneisenau*, then sheltering in Brest. That evening, he detached *Prinz Eugen* to continue the raid on the convoys alone, but we may note here that she had no success and after suffering engine-trouble, she too took refuge in Brest.

Thus *Bismarck* was alone when she suffered her next ordeal. Admiral Sir John Tovey, Commander-in-Chief of Britain's Home Fleet, had with him HMS *Victorious*, an *Illustrious*-class carrier that had been commissioned only two months earlier. He hoped her airmen might be able to slow down *Bismarck* as *Formidable*'s airmen had slowed *Vittorio Veneto* at Matapan. He therefore ordered her to steam to a position within 100 miles of *Bismarck* and then deliver a torpedo strike with every aeroplane she could muster.

Unhappily, *Bismarck*'s changes of course as she attempted to lose her shadowers meant that *Victorious* could only launch her strike at 2210, an hour later and 20 miles further away than planned. Moreover the formation leader, Lieutenant Commander Eugene Esmonde, had just nine Swordfish of 825 Squadron, one of which had to turn back with engine-trouble, and six Fulmars of 802 Squadron; almost all their crews were inexperienced. Nonetheless at about 2350, they unhesitatingly braved *Bismarck*'s flak to deliver their attack, somehow escaped serious harm, and returned to their carrier where, though few of them had made a night landing before, they all landed safely except two Fulmars that were forced to 'ditch', only one crewman being rescued later.

Esmonde's men received little reward for their efforts. Violent manoeuvres by the battleship enabled her to avoid all their torpedoes except one. This – it was probably dropped by Lieutenant Percy Gick – struck her starboard side amidships where her armoured belt was strongest. It caused very little damage but killed Chief Boatswain Kirchberg, first but horrifyingly far from last of *Bismarck*'s crew to die.

Victorious had no chance of delivering a further strike. In the early hours of 25 May, a sharp change of course by *Bismarck* shook off her shadowers. Yet it seems that Lütjens did not realize this – perhaps he simply could not believe his luck – because at about 0745, he transmitted a half-hour-long account of the sinking of the *Hood*. It was a fatal mistake, for the signal enabled British direction-finding stations to calculate his position.[2]

Unfortunately, the British then made a mistake of their own. On Tovey's flagship, battleship *King George V*, *Bismarck*'s position was plotted inaccurately, leading Tovey to believe that she was making for Germany, not France. By the time the error was corrected, in the late afternoon, both *King George V* and battleship *Rodney* which had been ordered to join Tovey were at least 125 miles north and north-east respectively of their quarry.

Dawn on 26 May presented a scene perfectly expressive of the British mood: cloudy grey skies; fierce grey winds; angry grey seas. Between *Bismarck* and safety there was just one obstacle. Somerville's Force H had left Gibraltar at 0200 on 24 May, to push northward into a rising gale. Neither the elderly battle-cruiser *Renown* nor light cruiser *Sheffield* could engage *Bismarck* with any hope of success. But *Ark Royal* carried three squadrons of Swordfish, Nos. 810, 818 and 820 and with these *Bismarck* could be located and then attacked, provided they could only get airborne.

This seemed far from certain. Huge waves were pouring right over the decks of *Renown* and *Sheffield* and even onto the front of *Ark Royal*'s flight deck, 62 feet above water level. Her stern was rising and falling by a minimum of 53 feet. Her two squadrons of Fulmars could not possibly operate in such conditions. Even the astonishingly reliable Swordfish needed parties of up to forty men just to hold them on the lurching, slippery flight deck. Nonetheless, at about 0845, ten of them somehow got into the air, to spread out in a wide arc of search, north, north-west and west.

Though *Ark Royal*'s Swordfish would have detected *Bismarck* anyway, the honour of first sighting in fact fell to a Catalina from Coastal Command's 209 Squadron. Piloted by Flying Officer Briggs[3], this spotted the battleship 70 miles north of *Ark Royal* at about 1030. It was severely damaged by AA fire but Briggs was able to radio his report before nursing the Catalina back to base and subsequently receiving a Distinguished Flying Cross. His signal was heard by the Swordfish and within the next 45 minutes, first Sub-Lieutenant Hartley, and then Lieutenant Callander located the German giant. Thereafter, these aircraft or other Swordfish that relieved them later remained in touch with *Bismarck*, their crews well knowing that in the event of engine failure, they would stand no chance of survival in violent, icy waters. Their quiet devotion to duty has rarely been acknowledged – or surpassed.

Those Swordfish not shadowing *Bismarck* returned to *Ark Royal* where they somehow managed to land on her heaving decks, though one was literally smashed to pieces when the carrier's stern reared up just as it was touching down. Miraculously, its crew were unhurt. And at 1450, Lieutenant Commander James Stewart-Moore, CO of 820 Squadron, led fourteen Swordfish armed with torpedoes towards the enemy. An hour later, these sighted a warship and since they had been told that any ship in the vicinity would be hostile, they attacked at once. Eleven of them dropped their torpedoes but the last three realized that something was wrong: their target had not fired a single shot at them. Their doubts were confirmed by the receipt of a desperate signal in plain English from their carrier: 'Look out for *Sheffield*!'

At the time that *Ark Royal* was recovering her scouts and was out of sight of the rest of Force H, Somerville had sent off his cruiser to assist in shadowing *Bismarck*. His signal was repeated to *Ark Royal* but only 'for information' and there was a delay in decoding it while other more immediate messages were dealt with. When Captain Maund did learn what had happened, he at once sent his plain English warning, but by then his pilots were already attacking the wrong ship. As a regular part of Force H, *Sheffield* should have been familiar enough to *Ark Royal*'s airmen; she had even acted as the target ship for their practice torpedo attacks. Nor was she anything like *Bismarck*, being much smaller and having for example two funnels to the *Bismarck*'s one.[4] Yet obvious as these differences might appear in retrospect, it is difficult to blame the airmen for this error, keyed up as they were to the height of tension.

A potential tragedy was averted by a strange twist of fate. The torpedoes the Swordfish carried had been fitted with those same 'Duplex' pistols used at Taranto that were detonated either by contact or by their target's magnetic field if they passed underneath it. They proved unsuitable in the violent waters of the Atlantic and at least five of them exploded prematurely. Superb ship-handling by Captain Charles Larcom avoided the others.

It was a dejected, humiliated group of airmen who returned to *Ark Royal* at about 1720, but their depression was quickly overlaid by a burning determination to try again and succeed. At 1910, the torpedo-planes took off once more, fifteen of them this time, four from 810 Squadron, four from 818, seven from 820; all led by 818's CO, Lieutenant Commander Trevenon 'Tim' Coode, with Stewart-Moore as his second-in-command. They were ordered to locate *Sheffield*, now in contact with *Bismarck*, and learn their target's exact position from her; their torpedoes had been fitted with the older but more reliable contact pistols. While they were on their way, at 2000, *Ark Royal* passed within point-blank range of an enemy submarine – but *U-556* had expended all her torpedoes in the course of her patrol. One more narrow escape to add to *Ark Royal*'s lengthy list – yet in fact even her destruction would not have altered *Bismarck*'s fate. That was sealed at 2035, when her Swordfish encountered *Sheffield* and learned that their enemy was 12 miles dead ahead. Less than 20 minutes later, Lütjens signalled to Naval Group West in Paris, under whose operational control he had now come: 'Am being attacked by carrier-borne aircraft.'

Lieutenant Commander Coode had divided his formation into five sub-flights of three aircraft each. His intention was that these should attack in quick succession from different directions, thereby splitting *Bismarck*'s fire and making it more difficult for her to escape all the torpedoes. Unfortunately, above the battleship was a wall of thick cloud in which the sub-flights lost contact with each other and were forced to go in separately.

All the attackers met vicious anti-aircraft fire but, surprisingly, only the one flown by Sub-Lieutenant Alan Swanton was seriously damaged, both he and his gunner being wounded; it returned safely with all the others. Not that their ordeal was over even then: landing on *Ark Royal*'s plunging, spray-soaked flight deck was perilous in the extreme. One Swordfish made seven circuits before touching down successfully; three were wrecked, though their crews were unhurt; and Swanton made what he called 'a bit of a controlled crash', his machine being rated as damaged beyond repair.

Exhausted both mentally and physically, the crews were far from clear as to what they had achieved and *Bismarck*'s survivors, to judge from their later accounts, were even more confused. For instance, her senior survivor, Lieutenant Burkard von Müllenheim-Rechberg, would declare that *Bismarck* was hit three times – twice forward and then a third hit aft when the attack was almost over – whereas signals by

Lütjens to Group West at the time of the attack report only two hits: the hit aft at 2105 and a hit amidships, not earlier but later, at 2115.

This last hit was almost certainly scored by the Swordfish piloted by Sub-Lieutenant Tony Beale. He made one of the final attacks because he had lost touch with the rest of his sub-flight in the clouds and had had to return to *Sheffield* for fresh directions. As he retired from it, both his observer and his gunner saw a column of water rise up on *Bismarck*'s port side amidships. They called out the news to the pilot who, by turning his machine quickly, was just in time to see this as well, as did one of the Swordfish 'shadowers'. Sadly, the torpedo struck *Bismarck*'s armoured belt and caused little damage. ·

It was the hit aft that was the crucial one. It tore a huge hole through which the sea poured into the steering-control rooms. Worse still, the impact jammed both *Bismarck*'s rudders hard to port. Unable to steer, she made two complete circles; then at a speed of only 8 knots she began to move north-westward – away from the safety of France.

Inevitably, as in the case of *Pola*, there has been much discussion as to who should receive the credit for this achievement. A Swordfish piloted by Lieutenant Stanley Keane reported a possible hit on *Bismarck*'s port side. If this was correct, the hit could have been made by Keane himself, but more probably by Sub-Lieutenant John Moffat who had attacked immediately before him. However, Keane described it as being 'about two-thirds of the way down from the bows'. *Bismarck* was 814 feet long, so a hit some 270 feet from her stern could not possibly have flooded her steering compartments or wrecked her rudders. Also Moffat has stated that *Bismarck* was 'turning away from my attack, rather than towards it'. In that case she was turning to starboard, yet the one point on which all the *Bismarck* survivors, and also the shadowing Swordfish, agree is that when the fatal blow was struck she was turning to port.

Finally in *Killing the Bismarck*, Iain Ballantyne reveals that the battleship's wreck has been located, and photographs taken by remotely controlled underwater vehicles have revealed a gaping hole at her stern on the starboard side, not the port. We have the testimony of Lieutenant Alan Owensmith (not Owen-Smith as it is usually and understandably recorded) that he saw 'a large column of water rise up on *Bismarck*'s starboard side right aft' just after two other Swordfish, flown by Lieutenant David Godfrey-Faussett and Sub-Lieutenant Ken Pattisson had attacked from starboard. *Bismarck* was then 'swinging round to port'. Pattisson's observer also reported this torpedo hit. It would seem therefore that the fatal attack was made by either Godfrey-Faussett or Pattisson, perhaps more probably the latter.[5]

In reality, though, as in the case of the *Pola*, it matters little. All *Ark Royal's* pilots were equally brave and determined if not equally successful. And between them they had won the conflict with the most powerful battleship then in service. All attempts to steer her by propellers alone failed; always the jammed rudders swung her back relentlessly onto a course that would lead her into the jaws of her pursuers. An immediate award of the Iron Cross was offered to any man who could free the rudders but in those high seas, the water, surging backwards and forwards in the flooded compartments, made it impossible to enter them. It was suggested that explosive charges might be employed but even if they could be placed in the right position, they would probably smash the propellers, so making the ship still more helpless. At 2140, Lütjens signalled once more to Group West: 'Ship unmanoeuvrable. We shall fight to the last shell. Long live the Führer.'

The remainder of the drama may be recounted quickly. Harried throughout the night by British destroyers, the crippled battleship was engaged next morning by *King George V*, *Rodney* and heavy cruisers *Norfolk* and *Dorsetshire*, and battered to a floating wreck, dead in the water, on fire from end to end and already desperately low in the water from flooding before she was mercifully finished off by scuttling charges. On the sufferings of her crew it is preferable not to dwell. The British ships rescued four officers and 106 men before reports of submarines in the vicinity caused them to withdraw. A U-boat saved three more men later and a German weather ship another two.

Despite the overwhelming odds against her, *Bismarck* did, as promised, fight until every one of her guns had been put out of action, and her flag was still flying when she capsized to port and sank. She was indeed a worthy final representative of an era – the era when the great battleship was 'Queen of the Seas' – a title now moving inexorably to the aircraft carrier.

Not that some sceptics were convinced even now. The hit that wrecked *Bismarck's* rudder would be dismissed as 'one in a hundred thousand', though a similar fate had all but overtaken *Vittorio Veneto* and would overtake *Prince of Wales* before the year was out. In the programme for an American inter-service war game of 29 November 1941, it was confidently related that 'despite the claims of air enthusiasts no battleship has yet been sunk by bombs'. The comment was illustrated by an impressive bow-on view of USS *Arizona*. Winston Churchill also seems to have been among the die-hards. On the day after *Bismarck*'s sinking, he reported gleefully to President Roosevelt that her destruction would have a 'highly beneficial' effect on the Japanese: 'I expect they are doing all their sums again.' He was probably right, but among Japanese calculations was surely one that surmised that if a single carrier equipped with obsolete biplanes could cripple the finest warship afloat, what might not be achieved by an entire task force of carriers equipped with the finest naval aircraft in the world?

For this was the situation the Japanese then enjoyed. Since their termination of the naval limitation treaties, they had built as many carriers as possible, and even before that termination, they had disregarded the limitations imposed. Following the conversion to carriers of *Akagi* and *Kaga*, already mentioned, the Japanese had begun work on two smaller carriers, *Soryu* and *Hiryu*. These were supposedly of 15,900 tons but in practice the former whose name means 'Blue Dragon' – the star constellation that the Western nations know as the Great Bear – was of 18,800 tonnage, while the splendidly named *Hiryu* – the 'Flying Dragon' – weighed in at 20,250 tons.

It might be mentioned that *Hiryu*, like *Akagi* before her, was unusual in that she had her island superstructure on the port side, though standard practice required it to be on the starboard side because experience showed that most pilots turned to port after take-off or in an emergency. This seems to have been good advice since on *Akagi* and *Hiryu* the number of serious accidents was double that of the usual rate and accordingly the port island was not repeated on later carriers. The reason for its adoption was to enable carriers with port and starboard islands to operate in close company without their aircraft causing too much interference or congestion; those of the former flying right-hand circuits and those of the latter left-hand circuits. The Japanese, in short, were already planning to use a number of carriers in one formation.

Before December 1941, this formation, the First Air Fleet, had been joined by Japan's finest carriers, *Shokaku* and *Zuikaku*, with a standard displacement of 25,675 tons, a speed of 34 knots, a strengthened flight deck, considerable armoured protection elsewhere, and the ability to operate seventy-three aircraft. Two other carriers, *Junyo* and *Hiyo*, were in the process of conversion from liners and would join the Imperial Navy in May and July 1942 respectively, while others were in the course of construction. Japan was also producing light carriers that could either provide fighter protection for non-carrier forces or support their larger sisters as circumstances decreed. These had their bridge on a low forecastle situated under and projecting beyond the flight deck, thus presenting the same 'Flat Iron' appearance as the old *Argus*. The first of them, *Ryujo*, was built between the wars, while two others, *Zuiho* and *Shoho*, would be converted from fast tankers by the end of 1940 and 1941 respectively.

By the end of 1941 also, all the larger Japanese carriers had been equipped with warplanes of superb quality. So effective were they that an officer as experienced as Somerville would declare that the Japanese attacks on Ceylon could not have been carried out with 'normal carrier aircraft'. He was unable to believe that the Val dive-bombers, Kate torpedo-planes and Zero fighters[6] were standard issue for the Japanese Naval Air Force.

Both the Aichi Val and the Nakajima Kate were of all-metal construction; the former being a two-seater, the latter carrying a crew of three. The Kate had a fully retractable undercarriage but in the Val, although it was produced two years later, this was fixed. Even so, it had a top speed of 267 mph, was highly manoeuvrable and could dive at a very steep angle without losing any of its stability; it could therefore deliver its 550-lb bomb with an exceptionally high rate of accuracy. The Kate's top speed was 235 mph, it could be used as a high-level as well as a torpedo-bomber and although, despite numerous accounts to the contrary, it could not carry the deadly 24-inch 'Long Lance' torpedo used by Japan's cruisers and destroyers, its 17.7-inch weapon was still more powerful than those used by the Allies and could be dropped at much higher speed from a greater, and therefore safer, height and range.

The Mitsubishi Zero was the last of the three types to reach the Japanese fleet carriers; indeed, on Japan's light carriers, Zeros would only begin to replace the older Claude naval fighters in March 1942. It was constructed of a special light alloy that gave it a speed of 335 mph – 60 mph faster than the Claude – an exceptionally long range, a high rate of climb and extreme manoeuvrability, especially at low speeds. As well as the two 7.7mm machine guns carried by the Claude, the Zero also mounted two 20mm cannon. Its only real disadvantage was that its lack of armour plate meant it could not sustain serious battle-damage; this would often literally tear it apart – though of course to hit such a small, agile aeroplane in the first place was by no means an easy accomplishment.

A war with Britain and the United States in late 1941 would therefore give Japan powerful initial advantages, and unhappily by that time war had become a virtual certainty. On 7 July 1937, fighting broke out between Chinese and Japanese troops on manoeuvres near Peking. This action had not been planned by the Japanese but it, and the massacre of over 200 Japanese civilians by Chinese militia at Tungchow on 2 August, gave the military extremists the justification they wanted. They embarked on a full-scale invasion of China, during which the cruelties at Tungchow were repaid with interest.

By late 1938, the Japanese had forced the Chinese leader, Chiang Kai-shek, to retire up the Yangtse River to Chunking. Yet he still refused to come to terms, being sustained by mounting aid, both military and financial, from Britain and the United States. So to put further pressure on him and his allies, the Japanese persuaded the Vichy French authorities to allow their troops to be stationed first in August 1940 in northern French Indo-China, then on 24 July 1941 in southern Indo-China as well.

On his part, from July 1940 onwards, President Roosevelt attempted to put pressure on Japan by forbidding the export to her of a steadily increasing number of strategic materials: first aviation fuel, lubricating oil and high-grade scrap; later, air frames, aero-engines, steel, copper and brass. Finally on 26 July 1941, he ordered the freezing of all Japanese assets in the United States, some £33,000,000 in value. Britain and the Netherlands government in exile followed suit.

This action meant that for want of funds, Japan faced a total halt to all her essential imports, in particular oil. In the words of her Chief of Naval Staff, Admiral Osami Nagano, she was 'like a fish in a pond from which the water is gradually being drained away'. In order to receive her vital raw materials in future, she would either have to submit to the orders of the United States or go to war and take these by force.

Since obeying the United States would entail abandoning the war in China, thereby suffering an immense loss of 'face', Japan's military chiefs would not consider it. Nor did it much concern them that the alternative was opposed by their country's moderate politicians, her commercial leaders, the Naval Commander-in-Chief, Admiral Isoroku Yamamoto, the Premier, Prince Fumimaro Konoye and the Emperor. Important conferences were always held in the Emperor's presence but the Japanese constitution and the advice of his counsellors combined to ensure that he invariably remained silent, so that he could not become embroiled in any controversial issues; his acceptance of the decisions reached was purely formal, like the signature of the British monarch to Acts of Parliament. Yet at an Imperial Conference on 6 September 1941, Emperor Hirohito – his name incidentally is pronounced 'Hiroshto' – did address his ministers, reciting a poem by his grandfather, Emperor Meiji:

'The four seas are brothers to one another.
Why then do the waves seethe and the winds rage?'

Cryptic though this utterance was, it was rightly understood by all present to be a plea to preserve the peace. It was therefore tactfully omitted from the Army records of the proceedings.[7]

On 16 October Prince Konoye resigned, to be succeeded by the Army's representative, General Hideki Tojo, who was not nicknamed 'The Razor' for nothing. On 26 November, Roosevelt refused to lift the embargoes in return for a Japanese promise to evacuate southern Indo-China forthwith and northern Indo-China once peace had been concluded with Chiang. Instead he declared that only a total Japanese withdrawal from China would be acceptable. That night Japan's six largest carriers left their anchorage at Tankan Bay in the Kurile Islands north-east of Japan on a mission of destruction.

The Pearl Harbour raid had been planned by Admiral Yamamoto, who believed that before commencing Japan's southward advance, it was essential to neutralize the American Pacific Fleet in Hawaii, and whose energetic and forceful personality, backed by the threat of resignation, had finally won the reluctant approval of the Naval General Staff. The operation was entrusted to Vice Admiral Chuichi Nagumo, whose six 'flat-tops' could boast 423 modern warplanes and an escort of battleships *Hiei* and *Kirishima*, heavy cruisers *Tone* and *Chikuma*, light cruiser *Abukuma* and nine destroyers, plus three submarines as long-range scouts and eight tankers to refuel them at sea.

By 2100 on 6 December, Nagumo had reached a point 490 miles north of the island of Oahu, which has Pearl Harbour on its southern coast. Here his flagship *Akagi* hoisted the battle-flag once flown by Admiral Togo before Japan's great victory over the Russians in 1905 at the Battle of Tsushima. Then, as night closed in, his carriers sped south at 26 knots so as to reach their planned launching position 275 miles north of Pearl Harbour on the following morning.

At 0600 on 7 December, Nagumo's force turned into the wind and the first strike wave began to leave the decks of the six carriers: forty Kates armed with torpedoes; forty-nine Kates carrying bombs converted from 16-inch naval shells; fifty-one Val dive-bombers; forty-three Zero fighters. They were led by Commander Mitsuo Fuchida, flying as observer in a high-level Kate marked with a distinctive red and yellow striped tail and wearing round his helmet a white scarf presented by *Akagi*'s maintenance crewmen. They reached Oahu's north coast at 0735 and shortly thereafter the clouds cleared away, leaving the island bathed in bright sunshine. As Pearl Harbour came into view, not one American fighter rose to intercept the raiders; not one anti-aircraft gun opened fire on them. At 0749, Fuchida ordered his men into action. At 0753, before they could even comply, he radioed to Nagumo the signal 'Tora, Tora, Tora!' (Tiger, Tiger, Tiger), indicating that complete surprise had been achieved.

It could easily have been otherwise. The Japanese had decided to keep within the letter, though scarcely the spirit, of international law by serving what amounted to a declaration of war – and was accepted as such by both Roosevelt and the Chief of the General Staff, General George Marshall – just before hostilities commenced. The inefficiency of their embassy staff in Washington in fact prevented it from being delivered in time, but the Americans had broken the Japanese diplomatic code and by the early hours of 7 December, they knew that this ultimatum was to be delivered at 1300 Washington time. It was pointed out that this would be dawn in Hawaii, and Marshall, who did not believe it was a coincidence, sent a message to the commanders at Pearl Harbour warning them to 'be on the alert accordingly'. American inefficiency ensured that this would not be delivered in time either.

Even without it, Pearl Harbour had two other chances of mitigating disaster. The Japanese had unwisely decided to support their air attack with a raid by five midget submarines. Early on 7 December, one of them was sunk by an American destroyer and another was attacked and possibly sunk by a patrolling Catalina. Unhappily, their reports were delayed and when received were treated sceptically: there had been so many 'false alarms'. And finally Fuchida's squadrons were detected by radar operators on Oahu but their message was disregarded since it was believed the sighting was of a dozen Flying Fortresses, due to arrive that morning from the mainland.

So it was into the quiet calm of a peacetime Sunday morning that Fuchida's warriors burst to hurl the United States into the Second World War. It had been intended that Lieutenant Commander Shigeharu Murata's torpedo-planes should attack first but, as a result of a misunderstood signal, the eager Lieutenant Commander Kakwichi Takahashi thought his dive-bombers had been detailed for this task. At 0755, his Vals, accompanied by strafing Zeros, began attacking the American aerodromes where the aircraft, lined up together in the centre of the field to prevent sabotage, made easy targets. In all, 188 of them were destroyed, 159 damaged.

Other dive-bombers joined with Murata's Kates in attacking the American warships, the primary targets being the Pacific Fleet's majestic battleships. Seven of these were moored off the south-east shore of Ford Island. Another, *Pennsylvania*, was in a dry dock in the Navy Yard that lay south of 'Battleship Row' and across the harbour from the island. Also present was *Utah*, formerly a battleship but now demoted to the role of target-ship; she was one of a much smaller number of vessels moored off the north-west shore of Ford Island.

Not that this saved them from attention. At the very start of the raid, five torpedo-bombers hurtled towards them to give a graphic illustration of the ruthless efficiency of Japan's naval airmen. One torpedo narrowly missed light cruiser *Detroit*. Another badly damaged light cruiser *Raleigh*. Two more hit *Utah* that heeled over and sank. The fifth Kate flew on over Ford Island to the Navy Yard before it released its weapon. This badly damaged light cruiser *Helena* and the shock wave also stove in the side of nearby minelayer *Oglala* which capsized.

On the other side of Ford Island, far greater harm was being inflicted. At the north-eastern end of 'Battleship Row', the machine-gunners on *Nevada* were in action with admirable promptness, shooting down three Kates, but at least one had already released its torpedo and this struck *Nevada* near the bow. At about the same time, two bomb hits caused further damage. *Arizona*, the next battleship in the line, was protected from torpedoes by repair-ship *Vestal* moored alongside her and she also received just one torpedo hit near the bow. But the Val dive-bombers attacked her in strength, scoring half-a-dozen hits that inflicted heavy casualties. Two of the bombs that missed *Arizona* hit *Vestal* instead, one of them tearing right through her before it exploded. She was later able to get under way, but had to be beached to stop her sinking.

Beyond *Arizona* were two pairs of battleships: first *Tennessee* and *West Virginia*; then *Maryland* and *Oklahoma*. *Tennessee* and *Maryland*, moored nearest to Ford Island, were protected by the outboard vessels and not harmed at this stage, but *West Virginia* took six torpedoes and two bombs, and *Oklahoma* three torpedoes. Both began to list but, curiously, *Oklahoma* was the more seriously hurt. Her port side ripped open, she was already heeling over when two more torpedoes completed her ruin. She continued to roll until she turned turtle, her superstructure resting on the mud of the harbour. Prompt counter-flooding saved *West Virginia* from the same fate and she sank slowly on a more or less even keel. At the south-western end of 'Battleship Row' came *California*. She was hit by two torpedoes that caused widespread flooding, and a dangerous list that again was only corrected by counter-flooding.

California was the last vessel to take a torpedo – at 0805, so swift had been the Japanese onslaught. But even as the torpedo-carrying Kates pulled away, the Kates armed with the converted 16-inch shells came in to drop these equally lethal weapons. Almost the first to fall brought about the most spectacular incident of the raid as a huge red cloud of flame and smoke billowed 500 feet into the air. The bomb had smashed through *Arizona*'s forecastle and detonated her forward magazine. The explosion blasted men overboard, not only from *Arizona* but from *Nevada*, *Vestal* and *West Virginia* and shook Japanese aircraft far overhead.

Elsewhere the Kates scored two hits and two very near misses on *Maryland*, two hits on *Tennessee* and two on *California*, one of which set off a magazine containing anti-aircraft ammunition. The fires that were started were eventually brought under control but *California*'s cumulative damage was too great. Like *West Virginia* before her, she slowly settled onto the seabed.

By about 0825, the first attack was over and most of the raiders were returning to their carriers. Five Kates, a solitary Val and three Zeros had been shot down. Fuchida remained behind to control the second wave of attackers, led by Lieutenant Commander Shigekazu Shimazaki, when this appeared at 0840. It contained no torpedo-planes, considered too vulnerable now the defences were alerted; but fifty-four high-level Kates, eighty Vals and thirty-six Zeros made a formidable proposition. They were directed primarily at the Navy Yard but many of them were diverted at the last moment towards a more tempting target.

In the brief lull between attacks, battleship *Nevada* had managed to get underway. Chief Boatswain Edwin Hill jumped onto the quay to which she was moored, cast off the lines, and then swam back to rejoin his ship as she was moving. Despite having no assistance from tugs, of which four were normally required, *Nevada* was able to make for the open sea. As she reached the narrowest part of the channel between Ford Island and the Navy Yard, however, the dive-bombers concentrated on her, hitting her at least twice and covering her with a curtain of spray from near misses. An attempt was made to anchor her on the south side of the channel but just as this was about to be done, another group of dive-bombers came in, scoring three hits near the bow, killing, among others, Chief Boatswain Hill, and so damaging her that she had to beach. She was later towed across to Ford Island but her flooding could not be contained and she too slowly settled.

Now the Japanese turned their attention to the only undamaged battleship, *Pennsylvania*, resting helplessly in dry dock. Her luck held, for only one bomb hit her, but other ships were less fortunate. Destroyers *Cassin* and *Downes* that shared the dry dock with *Pennsylvania* were both ravaged by fire and were wrecked beyond repair. In the floating dry dock, the forward magazine of destroyer *Shaw* exploded, blasting off her bows, though, amazingly, she was repaired later. A bomb falling between ship and quay badly damaged light cruiser *Honolulu*. Other raiders attacked the vessels to the north-west of Ford Island. They put up a resolute defence and shot down at least five Vals but one of these crashed into seaplane tender *Curtiss*, and both *Curtiss* and light cruiser *Raleigh* were also hit by bombs.

By 0930, the assault on Pearl Harbour was over. The second wave of attackers, though opposed by far heavier anti-aircraft fire and two gallant fighter pilots, Army Lieutenants Welch and Taylor who had taken off from a small undetected airstrip to down five enemy warplanes, lost only fourteen Vals and six Zeros. The American casualties in men as well as in ships were immense. There were 1,103 fatalities in *Arizona* alone, including Rear Admiral Kidd and Captain Van Valkenburg; 415 in *Oklahoma*; 105 in *West Virginia* including Captain Bennion; 98 in *California*; 50 in *Nevada*.

Commander Fuchida, after making a final check of the damage inflicted, finally left the scene at about 1100, accompanied by a couple of Zeros that had lost touch with their own squadrons. His pilot, Lieutenant Mutsuzaki, touched down on *Akagi* at 1300. By that time, the aircraft of the first wave had been rearmed and refuelled and Fuchida urged that another attack be delivered, declaring there were still plenty of targets available: the docks, power plants, repair shops and oil tanks without which Pearl Harbour could not continue as a base. To his great disappointment, though, Vice Admiral Nagumo, never enthusiastic about the operation, was not prepared to risk tempting fate any further and instead ordered an immediate withdrawal.

In fairness to Nagumo, the raid had already achieved its immediate short-term objective. Although *West Virginia*, *California* and *Nevada* were all later salvaged, Japan had secured a temporary command of the seas that became total on 10 December, when the British battleship *Prince of Wales* and battle-cruiser *Repulse*, attempting to intercept invasion convoys heading for Malaya, were sunk by land-based aircraft. During the next six months, the Japanese capitalized on their advantage by overrunning Malaya, Singapore, Hong Kong, Borneo, Sumatra, Java, New Britain, New Ireland, the American islands of Guam and Wake, Burma and the Philippines at an almost ridiculously low cost.

Throughout this period, the spearheads of Japan's assaults, the very symbols of her triumphs, were her aircraft carriers. The light carriers supported landings in the Philippines, Malaya and the East Indies but their finest achievement came on 6 April 1942, when *Ryujo*, accompanied by a squadron of heavy cruisers, fell on unescorted merchantmen in the Bay of Bengal, sinking eighteen of them totalling 93,000 tons and paralyzing sea traffic in the area until the end of the month. *Ryujo*'s airmen were responsible for two-thirds of the tonnage destroyed.

Japan's larger carriers, naturally, were still more successful. *Soryu* and *Hiryu* were detached from Nagumo's force to go to Wake Island, the defenders of which, on 11 December 1941, had thrown back an attempted landing and sunk two Japanese destroyers. They began their preliminary strikes on 21 December. Two days later, Wake Island was in Japanese hands.

Nagumo's carriers, in various combinations, were again in action in 1942. They raided New Britain, New Ireland and Amboina in January. On 19 February, they attacked Port Darwin in northern Australia, sinking US destroyer *Peary* and eight merchant ships, damaging ten other vessels and thoroughly wrecking the town. On 4/5 March, they turned their attention to the port of Tjilatjap in southern Java, all but destroying it and sinking or crippling the twenty-three merchantmen present.

April 1942 found Nagumo steering westward into the Indian Ocean, preparing to strike at Ceylon. Of his original Pearl Harbour Force, *Kaga* had retired to Japan with engine-trouble but he had gained two more battleships, *Kongo* and *Haruna* and two more destroyers. It seemed that his move might lead to history's first clash between carrier task forces because the British Eastern Fleet under Vice Admiral Somerville included *Formidable*, her sister-ship *Indomitable* and the small, elderly *Hermes*. Unfortunately, Somerville had been advised by the code-breakers that the Japanese would make their appearance on 1 April, and when by the following evening they had not done so, he retired to Addu Atoll, a secret base in the Maldive Islands 660 miles to the south-west, where his ships could take on fuel and fresh water. Accordingly, when at 1600 on 4 April, a Catalina reported Nagumo's force 350 miles south-south-east of Ceylon, there was nothing that the Eastern Fleet could do to help.

At 0740 on 5 April, the indefatigable Commander Fuchida appeared over Ceylon's great port of Colombo at the head of thirty-six Val dive-bombers, fifty-three Kate high-level bombers and thirty-six Zeros. Radar had failed to give any warning of his approach and although the thirty-six Hurricanes and six Fulmars that made up the harbour's air defence did their best to intervene, they were attacked as they climbed to engage and were most vulnerable. Seventeen Hurricanes were shot down or crash-landed, ten pilots being killed. Four Fulmars and their crews also perished. Fuchida lost six Vals and one Zero, with nine other aircraft damaged. Yet little harm was done to the shore installations, only an old First World War destroyer and a liner converted to an armed merchant cruiser were sunk, and just one of the twenty-one merchantmen in the harbour was even damaged. For the first time the Japanese were greatly disappointed by the results of a raid by their carriers – but they were soon to receive ample compensation.

It had been fortunate for the British Eastern Fleet that it had retired to Addu Atoll. Nagumo controlled 114 Vals, 128 Kates and about 100 Zeros, whereas Somerville had only forty-five Albacores, twelve Swordfish and twenty-three serviceable fighters. Moreover the difference in quality between the Japanese and the British had been horribly illustrated during the raid on Colombo. As the Japanese approached, they encountered six Swordfish from a squadron based in Ceylon. Six Zeros, led by Lieutenant Commander Shigeru Itaya, pounced on these from above, shooting them all down in a single swift attack. Among the airmen killed was Sub-Lieutenant Beale, the former *Ark Royal* pilot who had been one of those to torpedo *Bismarck*.

Indeed the main reason for regret was that not all Somerville's ships had accompanied him. *Hermes* and the Australian destroyer *Vampire* had headed for the Royal Navy's main base in Ceylon, Trincomalee, where they were to prepare for a planned operation against Vichy French Madagascar, while heavy cruisers *Dorsetshire* and *Cornwall* had been directed to Colombo to complete an interrupted refit and to be ready to escort a troop convoy respectively. This latter pair was now sighted by a Japanese reconnaissance aircraft. At 1340, all Nagumo's remaining Vals, led by Lieutenant Commander Takashige Egusa, hurtled out of the sun directly ahead of them, which meant that they could bring only a minimum of their AA guns to bear.

There followed another breathtaking example of the deadly effectiveness of Japan's naval airmen. The first three Vals to attack *Dorsetshire* all scored direct hits, one of which jammed her steering gear, forcing her to turn a complete circle, unable to manoeuvre. Then three more bombs tore into her, one of them detonating a magazine. Losing speed rapidly, listing ever more steeply to port and enveloped in flames, smoke and steam from bridge to stern, she was clearly doomed even before she was struck four more times in quick succession; after which she capsized and sank by the stern. Eight minutes had elapsed since the start of the raid.

Cornwall survived for little longer. When the assault began she immediately suffered one direct hit and two near misses and thereafter, enemy aircraft were diving on her almost continuously. She did manage to shoot down one Val in flames but was ravaged by seven more hits and shaken from end to end by innumerable near misses. Listing, burning furiously, her siren, struck by shrapnel, screaming deafeningly as if the ship was giving voice to her agony, she slowed to a halt, then sank bows first. Twenty-two minutes had elapsed since the start of the raid.

The warning was only too clear and the British Eastern Fleet ignominiously left the area. When at 1500 on 8 April, another reconnaissance Catalina sighted the Japanese task force east-south-east of Ceylon, steering at full speed straight for Trincomalee, the island's defenders were again on their own. At 0720 on 9 April, Fuchida was back with ninety-one Kates and thirty-eight Zeros. This time radar did give a warning but the sixteen Hurricanes and six Fulmars that tried to intercept were hopelessly outnumbered. Ten Hurricanes were shot down or crash-landed but mercifully only two of their pilots died. One Fulmar and its crew were lost. The Japanese lost two bombers and three Zeros; ten more Kates were damaged. They destroyed fuel tanks and an ammunition dump but again the harm inflicted was much less than they had hoped and expected – and again they were to be compensated elsewhere.

Nagumo had once more kept back Egusa's dive-bombers in case any British warships were sighted and at 0855, one of his scouts reported, some 65 miles south-east of Trincomalee, a number of vessels including a carrier. This of course was *Hermes* and as she had carried no fighters on board her, she was defended only by AA guns when, at 1035, eighty Vals escorted, it seems, by just nine Zeros, appeared overhead. She had not the remotest chance of surviving. Some forty bombs crashed into or all around her. One blew the forward lift into the air, to fall back half on the flight deck, half in the lift well. Another hit the bridge, killing Captain Richard Onslow and everyone else there. By 1050, *Hermes* was blazing from stem to stern and listing so heavily to port that the sea was washing onto her flight deck. Five minutes later, she sank, taking down with her sixteen officers and 283 men.

Next came the turn of destroyer *Vampire*. She had already been near missed three times before a bomb found a boiler-room and brought her to a halt. Another struck a locker containing potatoes that rattled about the superstructure like huge hailstones. Then three more bombs blew her bow off. Her crew abandoned her – just in time, for at 1102, a hit in the after magazine tore her to pieces. Amazingly, only eight men lost their lives, but among them was *Vampire*'s skipper, Commander Moran. Egusa's airmen also found and sank a Fleet auxiliary, a corvette and a tanker but the hospital ship *Vita* was spared and later rescued some 600 survivors from *Hermes* and *Vampire*.

By contrast, the counter-attacks by British aircraft based in Ceylon were inevitably feeble. Eight Fulmars of 806 Squadron engaged Egusa's men, though only after these had completed their work of destruction, shooting down four Vals and damaging two more for the loss of two of their own number. Nine Blenheims of No. 11 Squadron RAF attacked Nagumo's fleet at 1025, shortly before the assault on *Hermes* began. They were opposed by Zeros, two of which their gunners shot down, and five of the Blenheims were lost and all the other four damaged, one returning on a single engine. Nor was their courage rewarded, for though Japanese accounts report as many as six near misses on *Akagi*, four to starboard, two to port, these did her no harm.

Nonetheless, the near misses did carry a warning that the immunity of Nagumo's vessels might not last much longer. And while they had been operating in the East Indies and the Indian Ocean, the naval strength of their enemies had been building up in the Pacific. It was to the Pacific that the Japanese aircraft carriers now returned and there they would meet their most dangerous opponents: the aircraft carriers of the United States Navy.

Notes

1 This again was a somewhat ironical name for a vessel fighting against Britain, where the great soldier after whom she was named was known as Prince Eugene, the friend and companion-in-arms of Churchill's ancestor the Duke of Marlborough.

2 When the existence of the 'Ultra' Intelligence became common knowledge, there was a tendency to believe that this had made a decisive contribution towards *Bismarck*'s destruction. In reality, it did not, as Ronald Lewin makes clear in his *Ultra Goes to War: The Secret Story*. All signals to and from the battleship were made in a new operational cypher that Bletchley Park had not yet penetrated and signals from other sources were only decoded too late to be of value.

3 The Catalina's co-pilot was Ensign Smith of the United States Navy, there to gain operational experience. His presence was surely an unneutral act and has led to the tactful description of him, even in accounts written long after the war, as a 'passenger'.

4 It has been suggested that the pilots may have thought that *Sheffield* was *Prinz Eugen*,

but again there were several differences such as the number of funnels. *Prinz Eugen* bore a much closer resemblance to *Bismarck* than she did to *Sheffield*.

5 Further details of the various claims can be found in order of publication in: *The Bismarck Episode* by Captain Russell Grenfell; *Ark Royal 1939-1941* by Rear Admiral Sir William Jameson; *Pursuit: The Chase and Sinking of the Bismarck* by Ludovic Kennedy; *Battleship Bismarck* by Baron Burkard von Müllenheim-Rechberg; *I Sank the Bismarck* by John Moffat with Mike Rossiter; *Killing the Bismarck* by Iain Ballantyne.

6 The Allies avoided the difficulties of the complicated Japanese system of aircraft classification by giving each type an arbitary code-name: ladies' names for bombers; men's names for fighters. There was one exception in practice. Part of the Japanese system was a reference to the last two numbers of the year in which the machine had gone into production, counting from the legendary foundation of their country by the first emperor, Jimmu Tenno, in 660 BC. In the case of their most famous fighter this was the year 2600 (AD 1940) and it thus became Type 00 or Zero-Sen. Japan's enemies took up this designation and to them the aircraft was almost always called the Zero, or by RAF pilots the Navy Nought, rather than its official code-name of the Zeke.

7 It is important not to be misled by the protestations made by Army extremists both before and after the Second World War that they were passionately devoted to their sovereign. Professor Storry succinctly summarizes their real attitude: They 'were loyal to their conception of what the emperor ought to be. To the emperor as he was they were grossly disloyal – and a few of the more sophisticated among them were well aware of this fact'.

Chapter 4

The Fights of the Phantoms

As the Japanese fleet had closed in on Oahu in the late afternoon of 6 December 1941, it had received last-minute Intelligence that eight battleships were present at Pearl Harbour, but two aircraft carriers had recently left to ferry warplanes to bases further west. Commander Minoru Genda, Nagumo's brilliant young Operations Officer, was bitterly disappointed. If there had been a chance of sinking a pair of carriers, he declared, he would not have minded if none of the battleships were there. His reaction would soon prove justified: it was the aircraft carriers that would provide the means by which the Americans would gain their revenge for Pearl Harbour.

The two carriers that had escaped probable destruction at Pearl Harbour were *Lexington*, one of the original battle-cruiser conversions, and the smaller but later, faster and more modern 19,800-ton *Enterprise*. In late December, they were joined by *Enterprise*'s slightly older sister-ship *Yorktown* and in February and March 1942, one or more of these vessels attacked a number of Japanese or Japanese-occupied islands or bases with varying degrees of success.

For these raids the Americans employed two main types of strike aircraft. Their torpedo-plane, the miserably misnamed Douglas Devastator, had a top speed of only 206 mph, a poor range and insufficient armour protection; it was further handicapped by carrying a slow-running and frequently unreliable torpedo. The Douglas Dauntless dive-bomber, by contrast, was a worthy match for the Val and like it, was a single-engined two-seater that was highly manoeuvrable and extremely stable when diving, thereby ensuring accurate bombing. At a top speed of 275 mph it was slightly faster than the Val and it was also more rugged.

Equally rugged was the Americans' naval fighter, the Grumman Wildcat, and with a top speed of 330 mph and armament of four – later six – 0.5-inch machine guns, it quickly proved deadly against enemy bombers. On 1 February, seven land-based Betty bombers attacking *Enterprise* were all destroyed by her flak or fighters; her only damage being caused when a crippled aircraft made a suicide dive[1] but luckily only struck her flight deck a glancing blow before plunging into the sea. On 20 February, *Lexington*'s Lieutenant Edward 'Butch' O'Hare earned the first Congressional Medal of Honour awarded to a fighter pilot in the Second World War by engaging a formation of Bettys single-handed and shooting down five of them. The Wildcat was less effective in combats with the Zero, having a shorter range, a slower rate of climb and less manoeuvrability. It was, however, a very sturdy aeroplane that, unlike the Zero, could withstand a great deal of punishment.

The last, most famous of these early American carrier operations came on 18 April. It was delivered by different aircraft: sixteen twin-engined Mitchell bombers led by Lieutenant Colonel James Doolittle. They took off from a different carrier: the 20,000-ton *Hornet*, designed as a sister-ship of *Yorktown* and *Enterprise* but later extensively modified; and they attacked different targets: four cities in the Japanese homeland including Tokyo – after which they had to fly on to crash-land in China. Though rightly praised for its effect on American morale and its illustration of American courage and resourcefulness, its chief effect was to deprive the US Navy of *Hornet*, and of *Enterprise* that had formed part of her escort, at the crucial Battle of the Coral Sea. The material harm inflicted was slight and few of Tokyo's inhabitants knew that the capital had been bombed. Nor, contrary to oft-repeated claims, did it prompt the Japanese to adopt a calamitous course of action, because the plans for this had already been agreed.

It had never been the Japanese hope that they could conquer the United States, but they had believed that by a resolute defence of their newly captured territories they could persuade the United States to agree to a compromise peace that would leave many of these in their hands. American fury at the 'sneak attack' on Pearl Harbour had made it horribly clear that this was most unlikely and during March 1942, both Yamamoto's Combined Fleet and the Naval General Staff were desperately seeking a dramatic new move that might yet achieve their aim. Assaults on Hawaii, Ceylon and Australia were all rejected as impracticable but Captain Sadatoshi Tomioka, head of the General Staff's Planning Division, had raised a further intriguing possibility.

This was a major advance into the south-west Pacific. Japan was already occupying bases in the northern Solomons but Tomioka wished her to continue first to Tulagi in the southern Solomons, later to Fiji, Samoa and Free French New Caledonia. This would sever the American supply routes to Australia, making it very difficult to build up that country into a major base from which future Allied offensives could be mounted. In addition, Tomioka desired to capture Port Moresby on the southern coast of New Guinea, thereby depriving the Allies of a present base for their bombers and a future base for their land forces.

These moves, if successful, would not only greatly strengthen Japan's defensive perimeter in the area but, as Tomioka pointed out, would also isolate Australia, while Port Moresby would provide an ideal springboard for air attacks against her northern territories. There was thus just the possibility that the threat to Australia would appear so great that Britain and the United States might be tempted to discuss terms in order to protect her. Tomioka's plan won the support of both his superiors and the Japanese Army, so it was with some indignation that the Naval General Staff learned at the end of March that Admiral Yamamoto wished to adopt an alternative course of action.

Yamamoto's proposal was that his Combined Fleet should assault Midway Island, 1,100 miles north-west of Pearl Harbour, coupled with a diversionary operation to seize bases in the western Aleutian Islands. This he believed would force the US carriers to give battle and enable him to destroy them. As a conciliatory gesture to the Naval General Staff, he agreed that the capture of Port Moresby and Tulagi might be attempted before the move towards Midway but the capture of Fiji, Samoa and New Caledonia only after it.

Yamamoto's desire to sink the crucial US carriers has naturally been approved by American historians, but it has never been explained why it was so essential that the carriers be destroyed in the vicinity of Midway Island when this could equally well have been done elsewhere – in the waters north of Australia, for example. And it seemed far more logical that the Americans would risk everything to aid Australia, to which they were already sending land and air forces, than to protect Midway, the loss of which would have nothing like such severe consequences and which even if it was lost would be so remote from other Japanese-held islands that they could only supply and defend it at a ruinously high cost.

It would also suit the Japanese far more to try to fight their decisive engagement in the south-west Pacific. Here the supply lines of both sides would be equally long, whereas Midway was distant from Japan but dangerously close to Hawaii. Here the Japanese could receive the assistance of land-based aircraft from a whole number of airfields, whereas in an action off Midway only the Americans could be so supported. In short, Yamamoto's plan involved greater risks than did the threat to Australia and for the sake of a less important objective that was therefore less likely to provoke the major fleet action that he desired.

These arguments are not made merely in the light of after-knowledge. They are the ones put forward by the Naval General Staff at a conference in Tokyo on 2 April. They even won the support of some of Yamamoto's own subordinates, notably Vice Admiral Nobutake Kondo, who would take overall command of the Midway invasion force and Vice Admiral Shigeyoshi Inouye, who would be responsible for keeping Midway supplied if it were captured. Yet Yamamoto still insisted on his Midway project and by sheer force of personality and threat of resignation, he finally gained a reluctant acceptance. It almost seems that realizing the Pearl Harbour operation, for which he bore almost the sole responsibility, had been a moral and strategic disaster, he was desperate, consciously or unconsciously, to reverse its effects in the same theatre of operations.

Meanwhile on 4 May, under the overall command of Vice Admiral Inouye at Rabaul, New Britain, a number of Japanese formations moved into the Coral Sea, north-east of Australia, to initiate their southward thrust. There was a small transport group under orders to capture Tulagi and a larger one detailed to take Port Moresby. Both were under the protection of the Close Support Force of Rear Admiral Aritomo Goto, consisting of four heavy cruisers, a solitary destroyer and light carrier *Shoho* with fourteen Zeros and six Kates on board.

Finally, to provide long-range cover and to engage any US warships that might attempt to intervene, there was the Striking Force of Vice Admiral Takeo Takagi, who flew his flag in heavy cruiser *Myoko*. Heavy cruiser *Haguro* and six destroyers were also present to guard carriers *Shokaku* and *Zuikaku*. On board the former were nineteen Kates, twenty-one Vals and eighteen Zeros; *Zuikaku*, flagship of Rear Admiral Chuichi Hara, carried twenty-one Kates, twenty-two Vals and twenty Zeros.

Having broken the Japanese codes, the Americans were well informed of the enemy's intentions and, as Japan's Naval General Staff had anticipated, concentrated all available forces to thwart these. In late April, the only American Task Force in the Coral Sea had been carrier *Yorktown*, flagship of Rear Admiral Frank Jack Fletcher, which controlled thirty-eight Dauntlesses, thirteen Devastators and twenty Wildcats, escorted by three heavy cruisers and six destroyers. On 1 May, however, Fletcher was joined by Rear Admiral Aubrey Fitch in command of carrier *Lexington*, with thirty-six Dauntlesses, twelve Devastators and twenty-two Wildcats on board, two heavy cruisers and five destroyers, and by Rear Admiral John Crace, a Royal Navy officer, commanding a combined American-Australian force of two heavy cruisers, one light cruiser and two destroyers.

The scene was set for the Battle of the Coral Sea, the first naval engagement in which only one class of warship was of major importance, 'The fleets', declares Captain Andrieu d'Albas in *Death of a Navy: Japanese Sea-Power in the Second World War*, 'appeared to each other only as phantoms.' Not a single surface vessel of either fleet sighted a single surface vessel of the other fleet. The whole conflict was fought out by their carrier-aircraft, locating and then striking at an enemy often hundreds of miles distant.

In these circumstances, the battle was inevitably one of harsh trial and tragic error, redeemed by the courage with which it was fought by the young American and Japanese airmen. The preliminaries to it began at 0800 on 3 May, when Rear Admiral Kiyohide Shima's transport group, covered by fighters from *Shoho*, landed on Tulagi – without resistance, for the small garrison there had prudently been withdrawn. When this was reported by an American reconnaissance aircraft that afternoon, the *Lexington* Task Force was refuelling but Fletcher sped northwards with *Yorktown*, intending to strike at Shima early next day.

Starting at about 0630 on 4 May, Fletcher in fact launched three strikes during the morning and early afternoon. A 1,000-lb bomb, making a very near miss on one of Shima's two destroyers, *Kikutsuki*, blew open her starboard engine-room; she sank later. Three minesweepers were also sunk, five flying-boats destroyed at their moorings, and Shima's other destroyer, *Yuzuki*, was strafed by Wildcats with the loss of ten men killed and twenty wounded. Two of the Wildcats were so damaged by her AA fire that they had to 'ditch', though their pilots were later rescued. One Devastator and its crew of three were lost.

At 0816 on 5 May, *Yorktown* and *Lexington* were reunited and for two days of mounting tension they cruised backwards and forwards, sending out scouts to look for their elusive enemy but without success. Allied land-based aircraft did sight both the Port Moresby Invasion Force and Goto's Close Support Force, and at 1030 on 6 May, four Flying Fortresses made an ineffective attack on *Shoho* that they rather insultingly identified as a light cruiser. The big Japanese carriers, however, remained invisible and they for their part were strangely unadventurous; not sending out a single reconnaissance machine but relying on long-range Mavis flying-boats based at Rabaul. One of these did locate Fletcher on the morning of the 5th, but was shot down in flames by a Wildcat before it could make its report. Another spotted one of the American carriers next morning, but problems in transmission meant that its report only reached Takagi's Striking Force on the following day.

Consequently when dawn broke on Thursday, 7 May 1942, both Fletcher and Takagi – or perhaps one should say both Fletcher and Hara, to whom his superior had delegated responsibility for air operations – were aware that hostile warships were dangerously close but knew neither their position nor their strength. In view of the distances involved, only aerial scouts could provide the answers, but Fletcher had not yet appreciated this and sent Crace's ships off in advance to search for the Port Moresby Invasion Force. He thereby deprived himself of the protection of their AA gunners, though these did some useful work later, shooting down at least four of the Japanese land-based aircraft that attacked them.

These attacks were inspired by a Japanese seaplane that reported Crace's two heavy cruisers as battleships; only one of a number of incorrect identifications that would have been amusing if they had not had such dreadful consequences. The first of them came at 0736. Rear Admiral Hara had at last decided to use some of his Kates on reconnaissance and one now reported a carrier and a light cruiser some 200 miles to the south. Hara was understandably pleased – so much so that it never occurred to him that any US carrier would surely have had a larger escort. At 0810, he sent twenty-four Kates, thirty-six Vals and eighteen Zeros, led by Lieutenant Commander Takahashi who had commanded the first wave of dive-bombers at Pearl Harbour, to destroy this 'carrier', which was really tanker *Neosho*, detached after refuelling Fletcher's ships, escorted by destroyer *Sims*.

Their identity was quickly realized by Takahashi when he sighted them at 0935. He directed his Kates, armed on this occasion with bombs rather than torpedoes, against them while he took his dive-bombers to search for the carrier that he felt sure must be somewhere in the vicinity. *Neosho* and *Sims* escaped the Kates' attack unharmed but their fate was only postponed. At about noon, Takahashi reappeared, determined at least to destroy the American ships that he could find.

This was quickly and ruthlessly achieved. First, four Vals dived on *Sims*. Three bombs scored hits, two of them in her engine-room. She slowed to a halt and a moment later a violent explosion tore through her and she began to sink by the stern. As she disappeared, another great explosion – of her depth charges it was reported, though it is hard to believe that these had not been rendered safe – killed most of those who had survived the bombing. Of her crew of 393, there were fourteen survivors.

Next, the Japanese turned their attention to *Neosho*. Seven direct hits plus eight very near misses left her dead in the water. One Val was fatally damaged by her anti-aircraft fire, but added to her injuries by crashing, intentionally or involuntarily, into her stern. Air trapped in her empty fuel tanks kept her afloat but with all power gone and her rudder wrecked, she drifted helplessly until the afternoon of 11 May, when an American destroyer rescued her survivors and those of *Sims* and sank her with torpedoes.

Meanwhile the Americans had also been bedevilled by false sightings. The most extreme of these came at 0815, when a Dauntless from *Yorktown* reported two carriers and four heavy cruisers 225 miles to the north-west. Not until it landed did it transpire that the pilot had made an error when encoding his message; he had intended to refer to two heavy cruisers and four destroyers – and even that was in fact a considerable exaggeration. By the time Fletcher learned of this, twenty-eight Dauntlesses, twelve Devastators and ten Wildcats from *Lexington* and twenty-five Dauntlesses, ten Devastators and eight Wildcats from *Yorktown* were already racing towards the area where the 'carriers' had been sighted.

As they set out on their mission, a report was received from a Flying Fortress of a number of warships, including a carrier, some 60 miles distant from those located by *Yorktown*'s Dauntless. As it happened, the big bomber had made the same mistake as Hara's scout: the 'carrier' was really a tanker. Fletcher, however, was naturally unaware of this, so did not recall his airmen even when the error of the *Yorktown* pilot came to light. His decision was justified at 1100, when they sighted a real carrier – *Shoho* – which they immediately attacked.

First into action were the Dauntlesses from *Lexington*. They burst past three Zeros – the only Japanese fighters airborne – but *Shoho* took such violent evasive action that all the bombs missed, though one came so close that its blast hurled overboard the Kates drawn up at the rear of her flight deck. Captain Ishinosuke Izawa had so far handled his vessel admirably, but he now made the mistake of turning her into the wind in order to fly off his remaining fighters. This made her an easy target for *Lexington*'s torpedo-planes and the first wave of *Yorktown*'s dive-bombers that arrived almost simultaneously. Two bombs struck *Shoho* in almost the exact centre of her flight deck. With flames and thick black smoke pouring from her, she began to lose speed and immediately afterwards a torpedo hit on her starboard side aft seems to have disabled her rudder, since she made no further evasive moves.

Shoho was now almost helpless as the rest of *Yorktown*'s dive-bombers, quickly joined by her ten Devastators, swept down. The three Zeros made a courageous attempt to intervene, shooting down the Dauntless piloted by Ensign Leppla, which crashed into the side of *Shoho*'s flight deck, but could not prevent eleven more bombs from hitting her, two well forward, three aft, six amidships. Six more torpedoes also hit, three on each side. She slowed to a halt, flames spreading throughout her entire length. An officer took down the portrait of the Emperor that was kept behind a silk curtain, wrapped it carefully and carried it to the flight deck. Then Izawa gave the order 'Abandon Ship'. At 1135, *Shoho* went down, leaving only a huge pall of smoke across the blue sky and a great pool of oil fouling the beautiful Coral Sea.

On the American carriers, the news was received in a triumphant call from one of *Lexington*'s squadron commanders, Lieutenant Commander Robert Dixon: 'Scratch one flat-top! Dixon to carrier, scratch one flat-top!' American jubilation was justified. Though *Shoho* was only a light carrier, her destruction promised that Japan might now start to pay a heavy price for her conquests. Moreover it left the Port

Moresby transports without fighter cover, while the number of machines that had combined to sink her showed that at least two US carriers must be present. Vice Admiral Inouye accepted the warning. Both the Invasion Force and Goto's Close Support Force were ordered to return to Rabaul.

Rear Admiral Hara by contrast had no intention of withdrawing. He had learned Fletcher's position in the early morning but the attacks on *Neosho* and *Sims* had wasted so much time that he could only engage the American carriers if his already exhausted airmen flew through steadily worsening weather, with no prospect of returning to their own ships before nightfall. Nonetheless, at about 1615, Takahashi was airborne again at the head of fifteen Kates and twelve Vals, flown by the most experienced of Hara's pilots.

Hara's action, though undoubtedly daring, was most misguided. His scouts had lost touch with the US carriers and he estimated that these were almost twice as far away as the 150 miles that was really the case. Not surprisingly therefore, Takahashi's men failed to find their targets and after jettisoning their weapons, partly to conserve fuel, partly to avoid the risk of accidents in night landings, they set off on their return journey. By an unhappy coincidence, their course took them close to the Americans, who detected them on their radar.

At about 1815 in the last moments of daylight, the American interceptors fell upon the startled Japanese. The Val dive-bombers, superbly manoeuvrable now that they had dropped their bombs, turned to fight it out with the Wildcats, shooting down two of these and losing only one of their own number. The more ponderous Kates fared less well, six of them plunging into the sea in flames.

A number of other Kates had lagged behind their fellows and at about 1900, by which time night had fallen, three of them sighted *Yorktown*. Believing she was Japanese, they prepared to land on her. For their part, the Americans, hoping the Kates would fall into their hands, turned on the flight deck landing lights and flashed meaningless signals that were accepted by pilots no doubt too tired to think clearly. Then, just as it seemed the trap would work, an anti-aircraft gunner, unable to bear the tension, opened fire and the horrified Japanese sheered away into the darkness. Yet, unbelievably, 20 minutes later, three more stragglers also mistook *Yorktown* for one of their own ships. They too were greeted by a burst of gunfire that shot down one of them.

On the Japanese carriers, searchlights were switched on as the sound of aero engines was heard approaching, and their aircraft hurried to them in a state of almost total confusion, one further Kate being forced to 'ditch' by lack of fuel.[2] The Japanese had been humiliated but there was one more round of the battle still to be fought. On 8 May, those deadly phantoms, the opposing fleet carriers, would at last meet in mortal combat.

Because they were separated by vast tracts of water, the clash took the form of two combats following a parallel pattern. Both sides dispatched reconnaissance machines to find the enemy, after which Fletcher passed tactical command to Rear Admiral Fitch, an officer with far greater experience of handling naval aircraft. Soon after 0830, both sides were informed of the enemy's location. At 0915, twenty-four Dauntlesses, nine Devastators and six Wildcats from *Yorktown* set out towards their objective. In accordance with current American practice, fifteen Dauntlesses, twelve Devastators and nine Wildcats from *Lexington* followed in a separate formation 10 minutes later. Hara's Striking Force, coming from both his carriers, eighteen Kates armed with torpedoes, thirty-three Vals and eighteen Zeros, led by the indefatigable Takahashi, was on its way soon afterwards.

It was the Japanese carriers that were the first to be sighted – by *Yorktown*'s Dauntlesses at 1032. The Devastators and escorting fighters had not yet arrived and by the time they did at 1057, *Zuikaku* had taken cover under a convenient heavy rainstorm. *Shokaku* was not so fortunate – the Japanese were steaming in two formations nearly 10 miles apart – and was promptly attacked by the Devastators while the Wildcats prevented the Zeros of her Combat Air Patrol from intervening, shooting down two of them. Unfortunately the slow, unreliable American torpedoes scored no hits.

They were not wasted, however, because they helped to divert attention from the Dauntlesses that now hurtled down from 15,000 feet. Three of them were shot down and a fourth so damaged that it had to 'ditch' near its carrier. But two bombs struck home. One smashed through *Shokaku*'s flight deck forward of the superstructure striking a tank full of aviation fuel that exploded in a spectacular mass of flames. Another hit right aft, causing little damage but also starting a fire from which poured thick clouds of black smoke. This was the first time that a Japanese fleet carrier had been hit, but so efficient were *Shokaku*'s damage control parties that when *Lexington*'s airmen appeared, she seemed to be undamaged.

As a result, they attacked her as well. The Devastators as usual failed to live up to their name and one was shot down by the Zeros, as were three escorting Wildcats. An administrative error had resulted in the Dauntlesses' fuel tanks not being filled to capacity and all except four of them had therefore been compelled to turn back. Of the four, one was shot down by AA fire, two more bombed ineffectively; but Lieutenant John Powers who had vowed he would hit a carrier or not return, continued his dive well below the 700 feet that was considered the minimum safe height if the Dauntless was to escape the blast of its own bomb. It was at 300 feet that he at last released it, striking *Shokaku*'s flight deck just forward of the bridge and causing another spectacular fire. The Dauntless, minus parts of its wings, crashed alongside the carrier, killing its gallant pilot who was later awarded a posthumous Congressional Medal of Honour.

Equal though different valour was displayed by *Lexington*'s Air Group Leader, Commander William Ault. Wounded and with his damaged Dauntless rapidly consuming fuel, his radio calls showed no concern over his plight, only eagerness that the hit scored by Powers should be made known. His last words were: 'So long people.' He was never seen again.

Similar quiet courage must be recorded of Warrant Officer Kenzo Kanno, pilot of the Kate that discovered the American carriers. He remained in contact with them until forced to make for his parent ship, *Shokaku*, desperately short of fuel. On the way, however, he sighted the Japanese Strike Force that he felt was not proceeding in quite the right direction. He therefore turned his aircraft to fly alongside that of Takahashi. Only when he had guided the attackers to within sight of the American fleet did he break away to continue his return northward. Since he and his two crew-members were already doomed, it was perhaps merciful that he should have encountered a flight of Dauntlesses, acting in the role of interceptors, four of which would claim the sole credit for shooting him down.

Apart from this, the American Combat Air Patrol was ineffective at first. The Wildcats failed to catch the Vals and the Dauntlesses attempting to intercept the Kates were pounced on by Zeros which shot down four of them for the loss of one of their own number. At 1115, the

Japanese torpedo-planes attacked, seven of the eight sent out by *Zuikaku* heading for *Yorktown*, all ten of those from *Shokaku* targeting *Lexington*. *Zuikaku*'s Kates all approached from port, making it easier for *Yorktown* to elude their torpedoes, but her Vals proved more successful. A very near miss caused considerable underwater damage, including holing a fuel tank that left a long trail of oil in *Yorktown*'s wake. A direct hit burst through the flight deck, penetrating two more decks before it exploded, killing sixty-six men and starting a fierce fire.

Shokaku's Kates attacked *Lexington* in three waves from different directions. One, struck by AA fire that detonated its torpedo, disintegrated, flinging blazing debris in all directions, among which the bodies of its crewmen were glimpsed spinning through the air. Their companions pressed on unflinchingly and although *Lexington* somehow escaped two torpedoes that passed underneath her, two more found her port side, flooding three boiler-rooms and reducing her speed to 17 knots. At 1125, *Shokaku*'s dive-bombers also scored two hits, one well forward in an ammunition locker containing 5-inch shells, the other on the superstructure just beside the funnel. Both started fires.

By 1130, the raid seemed to be over. Yet 10 minutes later, the last of *Zuikaku*'s torpedo-bombers which had somehow lost contact with its fellows, came in alone, flying steadily and with astonishing resolution through a wall of anti-aircraft fire until it reached the prescribed position off *Yorktown*'s bow where it dropped its deadly 'fish'. Captain Elliott Buckmaster hastily altered course and again the torpedo missed. Every available gun continued to blaze away at the Kate but its pilot could manoeuvre now; twisting like a snipe, he sped fast and low towards the northern horizon, and the chances are that he escaped for the American interceptors were busy elsewhere, harrying the main group of enemy aircraft. Between them, they and the anti-aircraft gunners destroyed thirteen Vals and eight Kates besides that of Warrant Officer Kanno. Among the dead was the veteran Air Group Leader, Lieutenant Commander Takahashi.

As the last lone Japanese torpedo-bomber disappeared from view, damage control personnel were already hard at work. On *Yorktown* the fire was quickly quenched and her ability to operate aircraft was unaffected. *Lexington*'s situation was more serious but by 1245, her fires were also out, her speed had increased to 25 knots and her aircraft were starting to land on her, though they could not be lowered to the hangar

deck because the torpedo hits had jammed her elevators in the raised
position. Lieutenant Commander Healy telephoned from his damage
control centre to give Captain Frederick Sherman the good news and
suggest cheerfully that if the ship had 'to take any more torpedoes' this
should be done on the starboard side.

Two minutes later, Healy was dead and *Lexington* was doomed.
Fumes from aviation fuel tanks fractured by the torpedo hits had been
seeping, undetected, through abandoned compartments in the forward
part of the carrier. Sparks, said to have come from an electric motor,
now ignited them. A tremendous explosion shook *Lexington* from end
to end. A blast of air, accompanied by streams of flame, ripped through
her, tearing open watertight doors, starting scores of new fires,
rupturing the main fuel tanks, the contents of which leaked out to feed
the flames, and shattering the forward water mains rendering the
pumps useless just when they were most needed. Regrettably, the chaos
below decks was not apparent on the bridge, so *Lexington*'s aircraft
continued to land on her until 1415, when dense black smoke began to
pour across her flight deck; after which the fourteen Dauntlesses and
five Wildcats still airborne flew off to *Yorktown*.

Even now *Lexington*'s crew, many of whom had served on her since
she had been commissioned and all of whom adored 'Lady Lex',
struggled desperately to save her. At 1445, however, the ship was
wracked by another huge explosion and the flames spread beyond
control. Volunteers picked their way through blazing compartments to
bring out wounded who might otherwise have been trapped. Patients in
the ship's hospital were carried to the comparative safety of the flight
deck. At 1630, the engine rooms were evacuated and *Lexington*'s
escorting warships closed around her to assist in the work of rescue. At
1707, Sherman reluctantly ordered 'Abandon Ship'. Of her crew, 216
had died in the air attack or the first great explosion, but such was the
calm discipline of the survivors that not one of the 2,735 officers and
men who now began to evacuate her was lost. The ship's spaniel 'Wags'
was carried off safely in the arms of Ensign Martin.

By about 1830, only Sherman and his executive officer, Commander
Mortimer Seligman, remained on board, making a last inspection to
ensure that nobody had been left behind. While they were below decks,
Lexington's store of torpedoes blew up, hurling parts of the ship and
even entire aircraft high into the air. Sherman and Seligman hastily

reappeared, beating out live sparks that had settled on their uniforms. They then slid down a line into the sea. By 1853, all survivors were aboard other ships and a destroyer finished off the carrier with torpedoes. She sank at 1956; as she disappeared a final vast explosion shook vessels 20 miles away.

Had Rear Admiral Hara mounted another strike, he might have inflicted further harm on the Americans but luckily he was in no position to do so. *Shokaku* was unable either to launch or recover aircraft. A Val and a Zero which attempted to land on her had both crashed, while three other Zeros from her Combat Air Patrol had to 'ditch' with their fuel exhausted. When the strike aircraft returned therefore, all had to land on *Zuikaku* and since many were damaged or desperately short of fuel they had to land quickly. To accommodate them, *Zuikaku* jettisoned five of her own Kates, four Vals and three Zeros, and her accumulating losses were so great that she was no longer an effective fighting unit. At 1800, Inouye ordered the Carrier Striking Force out of the area.

The Battle of the Coral Sea was over and although not fully appreciated at the time, it was a great American success. While tactically the sinking of *Shoho* and the much heavier casualties inflicted on Japan's naval airmen could not fully compensate for the loss of a fleet carrier, strategically the American gains were immense. Port Moresby would never again be threatened from the sea. Neither *Shokaku* nor *Zuikaku* would fight at Midway where their presence could well have proved decisive. Even the American cryptanalysts benefited. Before Coral Sea they could read only a proportion of enemy signals but during it a vast number were intercepted and since the background to these was known, it was possible to deduce their contents. As a result, the Americans could discover virtually the whole of Yamamoto's plans for the Midway operation and knew exactly what action was needed to combat them.

After Coral Sea, *Yorktown* steamed at top speed for Pearl Harbour where she arrived on 27 May. She was hurriedly installed in dry dock where more than 1,400 welders, fitters, electricians and shipwrights swarmed over her, working day and night to render her fully fit for action again. Early on the 30th, she left Pearl Harbour to rendezvous some 350 miles north-east of Midway with a Task Force containing *Enterprise* and *Hornet* that had departed from Pearl Harbour on the

28th; all three then proceeded to a position about 200 miles north of Midway.

As senior officer present, Fletcher was placed in overall command but it was agreed that *Enterprise, Hornet* and their escorts should operate in a separate formation about 10 miles distant from *Yorktown* under the tactical control of Rear Admiral Raymond Ames Spruance, whose flag was in *Enterprise*. Under Spruance also were five heavy cruisers, one light cruiser and nine destroyers. *Yorktown* was guarded by two heavy cruisers and five destroyers. On 4 June, all were on station north of Midway where they would remain unseen until the moment came to strike from long range at an enemy who had dispersed his forces to a ridiculously wide extent.

It has been traditional to describe the Battle of Midway Island as one between the US Pacific Fleet's 'David' and Yamamoto's 'Goliath'. To give just one example, Walter Lord justifies the title of *Incredible Victory* for his detailed account of the battle in his opening passage: 'By any ordinary standard, they' – the Americans - 'were hopelessly outclassed. They had no battleships, the enemy eleven. They had eight cruisers, the enemy twenty-three. They had three carriers (one of them crippled); the enemy had eight.'

It is difficult to think of a more misleading assessment. *Yorktown*'s hasty repairs may have left her vulnerable should she receive further damage but by no stretch of the imagination could a carrier with its power sources intact and its ability to operate aircraft unimpaired be called a cripple. The only American vessels mentioned are the ones with Fletcher and Spruance, not for instance, the five cruisers that were vainly trying to intercept Yamamoto's diversionary move on the Aleutians. The Japanese strength, by contrast, is made to include every ship that left harbour – and even one that did not, light cruiser *Katori* which remained at Kwajalein in the Marshall Islands but is counted as the flagship of Vice Admiral Teruhisa Komatsu, commanding the Japanese submarines taking part in the operation.[3]

For a fair comparison then, the Japanese strength should also not include their forces involved in the Aleutian Islands diversion. These occupied the islands of Attu and Kiska without resistance, while aircraft from carrier *Junyo* and light carrier *Ryujo* raided the American base at Dutch Harbour on both 3 and 4 June, at a total cost of four Vals, one Kate and two Zeros. One of the Zeros flown by Petty Officer Tadayoshi Koga was struck in its petrol tank by a single bullet and since loss of fuel prevented it from returning to *Ryujo*, Koga attempted to land on a nearby island in the hope of being rescued later. The Zero tipped over, killing him but remaining virtually intact; it was later retrieved by the Americans who learned from it the secrets of Japan's most famous warplane.

The Japanese warships in the Aleutians, however, played no part in the fighting at Midway. Nor did those, four battleships among them, that took up a screening position about equidistant from Midway and the Aleutians under Vice Admiral Shiro Takasu. Nor did the Japanese Main Body, intended to act as a reserve, commanded by Yamamoto in person aboard Japan's latest and largest battleship, *Yamato*, with two other battleships and the elderly light carrier *Hosho* among her supporting vessels. Nor did Vice Admiral Kondo who gave distant cover for the Midway invasion force and whose command included light carrier *Zuiho* and another pair of battleships. A smaller covering force with four heavy cruisers under Vice Admiral Takeo Kurita would come under assault from the air, but only after the battle had already been decided. Even the warships escorting the troop transports would see action only to the extent of firing at three Catalinas from Midway that attacked during the night of 3/4 June and torpedoed a tanker, causing minor damage.

Indeed the only Japanese group that opposed Fletcher and Spruance on 4 June was Nagumo's Striking Force. This consisted of *Akagi*, *Kaga*, *Soryu*, *Hiryu*, battleships *Haruna* and *Kirishima*, heavy cruisers *Tone* and *Chikuma*, light cruiser *Nagara* and eleven destroyers. Its instructions were to eliminate resistance on Midway, then deal with any American ships that might appear, but it could not be supported in these tasks by other friendly formations because all were too far distant. Kondo was some 500 miles away to the south-west; Yamamoto was some 500 miles away to the north-west (and 500 miles north of Kondo); Takasu was a further 500 miles north-west of Yamamoto.

Thus at Midway Island on the fateful 4 June, the Americans outnumbered their opponents by twenty-five to twenty in all warships, by fourteen to eleven in destroyers, and by eight to five in surface vessels larger than destroyers. Admittedly two of the five were battleships but their heavier armament was of little significance at Midway where, as at Coral Sea, the surface warships on both sides never engaged or indeed saw each other and were of value only as anti-aircraft batteries.

Admittedly also, in the key aircraft carriers Nagumo did outnumber his enemies – though by four to three, not eight to three – but a mere count of ship numbers is again deceptive because the American 'flat-tops' embarked more aircraft.[4] Nagumo's four carriers controlled seventy-four Kates, eighty-one Vals and seventy-two Zeros. *Soryu* also had two Yokosuka Judys, the later marks of which would be excellent bombers but which at this time could only be used as fast reconnaissance machines. His battleships and cruisers could provide seventeen seaplane scouts. The three carriers with Fletcher and Spruance controlled one-hundred-and-twelve Dauntlesses, forty-three Devastators and seventy-nine Wildcats. To these should be added the aircraft based on the unsinkable carrier of Midway Island: thirty reconnaissance Catalinas, fifteen Flying Fortresses, ten torpedo-planes, twenty-eight dive-bombers, twenty-six fighters. In all combat aircraft the Americans outnumbered Nagumo's Striking Force by 313 to 227; in aircraft of any sort by 343 to 246.

Even allowing for the fact that most of the Japanese types had better performances than their opposite numbers, it is difficult to agree with Lord's judgement that the Americans 'had no right to win'. Indeed, when it is recalled that the Americans also had an exact and priceless knowledge of their foes' plans, what seems most incredible is not that the Japanese were defeated, but that despite Yamamoto's desperately ill-considered strategy and desperately unwise tactics, they nearly saved the situation by the sheer fighting abilities of their magnificent naval airmen.

These began their activities at 0430 on 4 June. Scouts set out to look for American warships and thirty-six Vals from *Akagi* and *Kaga*, thirty-six bomb-carrying Kates from *Soryu* and *Hiryu* and thirty-six Zeros, nine from each carrier, left to attack Midway. Their leader was Lieutenant Joichi Tomonaga from *Hiryu*, for Fuchida was in the sick-bay recovering from an emergency operation for appendicitis. Almost exactly an hour later, a Catalina from Midway flown by Lieutenant Howard Ady sighted the Japanese carriers and soon after that, another one piloted by Lieutenant William Chase encountered Tomonaga's formation. Midway's fighters hastily took off to intercept the raiders, followed by its bombers to seek out Nagumo's warships.

At 0616, the last machine was airborne and at almost the same moment, Tomonaga's men appeared. Midway's interceptors, hopelessly outnumbered, downed two Kates but lost three Wildcats and twelve aged Brewster Buffaloes, with two more Wildcats and six Buffaloes badly damaged. Midway's AA guns, however, claimed two Kates, one Val and two Zeros. Four more Kates were compelled to 'ditch', the crew of one of them being lost, another Kate was damaged beyond repair, Tomonaga's own Kate was hit, and Lieutenant Hiroharu Kadano landed on *Hiryu*, brought his Kate to a halt – and fainted from the pain of his wounded leg. Vulnerable fuel tanks and seaplane hangars were set on fire but by 0700, Tomonaga radioed: 'There is need for a second attack.'

Midway's own striking forces, unfortunately, were overeager and attacked Nagumo's fleet separately instead of in combination as had been intended. They suffered heavily in consequence. The fifteen Flying Fortresses, bombing from 20,000 feet, escaped harm but six brand new Avenger torpedo-bombers – fast, sturdy, adaptable machines designed to replace the Devastators – four Martin Marauders adapted to carry torpedoes, ten Dauntlesses and six old Vindicator dive-bombers were shot down, compelled to 'ditch' or damaged beyond repair. One of the Avengers was brought back to a crash-landing by Ensign Albert Earnest, although he and his radio operator had been badly wounded and his rear gunner killed; he was later awarded a Navy Cross.

Nagumo had lost only four Zeros and his carriers were untouched, though *Akagi* had had a narrow escape when a fatally-damaged Marauder piloted by Lieutenant Herbert Mayes attempted to ram her, missing her bridge by a fraction before crashing into the sea. Now, however, Nagumo had an important and difficult decision to make. He had brought a further strike force to his carriers' decks but the thirty-six Kates on *Akagi* and *Kaga* had been armed with torpedoes so that they might engage any US warships found. If they were to assault Midway instead as Tomonaga had recommended, the torpedoes would be valueless. He therefore ordered his Kates to be lowered to their hangars and rearmed with bombs.

Then at 0728, a seaplane from heavy cruiser *Tone* – ironically its take-off had been delayed by trouble with its catapult – reported 'ten ships, apparently enemy' about 200 miles to the north-east. There was no mention of any carrier though the scout had sighted Spruance's vessels which included both *Enterprise* and *Hornet*. Even so, Nagumo was understandably concerned. At 0745, he ordered that the change to the Kates' armament be suspended until the situation could be clarified. At 0820, it was – in the worst possible way: the seaplane confirmed the presence of a carrier. Ten minutes after that, it reported other ships some 20 miles distant from the first formation, thus strongly suggesting a second US Task Force and so probably a second carrier.

Rear Admiral Tamon Yamaguchi, an aggressive, independently-minded officer who flew his flag in *Hiryu*, urged that a strike be launched at once against the enemy carrier. This, though, could not be escorted by Zeros, for all had been drawn in to oppose Midway's raiders, and could not include Kates armed with torpedoes as any such were still in their hangars. Furthermore, Tomonaga's aircraft were now returning and if they could not land before the new raid took off, the Kates certainly and the Vals and Zeros possibly, would soon start to 'ditch' from lack of fuel.

At 0837 therefore, Nagumo gave instructions that any Kates on *Akagi* and *Kaga* now armed with bombs should be returned to their hangars and re-equipped with torpedoes. At the same time, Tomonaga's machines began to land on their carriers. The last one touched down at 0917, whereupon Nagumo changed course to the north-east to steam towards his enemies. One minute later, the American carrier-planes finally entered the battle.

On the advice of his Chief of Staff, Captain Miles Browning, Spruance had launched every available warplane, timing their arrival over Nagumo's 'flat-tops' for the moment when it was calculated these would be at their most vulnerable, receiving and refuelling the aircraft of their Midway raid. Fletcher, remembering the errors of Coral Sea, was more cautious, holding back half his Dauntlesses and most of his Wildcats as a reserve. Unfortunately as was the usual practice, the air groups of the three American carriers all operated separately, and as it took time for all the aircraft within each air group to be brought to the flight deck, the different types set off on their mission at intervals, the intention being that they would join up en route.

In practice, almost everything went wrong. *Yorktown*'s Dauntlesses lost touch with the rest of their formation in low clouds. The Dauntlesses and Wildcats from both *Enterprise* and *Hornet* never did locate their Devastators and those from *Hornet* failed to sight the Japanese either. Eight dive-bombers and all ten Wildcats were forced to 'ditch', eleven other Dauntlesses landed on Midway, and only sixteen got back to *Hornet*, where those on Midway rejoined them that afternoon after being refuelled.

The result was that the Devastators attacked the Japanese on their own and in successsion – and were easy prey for Nagumo's Zeros. All fifteen from *Hornet*, the first to attack, were shot down. Only one pilot survived, Ensign George Gay, who spent the rest of the day clinging to a life raft that he dared not inflate until darkness fell in case it attracted attention; he was rescued by a Catalina next day. *Enterprise* lost ten of her fourteen Devastators, with one more damaged beyond repair. *Yorktown* lost ten out of twelve, with the remaining pair having to 'ditch'. All three formation leaders, Lieutenant Commanders John Waldron, Eugene Lindsey and Lance Massey, were killed.

By 1020, the last of the torpedo attacks was over and the Japanese appeared triumphant. Yet the Devastators had not been sacrificed in vain. Every Japanese fighter pilot, of whom there were now forty in the air, every AA gunner, every look-out, every officer on the bridges of their carriers had his attention fixed on the slaughter going on at a very low level. No one looked up.

Of *Enterprise*'s Dauntlesses, engine trouble had caused one to 'ditch' and two more to return to their carrier but Lieutenant Commander Clarence Wade McClusky still commanded thirty-three of them when at 1022, he prepared to attack. He intended that his own flight of three and the squadron of Lieutenant Earl Gallaher should engage the nearest carrier, *Kaga*, while Lieutenant Richard Best's squadron attended to the one beyond her, *Akagi*. However, his orders were misunderstood and only five Dauntlesses made for the Japanese flagship while all the rest dived on *Kaga*. Only at the last moment was McClusky noticed but he and his wingmen, Ensigns Jaccard and Pittman all scored only near misses and the Japanese could still dare to hope that they might again escape serious harm.

Then Lieutenant Gallaher released his bomb. It crashed into the after part of *Kaga*'s flight deck, setting fire to the Kates gathered there. A second bomb struck near the forward elevator, starting a series of explosions. A third landed just forward of the superstructure, detonating a fuel truck serving *Kaga*'s Zeros and flinging a wave of burning aviation fuel over the bridge to bring a quick though horrible death to Captain Jisaku Okada and most of those with him. A fourth found almost the exact centre of the flight deck, bursting through it to a hangar from which the Japanese had not had time to remove the bombs unloaded from their Kates; this exploded into one great wall of flame.

Before anyone on the Japanese carriers had had time to react, the seventeen Dauntlesses from *Yorktown*, led by Lieutenant Commander Maxwell Leslie, plunged down on *Soryu* – though their crews would later strenuously deny this.[5] Only thirteen carried bombs since faults in the electrical equipment used for arming and releasing them had caused four, including Leslie's, to be dropped prematurely. Despite this, all seventeen made their dives so as not to disrupt their oft-practised attack formation, Leslie at their head as usual. Immediately behind him came Lieutenant Paul Holmberg whose machine did carry a bomb. This struck *Soryu*'s flight deck forward, crashed into a hangar and exploded, blasting the forward elevator out of its well.

Of the eight other bombs aimed at *Soryu*, two more found their mark, ploughing into eighteen Vals standing on her flight deck waiting to participate in the second Japanese strike. These disintegrated in a series of explosions that hurled parts of them and pieces of the flight deck high into the air, engulfing *Soryu* in flames. So terrible was the destruction that the last four Dauntlesses attacked escorting warships instead, though without results.

Literally one minute after Leslie dived on *Soryu*, Best dived on *Akagi*. Determined to make certain of a hit, he came down to 1,600 feet, lower than any of McClusky's or Leslie's men. One of his companions, thinking he was out of contol, released his own bomb first. It plunged past Best's machine to explode only yards from *Akagi*'s side, sending a huge column of water higher than her bridge. Then Best dropped his bomb. It smashed through the flight deck amidships and, like the last bomb to hit *Kaga*, it exploded in a hangar still packed with bombs not yet returned to the magazines and turned it into an inferno. Another bomb fell among the Kates massed near *Akagi*'s stern and now loaded with their torpedoes which began to detonate in spectacular fashion. It was 1028. Just six minutes had elapsed since the first Dauntless had dived on *Kaga*.

Though seven of the dive-bombers were shot down by the furious Zeros as they retired and ten more were forced to 'ditch', it was a small price to pay for their success. All Vice Admiral Nagumo could do was transfer his staff to light cruiser *Nagara* and watch the destruction of three of his famous 'flat-tops'. *Soryu* sank at 1913, taking down with her the bodies of 717 of her crew and the immensely popular Captain Ryusaku Yanagimoto who, resisting the pleas of officers and men alike, remained on his bridge to the end. About the same time, two vast explosions in her forward aviation fuel tanks ended *Kaga*'s agony. She sank at 1925. Some 800 of her crew were lost. *Akagi* lingered on until the early hours of 5 June, when she was finished off by torpedoes from her escorting destroyers; she suffered over 260 fatal casualties. His officers brought Captain Taijiro Aoki to safety, possibly by force, but it is reported that he never really recovered from the loss of his ship.

Tactical command of Japan's Striking Force now rested with the aggressive Rear Admiral Yamaguchi on *Hiryu*. At 1054, eighteen Vals that he had wished to launch some two-and-a-half hours earlier finally left her deck under the command of Lieutenant Michio Kobayashi, a veteran of Pearl Harbour, accompanied by just six Zeros, two of which unwisely allowed themselves to be diverted to attack the retiring American raiders. Shortly after 1200, they sighted Fletcher's Task Group, the massive bulk of *Yorktown* towering above her escorts.

Kobayashi had probably hoped that by following a group of American aircraft he might achieve surprise, but Fletcher was not to be caught napping. To assist their radar operators, the Americans had installed in all their warplanes electronic equipment known as IFF – Identification Friend or Foe – that sent out a coded signal. Thus warned, *Yorktown*'s crew took prompt steps. Her returning Dauntlesses were waved away to land on *Enterprise* instead; fuel lines were drained and filled with carbon dioxide gas; a petrol truck on the flight deck containing 800 gallons of fuel was simply thrown overboard.

In addition, *Yorktown* was able to direct the twelve Wildcats of her Combat Air Patrol to a perfect interception that resulted in the destruction of no less than ten Vals, including Kobayashi's, and three of the four remaining Zeros. Another Val was downed by her AA gunners before the rest, with reckless courage, plunged down to under 1,000 feet. One more was literally torn to pieces by anti-aircraft fire but seconds earlier it had released its bomb which ripped through *Yorktown*'s flight deck to set fire to three Dauntlesses in a hangar. Two other bombs also struck, one causing further fires, the other wrecking her boiler-rooms and her communications systems. Yet another Val was shot down by Wildcats as it retired and only five and a solitary Zero returned to *Hiryu*, radioing ahead the news that their target was dead in the water and 'burning furiously'.

Fortunately, *Yorktown*'s situation was far less serious than this report indicated. Though the loss of communications decided Fletcher to transfer to heavy cruiser *Astoria*, the carrier's damage control personnel, very experienced after Coral Sea, quickly got her underway again, gradually working up to 19 knots. Her fires were quenched; the holes in her flight deck patched. In fact, for her own sake, it was a pity she was restored to fighting efficiency so quickly.

At 1250, Rear Admiral Yamaguchi learned from one of his scouts that the Americans had three aircraft carriers on strength. Undaunted, he warned his pilots to concentrate on the two undamaged carriers and prepared to attack with his only available aircraft, ten Kates and six Zeros, the torpedo-planes flying in two waves of five so as to engage any target sighted from both flanks. One was to be led by Tomonaga; the other by his observer Lieutenant Toshio Hashimoto, transferred to the Kate piloted by Petty Officer Takahashi. It was a decision that saved Hashimoto's life, for Tomonaga now learned that his port fuel tank, holed over Midway, had not been repaired. Unhesitatingly, he ordered the protesting mechanics to fill up the starboard one only and at 1331, led off his men on a mission from which he could not possibly return.

It was an hour later that the Japanese found a carrier. This was *Yorktown* but since she seemed undamaged and even flew a brand new battle ensign, they did not realize that she was the 'cripple' they had been told to avoid. American radar had reported them 20 minutes earlier and the Combat Air Patrol engaged Tomonaga's group, shooting down two Kates and three Zeros. Four Wildcats fell, one to 'friendly' AA fire; fortunately for everyone's peace of mind its pilot escaped by parachute. Anti-aircraft guns also shot down all Tomonaga's remaining Kates, one disintegrating when a shell struck its torpedo. Both the others did release their weapons first, but without success.

Hashimoto's group had better fortune. One lost contact with its fellows and later jettisoned its torpedo, but the other four, defying the anti-aircraft barrage, raced in at 150 feet to within 500 yards of *Yorktown* before launching their torpedoes. Two of these struck her, only 30 seconds apart, tearing open 65 feet of her port side. Thousands of tons of seawater poured in, flooding engine-rooms and boiler-rooms and robbing her of all power, thus depriving her of the ability to counter-flood. As Hashimoto's Kates sped away, *Yorktown* was already slowing to a halt with a terrifying list to port. At 1458, Captain Buckmaster, fearing she would capsize, ordered: 'Abandon Ship.'

Yorktown would soon gain her revenge. At 1420, one of her Dauntlesses, flown by Lieutenant Samuel Adams, had sighted *Hiryu*. At 1530, fifteen of her Dauntlesses that had landed on *Enterprise* took off in company with ten of *Enterprise*'s own dive-bombers against the last of Nagumo's carriers. Their assault began at 1703. This time surprise was not achieved. A desperate defence by the Zeros shot down two Dauntlesses and damaged three more beyond repair, while violent evasive action enabled *Hiryu* to escape the bombs dropped by the first wave of her attackers.

Then a bomb fell squarely on *Hiryu*'s forward elevator, hurling it out of its well and against the superstructure. Three more hits, one forward, two amidships, followed in rapid succession, tearing open the flight deck, setting the aircraft on it ablaze and ironically destroying most of *Hiryu*'s fire-fighting equipment. As flames and explosions wracked her, the last two Dauntlesses unsuccessfully attacked other Japanese warships instead, as did sixteen dive-bombers from *Hornet* and six Flying Fortresses from Midway that arrived at about 1730. *Hiryu*'s engineers, heroically remaining at their posts as the flames cut off every avenue of escape, kept her moving at a full 28 knots until the decks above them became white-hot and they dropped in appalling agonies. By 2123, she had come to a halt. She lingered on until the early morning of 5 June, when she was finished off by torpedoes.

After all known survivors had been taken off, Yamaguchi and Captain Tomeo Kaku retired to their cabins where it is believed they committed 'seppuku' – the traditional Japanese ritual suicide by disembowelment. Of *Hiryu*'s crew 416 died but the Americans later rescued thirty-five men who had been trapped below decks and escaped only after the escorting vessels had left. They politely asked their captors to keep the news of their shameful survival secret. Even before *Hiryu* went down, Yamamoto, at 0255 on 5 June, signalled to all his forces: 'The Midway Operation is cancelled.'

All else was anti-climax. On 5 June, Spruance sent thirty-two Dauntlesses from *Enterprise*, of which nineteen originally came from *Yorktown*, and twenty-six more from *Hornet*, to harry the retreating Japanese. Sadly, they found only destroyer *Tanikaze*, detached to ensure that *Hiryu* had finally gone down, and scored only one near miss, splinters from which killed six men. *Tanikaze*'s gunners shot down one Dauntless, piloted by Lieutenant Adams whose sighting the previous day had resulted in the destruction of *Hiryu*.

Midway's aircraft were also in action. During the previous night, one of Vice Admiral Kurita's four heavy cruisers, *Mogami*, had accidentally rammed her sister-ship *Mikuma*. Surprisingly, the latter suffered only minor damage but *Mogami* had 40 feet of her bows twisted to port nearly at right angles and her speed reduced to 12 knots. Kurita made off at full speed, after leaving only *Mikuma* and destroyers *Arashio* and *Asashio* to look after the cripple. At 0808 on the 5th, this group was engaged by six Dauntlesses and six Vindicators from Midway. The big Japanese cruisers fought back viciously but ironically *Mikuma*'s gunners brought about her own ruin. Marine Captain Richard Fleming's Vindicator was set on fire and instead of baling out, he deliberately steered into one of *Mikuma*'s turrets, an action for which he was awarded a posthumous Congressional Medal of Honour. *Mikuma*, badly damaged and her speed too reduced to 12 knots was now in as much trouble as *Mogami*.

This luckless pair, with their faithful destroyers still in attendance, were the only targets offered to the Americans on 6 June. Three strikes were delivered against them during the day, two from *Hornet*, one from, *Enterprise*. *Mikuma*, shattered by ten bombs and ablaze from bow to stern, sank just after sunset with the loss of over 640 of her crew. Both destroyers were hit but suffered no serious damage. *Mogami*, struck five times, was battered almost beyond recognition but, with some 300 of her crew dead, was still able to crawl out of the danger zone, to spend the next 12 months undergoing repairs in a shipyard in Japan.

Ironically, the last vessel lost in this great American triumph was American. Despite her injuries, it soon became clear that *Yorktown* was far from mortally hurt and had been abandoned prematurely. For all the remainder of 4 June, all the next night and all the next day, she drifted without a man on board her. At about noon on the 5th, a minesweeper arrived to tow her, if agonizingly slowly, towards Pearl Harbour. A number of destroyers also appeared and at daybreak on 6 June, a salvage party from these, headed by Captain Buckmaster, boarded her. By 1330, they had made definite progress, epitomized by a slight but distinct reduction in *Yorktown*'s list – but at 1336, Japanese submarine *I-168* that had sighted her some hours earlier, at last reached a perfect firing position. Four torpedoes streaked through the water. The first missed. The next two tore open *Yorktown*'s side. The fourth struck destroyer *Hammann* squarely amidships.

One submarine in the right place had done more damage than the whole of Yamamoto's scattered fleet put together. *Hammann*, her back broken, sank in three minutes with the loss of 107 of her crew. The salvage party, all amazingly unhurt, hastily left *Yorktown*, this time with good reason. It is a sad comment on the earlier abandonment, though, that even now the carrier remained afloat through the rest of the day and the following night. She was still afloat at first light on 7 June, if only just, for she had listed so far to port that her flight deck was almost touching the water. At 0501, her brief but dramatic career came to its appointed end as she disappeared forever beneath the waves.

Notes

1 Japanese airmen normally flew without parachutes when operating against enemy vessels or over enemy territory, preferring death to the disgrace of being taken prisoner. It was therefore common practice for a pilot whose machine was fatally injured to dive onto any worthwhile target. During the Pearl Harbour raid, Lieutenant Fusata Iida deliberately flew his damaged Zero into an aircraft hangar and it is possible that the action of Lieutenant Mimori Suzuki whose Val crashed into seaplane tender *Curtiss* was also intentional.

2 Most Allied accounts declare that the Japanese lost no less than eleven aircraft in this way but it seems that this was the number rendered unserviceable from a variety of causes other than combat throughout the whole day.

3 In fact just one of Japan's submarines, *I-168*, played any part in the Midway drama – though very effectively. The Americans also ordered submarines into the area but only *Nautilus* and *Tambor* participated in the action, the former making two unsuccessful attacks, the latter sighting the enemy but being unable to attack.

4 The figures given for the aircraft available to each side come from *The Barrier and the Javelin: Japanese and Allied Pacific Strategies February to June 1942* by H.P. Willmott who made a special study of this aspect of the battle.

5 There has been heated argument over the identity of the carrier attacked by *Yorktown*'s dive-bombers. That it was *Soryu* is the verdict of Professor S.E. Morison in Volume IV of the US Official Naval History, *Coral Sea, Midway and Submarine Actions, May 1942 - August 1942*. The evidence for this is set out in most detail in an Appendix to Walter Lord's *Incredible Victory* entitled 'The Riddle of the Dive-Bombing Attack'. The view that *Yorktown*'s men attacked *Kaga* is best summarized by Professor Thaddeus Tuleja in an Appendix to his *Climax at Midway* entitled 'Who Sank the *Kaga*?'

Chapter 5

To the Aid of Malta

One of the most remarkable aspects of the American aircraft carriers' early successes is that they were achieved by so few vessels. While the Japanese at various times had employed seven fleet carriers and four light carriers, three of which were capable of performing any front-line duty, the Americans had been able to use only four: *Yorktown*, *Lexington*, *Enterprise* and *Hornet*. Officially there were eight US carriers then in commission but the little escort carrier *Long Island* could not take part in fleet operations – though her class was later to prove invaluable protecting convoys or amphibious landings. Nor could the 14,500-ton *Ranger*, slow, inadequately armoured and lacking sufficient anti-aircraft guns, though she too would form part of later invasion forces. And the large carrier *Saratoga* had been torpedoed by submarine *I-6* on 11 January 1942, when some 500 miles west of Hawaii and spent the next five months undergoing repairs in dry dock.

That left *Wasp*, of only 14,700 tons but well capable of performing front-line duties. She, however, had been in the Atlantic, becoming the first American warship to participate in the war in the Mediterranean. This she had done to some purpose and has been hailed in American accounts as 'the ship that saved Malta'. It was a somewhat exaggerated attribution: *Wasp* had certainly played a large part in saving Malta but there were many other vessels of which this could be said and a fair number of these were aircraft carriers.

First and most surprising was the old 'Flat Iron', HMS *Argus*, recalled from retirement in the hour of her country's need. As early as 2 August 1940, she would be found south of Sardinia, carrying twelve RAF Hurricanes and with an impressive escort that included *Ark Royal*. The intention was that the fighters should take off from her and fly some 200 miles to land in Malta.

The importance of that vital island arose from its geographic position and the effect that this had on the campaigns being fought in the deserts of North Africa. After Italy's entry into the war, the only way in which the British forces in the Middle East could be supplied was by convoys steaming some 14,000 miles round the Cape of Good Hope. By contrast, the distance between the port of Messina in Sicily and Tripoli, capital of Italy's colony of Libya, was only 350 miles. The Axis powers had, it seemed, every advantage – except that 60 miles south of Sicily, right in the path of their supply routes, was a British base, from which aircraft, surface vessels and submarines could and did decimate their convoys. 'Malta', reflects the Italian Official History sadly, 'was the rock upon which our hopes in the Mediterranean foundered.'

Yet if Malta was to survive as a base, she would have to be provided with necessities such as food and fuel and be defended from enemy bombers based so near at hand in Sicily, and by August 1940, it was clear the handful of Hurricanes and Sea Gladiators on the island[1] must be reinforced as a matter of urgency. Hence the mission of *Argus*, code-named with delightful double-meaning, Operation HURRY. It succeeded with rather deceptive ease. Guided by two Skuas that took off with them, all twelve Hurricanes reached Malta safely, though one crash-landed without injury to its pilot, and there they amalgamated with the existing Station Fighter Flight to form 261 Squadron RAF.

No further attempt was made to reinforce Malta for more than three months. During these, the Battle of Britain was being fought and Hurricanes – which, it is too often forgotten, bore the brunt of this, if only because they were numerically by far the RAF's most important fighter – were much too valuable to be spared even for Malta. Sadly, when the next supply mission, Operation WHITE, did take place, on 17 November, it proved very different from Operation HURRY. Once again twelve Hurricanes and two Skuas took off from *Argus* but they had been given a dangerously long distance to cover and the following wind at the time of take-off promptly veered to blow directly against them. Two of the first wave of six Hurricanes ran out of fuel and 'ditched', one of the pilots being rescued by a Sunderland flying-boat. The observer in the Skua guiding the second wave was on his first flight out of training school. As the weather grew worse, he was unable to find his way to the island. The Skua eventually reached Sicily where it was shot down. The Hurricanes were never seen again.

Despite this tragedy, *Argus* had demonstrated it was perfectly possible to supply fighters to Malta provided proper precautions were taken. She now withdrew from centre-stage, though she continued to play her part in the salvation of Malta, being among the vessels bringing Hurricanes to Gibraltar, where they were transferred to larger carriers for the final passage to their launching positions. During 1941, as it seems almost unnecessary to say, *Ark Royal* was the carrier that contributed most to the preservation of Malta – and she would do so in more than one way.

Early January saw *Ark Royal*'s fighters covering a convoy bringing stores to the island. In early April, twelve of the later Hurricane Mark IIs flew from her decks, all of them reaching Malta safely. On 27 April, twenty-four others followed, all but one getting to the island. In late May and early June, *Ark Royal* made two more ferry trips, being joined on both occasions by *Furious*, and in mid-June, she was back again, this time in company with *Victorious*. A total of 140 Hurricanes were carried on these missions, of which only five failed to arrive. Some of the fighters were staged on to Egypt but three full squadrons were established on Malta, just at the time when Fliegerkorps X was withdrawing from Sicily to the Balkans in readiness for operations further east.

On 22 June, German forces poured into Russia. As with the Japanese attack on America at the end of the year, the whole aspect of the war was altered, but for *Ark Royal* it was 'business as usual'. On the 27th, twenty-two Hurricanes left her deck, all except one making it to Malta. On the 30th, she flew off twenty-six more Hurricanes, all of them successfully, though *Furious*, accompanying her again, had a more trying experience. The aircraft of Sergeant Hare swerved when halfway along the deck and crashed, fatally injuring Hare and disabling six other pilots whose machines could not therefore be launched. Only nine Hurricanes got off *Furious* and duly landed on Malta.

In late July, *Ark Royal* along with the rest of a strengthened Force H formed the escort to six merchantmen carrying stores for the island-fortress. It should be noted that on this and similar occasions, it was intended that the majority of the covering warships should proceed only as far as the Narrows – the waters between Sicily and Cape Bon,

Tunisia. Here they would turn back, leaving only cruisers – on this mission these carried troops for Malta's garrison – and destroyers to guard the freighters as they made their final dash for the island. It was appreciated that air-attacks were likely to inflict losses during this last stage, but it was hoped that the protection of the carrier's fighters would have provided a sufficiently 'good start' to ensure that the bulk of the supplies got through.

As it happened, the heaviest casualties occurred during the early part of the operation, and among Royal Navy ships; Italian torpedo-bombers sinking destroyer *Fearless* and badly damaging light cruiser *Manchester*. Most of the attacks, however, were beaten off by *Ark Royal*'s Fulmars and all the precious merchantmen reached their destination. Similar results attended the passage of another convoy to Malta guarded by Force H in late September. Again both troops and supplies were carried. Again most of the early attacks were directed against the escorting warships, battleship *Nelson* being damaged. And again *Ark Royal*'s Fulmars prevented any losses among the supply ships at least until after Force H turned back. One of them was sunk by a later air-attack but eight others arrived safely.

Prior to this on 9 September, fourteen more Hurricanes had reached Malta from *Ark Royal*, only to fly on to Egypt. Four days later, *Ark Royal* and *Furious* sent off forty-six more, but again one crashed on take-off from *Furious*. The rest duly got to Malta, twenty-two staying to strengthen the island's defences, the rest proceeding to Egypt. In mid-October, *Ark Royal* sent off ten Albacores and two Swordfish to join Malta's striking forces. Finally a month later, *Ark Royal* would again accompany the elderly *Argus* but this time both were carrying Hurricanes, thirty-four of which got through to boost Malta's fighter squadrons.

It was the noble '*Ark*'s' last contribution towards aiding Malta. The following day was the 13th (though Thursday, not Friday), and on it her astonishing luck finally ran out. At 1541, as she headed back to Gibraltar, a torpedo fired by *U-81* struck her starboard side, flooding two boiler rooms, killing one man, Able Seaman Mitchell, and destroying all power in the rear half of the vessel, thereby preventing the pumps from working. As she heeled over alarmingly, orders were given for all except some 250 men to 'Abandon Ship'.

Unfortunately, while the evacuation of the crew was orderly and disciplined, it does seem that some key engine room and damage control personnel were evacuated prematurely, probably because of confusion caused by the ship's communication system having been put out of action. Since the lives of some 1,700 men were at stake and the high losses suffered when *Courageous* had capsized had not been forgotten, it is easy to understand this action but it did cause a costly delay in restoring power and in attempting to correct the list by counter-flooding.

Not that everyone concerned did not make strenuous efforts to save the great carrier. Somerville personally hastened to Gibraltar where he ordered out motor launches to help rescue her crew and tugs to take her in tow. Sadly, only one managed to do this and it was able to make very little, if any, headway against a strong current – as would be confirmed when the wreck was located long after the war. *Ark Royal*'s engineers, working in increasingly unpleasant and dangerous conditions, managed to restore some power in the port boiler room but the flooding increased, imperceptibly yet remorselessly. By about 0200 on the 14th, it reached the vents from the boiler, blocking the escape of the hot gases and so setting the boiler on fire. As smoke and fumes filled the room, the engineers were forced to withdraw. The carrier's list began to increase sharply. At about 0400, it was accepted that nothing more could be done and the remainder of the crew left her.

At 0613, the end came. 'It was the blackest of days when I saw my poor *Ark* sink', Somerville told his wife. 'Just a blur in the dark as she lay on her side for some time and then slowly, slowly she turned over like a tired and wounded ship going to sleep.' Apart from Able Seaman Mitchell every man of her crew was saved, as were her two cats, one brought off at the time of the first evacuation in the arms of a Royal Marine, the other found by a motor launch 20 minutes after she had gone down, clinging to a piece of wood, quite unhurt but, with some justification, furiously angry.[2]

He was not the only one. 'I can't understand,' lamented Somerville, 'how one torpedo should have caused the loss of this fine ship.' It was natural that questions should be asked in the anguish and disappointment that followed *Ark Royal*'s sinking and perhaps not too surprising that the luckless Captain Maund was court-martialled, found guilty of negligence and reprimanded. He was later entrusted with important duties ashore but never commanded another major warship.

While some mistakes had admittedly been made, it is difficult to agree that they amounted to negligence and considering his past achievements and the fact that *Ark Royal* may well have gone down whatever happened[3], it does seem that he was treated ungenerously to say the least.

It may have caused further heartache that *Ark Royal* had perished during what was in effect a transport mission rather than in the sombre magnificence of a naval battle as *Lexington* and *Yorktown* were to do, but that would underrate the importance of such missions. As Captain Roskill declares in his Official History, it 'cannot be doubted' that the 'three convoy operations and the frequent aircraft ferrying trips made by Force H saved Malta in 1941'. And how crucial Malta was in influencing the war in North Africa would be demonstrated by a British offensive that began just four days after the end of *Ark Royal*.

Early in 1941, Hitler had come to the help of his Italian allies by sending to North Africa German troops under General Erwin Rommel who, taking full advantage of the diversion of British forces to Greece, had recovered the whole of Cyrenaica apart from the port of Tobruk. During the summer, the British were painstakingly preparing for a major counter-attack code-named Operation CRUSADER, and the success of this would owe much to the activities of Malta's striking forces.

In September 1941, 28 per cent of all supplies sent to Rommel failed to reach him. In October, the proportion lost was 21 per cent. In November, it rose to 63 per cent and when on the 18th of that month, CRUSADER was launched every advantage lay with the British Eighth Army and Desert Air Force. Despite frankly muddled tactics, by 7 December – the day the Japanese struck at Pearl Harbour – they had compelled Rommel to retreat in his turn, ultimately to the western border of Cyrenaica.

Though, astonishingly, General Sir Claude Auchinleck, the Commander-in-Chief, Middle East, had so little appreciation of Malta's value that as late as August 1942, he could declare that the retention of the island was not absolutely necessary for his plans, Hitler was much better informed. On 2 December, Fliegerkorps II was transferred from the Moscow front to Sicily, joining with Fliegerkorps X in the Balkans to form Luftflotte (Air Fleet) 2. Its commander, the redoubtable Field

Marshal Albert Kesselring, was also given overall control of Luftwaffe forces in Libya and in practice of the Regia Aeronautica as well: a total of 2,000 warplanes. His orders from Hitler were to 'ensure safe lines of communication' with North Africa by achieving 'the suppression of Malta'.

Kesselring set about his task to the utmost of his very considerable ability. As the number of enemy raids and the weight of enemy bombs mounted inexorably, Malta was compelled to look to her own defence rather than to conduct offensive operations. Supplies and reinforcements began to reach Rommel again, enabling him, by early February 1942, to regain over half of Cyrenaica, including the airfield complex at Martuba near Derna. The loss of this meant that the RAF could no longer provide fighter cover for convoys making to Malta from Alexandria and caused the waters between Cyrenaica and Crete to be known henceforth as 'Bomb Alley'. In mid-February, two merchantmen in a convoy of three were sunk and the third so damaged that she had to return to Alexandria. Next month, only two of a convoy of four reached Grand Harbour and they were subsequently sunk at their moorings after just 5,000 tons of supplies had been unloaded.

During 1942, Force H, now under Somerville's successor, the South African Sir Neville Syfret, continued to do its best to mitigate Malta's ills. On 7 March, it was back in the western Mediterranean, among its numbers being *Argus* whose Fulmars were there to provide protection, and *Eagle* from which fifteen fighters were to reinforce Malta. These, though, were not Hurricanes but Spitfires, the first apart from a few reconnaissance machines to operate outside the British Isles. All reached the island safely, as did a total of sixteen more from *Eagle* in two instalments on the 21st and 29th.

Though with their greater speed and faster rate of climb, the Spitfires, by this stage of the war, were clearly superior to the Hurricanes, they lacked the Hurricanes' ruggedness and by mid-April virtually all of them had been rendered unserviceable, mostly by attacks on their own airfields. On 15 April, Malta was honoured with the award of the George Cross but during that month the island endured its worst ordeals and its bombers, surface vessels and submarines were all compelled to withdraw to less exposed locations.

It was clear that Spitfires for Malta, in the words of the Air Officer

Commanding, 'must come in bulk and not in dribs and drabs'. The trouble was that no British carrier could accommodate large numbers of them. It was now that United States aircraft carrier *Wasp* made her appearance. With her broad lifts and long flight deck she could provide Spitfires 'in bulk' and after a personal appeal from Churchill, President Roosevelt generously replied: '*Wasp* is at your disposal.'

At 0518 on 20 April, Squadron Leader Edward Gracie took off from *Wasp*'s deck in the first of forty-seven Spitfires, all except one of which arrived safely. Unhappily, they also arrived in a very poor condition. As Ian Cameron summarizes the situation in *Red Duster, White Ensign: the Story of the Malta Convoys*: 'ninety per cent of their long-range tanks were defective (and caused serious flooding in the carrier's hangar); ninety-five per cent of their guns were dirty and unsynchronized; seventy per cent of their radios were inoperative.' To which it may be added that nearly 50 per cent of the pilots were totally inexperienced. By the evening of the 21st, only seventeen were still serviceable. Within three days all had been grounded.

It seemed catastrophic but help was at hand from an unexpected source. By the end of April 1942, as the RAF Official History rather unkindly notes: 'Hitler, with that improvidence characteristic of the master-plotters of war, was short of aircraft.' To him, other theatres, chiefly Russia and North Africa, seemed 'more important' than Malta, and to them in early May, 'the greater part of Kesselring's bombers departed'.[4]

In late June, it appeared that this action had been justified, at least in North Africa, where Rommel's capture of Tobruk had owed everything to a crushing onslaught on its defences by Kesselring's Stukas, delighted to find there were 'no "Huren-kähne" to harass them'. But then, intoxicated by his achievement and the award of his Field Marshal's baton, Rommel persuaded Hitler to let him race for the Suez Canal instead of pausing on the Egyptian frontier until Malta had been secured, as had previously been agreed. As a result, in July, by which date Wellington bombers, Beaufort torpedo-planes and a number of submarines had all returned to Malta and were again striking at his supply lines, he found himself desperately over-extended, heavily out numbered and saved from destruction only by the abysmally poor tactics of General Auchinleck who had now taken personal command of Eighth Army.

Meanwhile, Malta's fighter strength had also been restored. Roosevelt again made *Wasp* available and she once more headed for the Mediterranean with forty-seven Spitfires on board, being joined off Gibraltar by HMS *Eagle* with another seventeen. When the fighters took off in the dawn of 9 May, one of those from *Wasp* crashed into the sea and the carrier then trampled it under, killing the pilot. A few others also failed to reach Malta for various reasons but the reception of the remainder was so well arranged that the splendid ground crews had many of them ready for action within five minutes of their touching down.

It was the end of any prospect that Malta might be battered into submission but not the end of ferry trips by aircraft carriers. *Wasp* now left for the South-West Pacific but British carriers took over her task and if they were never able to carry the great number of Spitfires that she had done, as they gained experience, they did manage to handle much larger groups than had previously been thought possible.

There were eight such missions in all. The first five were executed by *Eagle* which, as we have seen, had already provided Malta with Spitfires on four previous occasions including the one where she had accompanied *Wasp*. The last three were the responsibility of *Furious*. Not all the Spitfires they carried got to Malta – on two separate occasions four of them failed to do so – but the importance of these operations can be judged from the numbers that did. From *Eagle*: seventeen Spitfires on 18 May; fifty-nine from two different missions in early June; sixty-one from two more missions in mid-July. From *Furious*: sixty-five from two missions on 11 and 17 August and twenty-eight from a final one in late October.

Nor was the delivery of Spitfires the most important duty performed by carriers during this period. 'All too close ahead', in the words of the RAF Official History, loomed 'the day when, failing the arrival of a convoy, the last reserves of fuel, food and ammunition would be exhausted.' The scanty rations issued to troops and civilians alike had been cut to an absolute minimum and unpleasant skin diseases, the evidence of malnutrition, had started to appear. The shortage of oil and of kerosene – source of all heat and light on a small treeless island – was equally great and the Governor, General Lord Gort VC, had to tour his capital, Valletta, on a bicycle. Malta, in short, was under siege and could not hope to hold out much longer without relief.

To provide that relief, it was decided to send not one convoy but two, in the hope that this would divide the enemy's attention and resources. Eleven merchantmen would sail from Alexandria in Operation VIGOROUS, while six more would set out from Gibraltar in Operation HARPOON. The generous Americans provided HARPOON with two of its ships, one of them the fast new 9,300-ton tanker *Kentucky*. This convoy had the advantage of being escorted as far as the Narrows by Force H, containing both *Eagle* and *Argus* to provide fighter cover. *Argus* controlled only a handful of Fulmars and Swordfish but *Eagle*'s four Fulmars were at last supported by single-seat monoplane fighters.

The Sea Hurricanes that served on *Eagle* and other carriers were not new aeroplanes off the production line, but conversions of existing ones by the addition of such items as arrester hooks, and they lacked the folding wings of those machines specifically designed for naval-air use. Their top speed was 315 mph at 7,500 feet and their armament at this time was usually eight machine guns, though later versions would have twelve machine guns or four 20 mm cannon. There were sixteen of them on *Eagle*, twelve from 801 Squadron, four from 813 Squadron and despite their scanty numbers they would do much to ensure that by the time Force H turned back, the HARPOON convoy would have had the 'good start' it needed.

Their contribution began late on 13 June, when Sub-Lieutenant Michael Crosley of 813 Squadron shot down an Italian shadower. Next morning, he also destroyed a German Junkers Ju 88 trailing the convoy and there were other clashes before, at about 1000, the Regia Aeronautica based in Sardinia made the first raid of the day. The Hurricanes of 801 Squadron dispersed a group of Savoia Marchetti SM 79 torpedo-planes, Sub-Lieutenant Duthie downing one of them, but eight Fiat CR 42 fighter-bombers were able to attack *Argus*. Happily, all their bombs missed and two of them fell to the carrier's Fulmars.

Some 40 minutes later came a major raid by both Italian high-level and torpedo-bombers, escorted by Macchi MC 200 fighters. By ill luck, the wind was blowing from astern which meant that the carriers had to reverse course in order to launch their aircraft. There were thus only a small number of fighters airborne to oppose the raid. Though they attacked most gallantly to bring down four SM 79s and three Macchis, the bulk of the raiders broke through to the convoy, losing three more torpedo-planes to AA fire but sinking one merchant vessel and badly damaging light cruiser *Liverpool* which had to be towed back to Gibraltar.

That afternoon from about 1820, both German and Italian aircraft from Sicily made a series of attacks but these achieved no successes at all, though *Argus* was narrowly missed by several torpedoes. In all during 14 June, nearly 150 bombers of various types and over 100 escorting fighters had struck at the HARPOON convoy. The Sea Hurricanes had shot down ten enemy aircraft, the Fulmars four and AA fire several others. Three Hurricanes and four Fulmars had been lost.

At dusk, Force H turned back towards Gibraltar, its Hurricanes gaining a further victory on the return journey. Spitfires and Beaufighters from Malta attempted to compensate for the carrier fighters' absence but they did not prove nearly so effective. Two more freighters were sunk by air attack on 15 June and, worse still, the tanker *Kentucky* was crippled and although taken in tow, proved impossible to save and was finished off by a destroyer's torpedoes. Only two vessels, *Troilus* and *Orari*, reached Grand Harbour early on the 16th, where their 15,000 tons of flour and ammunition were at least sufficient to postpone Malta's fate.

It was little more than a postponement, however. By the evening of the 15th, the VIGOROUS convoy, ceaselessly assaulted in 'Bomb Alley', was compelled to abandon its attempt to reach the island and returned to Alexandria. Malta now had only enough food, oil and kerosene to last until 7 September. After that there would be no alternative but to surrender.

If Malta were to survive therefore, the largest possible convoy had to be sent to her aid and it would have to come from the west so that carrier-based fighters could guard it for at least part of the way. It was indeed suggested that they should accompany it all the way to the island. The idea was eventually rejected since in the Narrows the movements of the major naval vessels would be so restricted that they were almost bound to suffer heavy casualties. Nonetheless, there must have been many anxious reflections when this decision became known. The convoy would make its attempt in August. If enough ships did not get through to Malta, there would be no time to organize another one before the fateful 7 September.

So a tremendous burden was laid on the crews of thirteen big fast freighters, two of them American, that assembled for Operation PEDESTAL, loaded with a strange and potentially lethal mixture of flour, ammunition and aviation fuel in cans. To join them and carry the oil and kerosene that Malta had to have came the American tanker *Ohio*, 14,500 tons and capable, as no British tanker then was, of making the 14 knots needed to keep up with the convoy. She was provided with additional AA guns and the gunners to man them, and entrusted to a new British crew that had been hand-picked, as had the Master, Captain Dudley Williams Mason, a quiet, retiring man who took his crew fully into his confidence, explaining exactly what they would have to do and what would be expected of them. When the vessels that helped to save Malta are recalled, a special place must be found for these merchant seamen who displayed, in the words of Vice Admiral Syfret, 'conduct, courage and determination' that would 'remain an inspiration to all who were privileged to sail with them'.

To provide an adequate escort and the necessary 'good start', Force H had been given two battleships, seven cruisers, twenty-six destroyers and, most important, three aircraft carriers, *Indomitable*, *Victorious* and *Eagle*.[5] This was the first time so many British fleet carriers had formed one task group and they spent three days in the Atlantic getting used to operating together and ironing out any problems that arose. They then joined the convoy on 9 August for a final practice, before entering the Mediterranean next day. Between them they controlled seventy-two fighters: twenty-two Sea Hurricanes from 800 and 880 Squadrons and nine Martlets – the Royal Navy version of the Wildcat – from 806 Squadron on *Indomitable*, five Sea Hurricanes of 885 and sixteen Fulmars of 809 and 884 Squadrons on *Victorious* and twenty Sea Hurricanes, including four held in reserve, from 801 and 813 Squadrons on *Eagle*.

This was naval air-power on an impressive scale by British standards – though certainly not by those of the United States or Japan – but it was never to operate at its full strength. At 1315 on 11 August, *U-73* put four torpedoes into the port side of *Eagle*, the columns of water from the explosions rearing up to three times the height of her mast. A flight of four Hurricanes had just taken off from her. Looking back, their pilots could see that she was already heeling over to port so steeply that aircraft were sliding off her deck. In less than eight minutes, she had fallen over on her side and disappeared, leaving only a dark stain of oil on the sea. The other sixteen Hurricanes went down with her, as did some 260 of her crew; happily, some 900 were saved by the escorting destroyers.

Axis Intelligence was well aware of the PEDESTAL convoy and its importance. A number of other German and Italian submarines had been sent to intercept it and would later cause further casualties. Italian motor torpedo boats were lying in wait for it at the Narrows. More significantly from the point of view of the British carriers, in Sardinia and Sicily the Luftwaffe and the Regia Aeronautica between them had mustered about 500 aircraft, not counting reconnaissance machines. *Indomitable* and *Victorious* would soon need every interceptor that they had aboard them.

Throughout 11 August, the convoy was dogged by shadowers and that morning one of these, a Junkers Ju 88, was engaged by Lieutenant Richard Cork of 880 Squadron, a veteran Hurricane pilot who during the Battle of Britain had served in the squadron commanded by the celebrated Douglas Bader, winning a Distinguished Flying Cross, later amended to a Distinguished Service Cross by order of the Admiralty. He claimed a 'probable' but in fact the enemy aircraft managed to get back to base on one engine with a dead gunner in the rear turret. Another Ju 88 was still less fortunate in the afternoon, being destroyed by Cork's CO, the red-bearded Lieutenant Commander Judd.[6]

Not until darkness was falling did an enemy raid take place and the Junkers Ju 88 bombers and Heinkel He 111 torpedo-planes made no hits, although two bombs narrowly missed *Victorious*. Unfortunately, in the gathering gloom and with the convoy's AA gunners firing at everything that flew, the pilots of the defending fighters, few of whom were experienced in night operations, found it difficult to discover their own carriers or land on them when they had done so. Captain Troubridge took the risk of displaying lights on *Indomitable* in order to assist them and consequently received a number of aircraft from *Victorious* as well as his own. On both *Indomitable* and *Victorious* there were crash-landings that destroyed or damaged not only the machine in question but others also. By dawn on 12 August, of the original seventy-two fighters on three carriers, less than fifty on two carriers remained serviceable.

It was little enough to oppose the massive raids that would be mounted throughout the day. At 0900, a force of Junkers Ju 88s began the assault but the Hurricanes from *Indomitable* intercepted them some distance from the convoy, destroyed several and so harried the others that only four reached the convoy, bombing it ineffectually. As the raiders turned away, the Hurricanes from *Victorious* joined in the fight and Lieutenant Rodney Carver, though handicapped by having an arm in plaster as the result of an earlier incident, shot down two of them.

Throughout the morning and early afternoon, waves of enemy aircraft, Italian torpedo-planes with fighter escort and German Junkers Ju 88 bombers and torpedo-carrying Heinkel He 111s guarded by Messerschmitt Bf 110s, continued to strike at the convoy, but its interceptors and AA gunners broke up raid after raid. Only one group of Ju 88s was able to attack the merchantmen. Damaged by one bomb that passed right through her before exploding and several near misses, the freighter *Deucalion* was forced to leave the convoy and try to make her own way to Malta at greatly reduced speed. That evening, a pair of Italian torpedo-bombers finished her off. Her crew had just enough time to abandon her before she blew up; they were rescued by her escorting destroyer, *Bramham*, which then rejoined PEDESTAL.

As well as their orthodox assaults, the ingenious Italians had devised some new surprises. One was to drop 'motobomba' in front of the convoy. These were a type of torpedo that came down by parachute and on hitting the water set off on a zigzag course that could not be predicted. Happily, the merchantmen, 'answering every manoeuvring order like a well-trained fleet' according to Vice Admiral Syfret, avoided them all. Another was a Savoia Marchetti SM 79 packed with explosives. The pilot of this baled out after take-off, leaving it to be directed towards the convoy by a radio guidance system. This failed to function and the SM 79 flew on to crash in Algeria, to the great indignation of the Vichy French authorities.

The most daring Italian scheme, though, concerned a couple of Reggiane Re 2001 fighters. A number of these had accompanied the Italian torpedo-planes, one being shot into the sea by Sub-Lieutenant Peter Hutton of 801 Squadron who had landed his Hurricane on *Indomitable* after *Eagle* had been sunk. The Re 2001 bore a considerable resemblance to the Hurricane and like the Hawker fighter could be used to carry bombs. The Italians had armed the pair mentioned with fragmentation bombs and camouflaged them in British-style colours. As *Victorious* prepared to land her Hurricanes the two Reggianes joined them, then suddenly roared in low upon the carrier. They caught her completely by surprise but luckily their light weapons had little effect on her armoured deck and only six men were killed by splinters. Both Reggianes escaped unharmed – as, it must be admitted, they thoroughly deserved to do.

A lull in the afternoon gave some relief to the hard-pressed defenders of PEDESTAL, but at about 1800, further waves of enemy aircraft started to attack one after the other: Savoia Marchetti SM 79s armed with torpedoes, Junkers Ju 87 Stuka dive-bombers flown by both German and Italian crews, Junkers Ju 88s, even old Fiat CR 42 biplane fighters converted to carry bombs. All these formations were provided with strong escorts of Reggiane Re 2001s, Macchi MC 202s or Messerschmitt Bf 109s. These alone considerably outnumbered the Royal Navy's interceptors, the pilots of which were by now very tired, having already flown at least two sorties during the day.

In these circumstances the carriers' fighters naturally found it difficult to get at their priority targets, the enemy bombers and torpedo-planes, and were usually promptly counter-attacked by the escort if they did. Sub-Lieutenant Thomson of 800 Squadron, for instance, dispersed a group of Italian Stukas, destroying one and forcing the others to jettison their bombs; but he was then compelled to defend himself against the determined attentions of some Messerschmitt Bf 109s, admittedly with good effect, for he out-turned one which he shot down. Lieutenant Cork who, as we saw, had claimed a 'probable' on the previous day, won a DSO on 12 August. Earlier he had downed two Junkers Ju 88s and a Messerschmitt Bf 110. He now added two Italian torpedo-bombers to his score, only to be engaged by two Reggiane Re 2001s, his Hurricane being hit in its radiator and rudder and so damaged that it would be considered beyond repair.

In these later assaults, the raiders inflicted serious damage on the British warships, though not on the more important merchantmen. A torpedo struck the stern of destroyer *Foresight*, so injuring her that she had to be sunk later. The German Stukas concentrated on *Indomitable*. Diving out of the sun, they scored two direct hits and three very near misses, reducing her speed, damaging both her aircraft lifts, buckling her flight deck and causing fires fore and aft. She fell astern of the convoy with flames and smoke pouring from her, and blazing petrol cascading from her deck into the sea. Yet already her damage control parties were taking the necessary steps to restore her speed and master her fires. Just before she was attacked *Indomitable* had managed to launch four more Hurricanes and Sub-Lieutenant Blyth Ritchie of 800 Squadron was able to take some revenge by shooting down two of the Stukas.

At about 1900, the main British force turned back for Gibraltar, leaving four light cruisers and eleven destroyers to take the convoy the rest of the way to Malta. *Indomitable*'s wrecked flight deck made it impossible for her to operate her aircraft, any still airborne being compelled to land on *Victorious*. Since *Victorious* was not able to accommodate them all, a number of damaged machines had to be pushed overboard to make room for those still serviceable. When the convoy had entered the Mediterranean, *Victorious* had carried five Sea Hurricanes and sixteen Fulmars. By the end of 12 August, she still carried twenty-one aircraft but this number was made up of eight Sea Hurricanes, among them that of Sub-Lieutenant Hutton who had originally set out on *Eagle*, ten Fulmars and three Martlets.

During the day, the pilots of four Sea Hurricanes, three Fulmars and one Martlet had lost their lives, among them Lieutenant Commander Judd, shot down by the rear-gunner of a Heinkel He 111. In return it was believed that the naval interceptors had brought down thirty-five enemy machines – the Martlets four, the Fulmars seven, the Sea Hurricanes twenty-four – and several others had fallen to the AA gunners. These figures cannot be confirmed in enemy records but, though there may well have been some exaggerated or duplicated claims, it should be stated that the records are clearly not complete. For example, the Bf 110 claimed by Cork is not recorded, yet not only did this crash close to *Indomitable* where there were numerous witnesses to testify to Cork's success but its pilot baled out and was later rescued by a destroyer. Cork's last victim, a Savoia Marchetti SM 79, was not recorded either, yet he photographed its crew in their dinghy with his camera-gun; it was while doing so that he was attacked by the Reggianes.

In any event, whatever the correct number of 'kills', no one could disagree with the verdict of David Brown in his *Carrier Fighters* that 12 August 1942 was 'a significant day in the history of air warfare' and during it 'by any standard the shipboard fighters had scored a victory'. This was reflected not so much in the losses they had inflicted as in the losses they had prevented their enemies from inflicting. *Indomitable* had to follow *Illustrious* and *Formidable* to a repair yard in the United States but the damage to her had come too late to have any influence on the attempted relief of Malta. The really crucial strategic prizes for the enemy were the merchantmen and of them only *Deucalion* had been sunk, and that after she had had to leave the protection of the convoy. The 'good start' had been achieved.

It was just as well. The agonies endured by the PEDESTAL ships during the night of the 12th/13th and on the following day under a combined assault by submarines, aircraft and motor torpedo boats make heart-rending reading. The escort lost cruisers *Manchester* and *Cairo*. The convoy lost eight more supply ships. But on the evening of 13 August, three merchantmen, *Port Chalmers*, *Melbourne Star* and *Rochester Castle*, the last-named low in the water from a torpedo-hit, all reached Grand Harbour. Next day, *Brisbane Star*, which had proceeded independently after a torpedo had blown a good deal of her bow away, joined them there.

Her arrival ended the travails of Operation PEDESTAL apart from those of four small warships some 70 miles to the west, clustered protectively around the most vital, most vulnerable of all the vessels in the convoy. As the only tanker, *Ohio* had received particular attention from the enemy and was now totally disabled, very slowly sinking, a vast hole from a submarine's torpedo gaping in her side, her engine room blown to pieces by a bomb, her stern split open by one of some twenty near misses and with the remains of a Junkers Ju 88 and a Junkers Ju 87 Stuka littering her deck. It seemed impossible that she could be saved – except that the escort vessels, her own crew and volunteers from other ships that had gone down earlier were all absolutely determined that she should be.

Their resourcefulness matched their resolution. Destroyers *Bramham* and *Penn* were lashed on either side of the tanker to keep her afloat. Destroyer *Ledbury* was secured to her stern to assist in steering her. Minesweeper *Rye* doggedly set about towing her. All through 14 August and all the following night the little group made its painful way towards Malta and at 0800 on the 15th, British seamanship and American ship-building skill finally triumphed as the unconquerable

Ohio, the sea washing over her main deck but her cargo virtually intact, entered Grand Harbour. Captain Mason was awarded the George Cross – the same decoration as the island he had done so much to save.

For saved she had been until great events in North Africa completely altered the situation. On 15 August, the same day that *Ohio* reached Malta, General Sir Harold Alexander replaced Auchinleck as Commander-in-Chief, Middle East. Lieutenant General Bernard Law Montgomery, warned by Intelligence that an enemy offensive might be only a fortnight away, had ignored Auchinleck's orders and assumed command of Eighth Army two days earlier.

These officers did not have an easy task before them. It has been stated that their arrival coincided with that of large reinforcements. In reality, before the coming Axis offensive that would become known as the Battle of Alam Halfa, no new troops or equipment reached Allied forces in the Middle East. On the contrary, it was Rommel who had recently received large numbers of men, equipment, tanks superior to any in Eighth Army, anti-tank guns and artillery, to such an extent that, as Captain B.H. Liddell Hart points out in his *History of the Second World War*, 'the strength of the two sides was nearer to an even balance than it was either before or later'.

In these circumstances, the new commanders could well be grateful to Malta's Striking Forces whose attacks on the Axis supply-lines prevented the situation becoming still more unfavourable. They also helped to postpone Rommel's assault until the night of 30/31 August, when it was repulsed by Montgomery decisively and with relatively few casualties. Alam Halfa thwarted Rommel's last attempt to reach the Suez Canal and enabled Montgomery to begin preparations for an offensive of his own at El Alamein.

For this, Montgomery was able to build up a considerable numerical superiority. Yet in July when Eighth Army's advantage had been much greater, General Auchinleck had mounted five offensives and all had failed miserably. Moreover at that time Rommel had had virtually no fixed defences, whereas now these were immensely strong, could not be outflanked and were guarded by a little matter of half-a-million mines.

In short, Eighth Army's victory was by no means as certain as would be declared after it was safely won, and again one factor that ensured it would be was Malta. Aircraft and submarines from the island, together with Allied bombers based in Egypt, between them sank 44 per cent of Rommel's supplies in October 1942. If less than the percentage sunk immediately prior to Operation CRUSADER, it was still, as Montgomery acknowledged, 'a wonderful achievement' that greatly aided his Eighth Army.

On the evening of 23 October, the Battle of El Alamein began and at the end of twelve days of ferocious fighting, the Axis forces were either surrendering or in full flight. Malta's reward came on 15 November, when Eighth Army recaptured the Martuba airfields. Rain prevented these from coming fully into use until the 19th, but that was just soon enough. On that day, four supply ships from Alexandria, suitably escorted, entered 'Bomb Alley'. They were subjected to the inevitable Axis air attacks but, records Captain Roskill, these were all 'broken up by the excellent fighter cover sent from the desert airfields'. In the early hours of the 20th, the convoy entered Grand Harbour. Operation STONEAGE, as it was code-named, had finally raised the siege of the island. The four merchantmen were the British *Denbighshire*, the Dutch *Bantam* and the American *Mormacmoon* and *Robin Locksley*. They were the last of all those fine ships that came to the aid of Malta.

Notes

1 The charming myth that the air defence of Malta before August 1940 rested on three Gladiators called 'Faith, Hope and Charity' by 'the grateful people of Malta' is, alas, only a charming myth. The names were invented by enterprising pressmen in Britain and the Air Officer Commanding in Malta during this period has confirmed that he first heard them after he had left the island in the following year. More to the point, there were half-a-dozen Gladiators on hand (though probably no more than three airborne at any one time) and as early as 28 June, four Hurricanes had joined them.

2 Amazingly, this cat had also been a *Bismarck* survivor. He had been found on some wreckage, shaking with cold and with his fur matted with oil, by destroyer *Cossack* after the German battleship had been sunk and was rechristened 'Herr Oscar'. When *Cossack* was sunk by a U-boat in late October 1941, he was again among those saved, was taken to Gibraltar and there joined *Ark Royal*. When she too was sunk, according to Iain Ballentyne who recounts his story in *Killing the Bismarck*, 'Herr Oscar' 'was regarded as a bit of a Jonah and was therefore sent ashore for good'. The last of his nine lives ended peacefully in 1955.

3 Eye-witnesses on the motor launch nearest to *Ark Royal* have stated that the hole in her side was 130 feet long by 30 feet wide. Even allowing for exaggeration, it seems clear that that one torpedo had inflicted terrible damage.

4 *Royal Air Force 1939-1945' Volume II 'The Fight Avails* by Denis Richards and Hilary St George Saunders. Kesselring had advised his Führer that Malta had been neutralized, but it appears that Hitler would have taken this action in any case and had, indeed, reached his decision before receiving this assurance.

5 For a time *Furious* also sailed with the convoy but her task was not to guard it but to fly off Spitfires for Malta on 11 August. As mentioned earlier, she duly did so, after which she and her destroyer escort returned to Gibraltar.

6 A year earlier and hundreds of miles away, Lieutenant Commander Judd and another of his pilots, Sub-Lieutenant Howarth, had made the first 'kill' credited to the Sea Hurricane. On 30 July 1941, Albacores from *Victorious* and *Furious* had attacked Kirkenes in northern Norway and Petsamo in Finland in an attempt to disrupt the supply lines of German troops advancing towards the ports of northern Russia. The raids achieved only meagre results at the high cost of twelve Albacores and four Fulmars, but at least the threat of counter-attacks next day was ended by Judd and Howarth who shot down a Dornier Do 18 flying-boat that was shadowing the carriers.

Chapter 6

The Fiercest Campaign

From the small but strategically vital island of Malta, it seems appropriate to turn to another, much larger island of equal strategic value. This one was in the South Pacific, so judging from romantic fiction, we might expect to find it bathed in permanent sunshine and blessed with golden sands, vivid flowers and luscious fruits.

Sadly, the island around which for six months would be fought a naval campaign of a ferocity unequalled in history, bore no resemblance to the picture thus painted. On it rainfall was almost incessant, at its worst from November to March, the summer months in the southern hemisphere. Covering it was dense jungle, broken by vile swamps or expanses of kunai grass, 7 feet tall and as sharp as a razor. In it lived enormous crocodiles, lizards, leeches, centipedes, scorpions, snakes, ants with incredibly vicious bites, spiders of nightmarish appearance, wasps 3 inches long and, smallest but most deadly of all, malarial mosquitoes. From it a sickening stench of decaying vegetation drifted over depressing grey seas, teeming with sharks that, horrible to relate, would feast well on human flesh on many a day in the near future. This was Guadalcanal in the southern Solomons, called by the Japanese 'The Island of Death'.

It is a sufficient comment on Yamamoto's move towards Midway that the notoriously stubborn Japanese made no attempt to repeat it, but instead redirected attention to their southward advance from which they should never have been diverted. It will be recalled that their initial objectives had been Port Moresby and Tulagi, but the Battle of the Coral Sea had meant that only the latter had been achieved. They now determined to resume the attempt on Port Moresby, while at the same time strengthening their position in the southern Solomons.

On 12 June 1942, these tasks were entrusted to Lieutenant General

Harukichi Hyakutake, younger brother of the Emperor's Grand Chamberlain. On 21 July, his troops landed on the northern shore of New Guinea's Papua Peninsula from which they struck south over the 8,500-feet-high Owen Stanley Mountains under orders to take Port Moresby from its landward side. Meanwhile on 19 June, a Japanese survey party had gone ashore on Guadalcanal that lies to the south of Tulagi across Savo Sound as it was then called. Their mission was to examine a site on Lunga Plain for a proposed aerodrome, from which the whole of the southern Solomons could be dominated.

By the end of the month, work on its construction was well underway. The news of this, first sent by 'Coastwatchers' – Allied agents who had remained in or been brought back to Japanese-occupied islands – and confirmed by aerial reconnaissance on 4 July, caused considerable alarm. The Americans had intended their own counter-offensive would commence in the southern Solomons and it was realized that an enemy airfield on Guadalcanal might make this impossible. Plans were hastily brought forward and early on 7 August, American troops led by Major General Alexander Vandegrift USMC, under cover of naval bombardments and strikes by carrier aircraft, landed on both Guadalcanal and Tulagi.

The aircraft in question came from *Enterprise*, already a veteran after eight months of war; *Saratoga*, recovered from the wounds inflicted by the submarine's torpedo, and *Wasp*, back from her services in the Mediterranean. All were under the command of the recently promoted Vice Admiral Fletcher, who in turn answered to Vice Admiral Robert Ghormley, controlling all forces in the South Pacific Area from Noumea in New Caledonia. Between them they carried one-hundred-and-three Dauntlesses, forty-one Avengers and ninety-nine Wildcats.

In addition to supporting their ground troops, Fletcher's men were soon in action defending the invasion force from the inevitable aerial counter-attacks. The first of these was detected by radar at 1315. The Wildcats, joined by some Dauntlesses in the interceptor role, prevented the bomb-carrying Bettys from scoring a hit and shot down four of them plus two escorting Zeros. Eight Wildcats and one Dauntless were also destroyed, the Dauntless by Petty Officer Saburo Sakai, Japan's leading fighter-pilot. He was then hit by the gunner of another Dauntless, terribly wounded in the head and permanently blinded in his right eye – yet somehow he brought his Zero back to Rabaul and landed safely before collapsing from loss of blood. He would recover, fight again and ultimately survive the war.

A second raid at about 1500 caused little damage and cost the Japanese ten of the fourteen Vals taking part. At noon on the 8th, another raid by Bettys, now armed with torpedoes, proved equally costly, five of them being downed by interceptors, thirteen more by flak. This time, though, their efforts were not in vain. A torpedo hit destroyer *Jarvis* near the bow, damaging her sufficiently to ensure her retirement from the area – and ultimately dooming her, for on the following afternoon, another group of Betty torpedo-bombers sent her to the bottom with every man of her 247-strong crew. Two of the Bettys, fatally hit, tried to ram their targets. One was blown to pieces by AA fire but the other struck transport *George F. Elliott*, setting her ablaze, later to sink with most of her valuable supplies still on board.

Despite these blows, the Americans could feel satisfied as the evening of 8 August approached. On Tulagi, the Japanese had demonstrated a determination to fight almost to the last man that would soon become very familiar; only twenty-three prisoners would be taken, all of them wounded. Yet the Americans had by now gained control, though resistance in some strongpoints would not be eliminated until the afternoon of the 9th. On Guadalcanal, the supreme prize of the almost-completed airfield was in American hands; it was named Henderson Field as a memorial to Major Lofton Henderson, a Marine officer who had died in action leading Midway's Dauntlesses against Nagumo.

At 1807, however, all satisfaction vanished. Vice Admiral Fletcher announced that he was withdrawing his carriers from the combat area. It seems that the strain of his responsibilities at Coral Sea and Midway had taken their toll and he remembered the loss of *Lexington* and *Yorktown* more than their achievements. He was also well aware that the priceless advantage of knowing his enemy's plans would temporarily be denied to him because the Japanese had just changed their main naval code.

All the same, it seems curious that Fletcher's recent victories apparently discouraged him more than they did his enemies. Even the Japanese naval airmen were not too disheartened by Midway where a majority of their highly-trained pilots had survived, including all those above the rank of lieutenant. The Imperial Navy's surface vessels were still more confident of their abilities, particularly at night, where they considered they could display their 'traditional qualities: skill, courage, surprise, daring and indifference to losses'. From a more practical aspect, night-fighting might be a way of countering the Americans' numerical superiority.

With this aim in mind, the Japanese had carried out intensive training for operations at night, heedless of risks and of casualties. They had also created many valuable aids such as reliable starshells and searchlights; huge, powerful night binoculars for their specially selected and, in ironical contrast to the Allies' belief that the Japanese suffered from poor night-vision, exceptionally capable lookouts; and above all, their 'Long Lance' torpedoes, true 'secret weapons' propelled by oxygen-enriched fuel carrying warheads twice the size of the American ones.

How deadly this combination of assets could prove was made horribly clear when a Japanese force of five heavy and two light cruisers plus a single destroyer, led by Vice Admiral Gunichi Mikawa, fell on the Allied warships guarding their transports in the early hours of 9 August. Before daylight Savo Sound had acquired a new, sinister name: Ironbottom Sound. The American heavy cruisers *Quincy* and *Vincennes* had sunk already; *Astoria* and the Australian *Canberra* followed them next day.[1] Heavy cruiser *Chicago* and two destroyers were damaged. Over 1,000 seamen died. The Japanese suffered only minor injuries.

Though this Battle of Savo Island was thus a shattering defeat, the Americans could take consolation from the knowledge that it might have been far worse. They continued unloading supplies until about 1600 on 9 August. They then withdrew, taking with them much unloaded cargo including all heavy artillery pieces, all construction material except one bulldozer, and a great deal of food and ammunition. Nonetheless, Vandegrift's men were left with enough supplies to maintain their position, if precariously. Had Mikawa followed up his success by destroying the American transports, he could have wrecked the whole operation. Moreover, early on 10 August, submarine *S-44* achieved some revenge for the defeat by putting four torpedoes into one of Mikawa's heavy cruisers, *Kako*, which sank within five minutes.

Mikawa's premature retirement had been caused by a fear that early next morning he would be subjected to attacks from the American carriers – which had thus yet again had a profound effect on events by their very existence. This also influenced the extraordinary pattern of the campaign that now emerged. The Americans held command of the seas during the hours of daylight because their carriers enabled them to dominate the air. This dominance would increase if they could develop Henderson Field so as to provide them, as at Midway, with an unsinkable aircraft carrier. On 20 August, twelve Dauntless dive-bombers and nineteen Wildcats left the deck of escort carrier *Long Island* to fly to Guadalcanal. Major General Vandegrift declares that their arrival was 'one of the most beautiful sights of my life'.

If the Americans could bring in fresh supplies by day, the Japanese were equally able to provide reinforcements of men and material after dark. These operations that began on the night of 18/19 August, and were collectively dubbed 'The Tokyo Express' by the Americans, were normally entrusted to Destroyer Squadron 2 under Rear Admiral Raizo Tanaka. A small, slim young man with a solemn face, his unshakeable determination won the respect even of his enemies who gave him the admiring nickname of 'Tenacious Tanaka'. They were also at first reluctant to oppose him. The lessons of Savo Island were confirmed in the early hours of 21 August, when a clash between Japanese destroyer *Kawakaze* and US destroyer *Blue* resulted in the latter's stern being shattered by a 'Long Lance' and her having to be scuttled two days later.

Tanaka's early missions brought to Guadalcanal a 900-strong infantry regiment commanded by Colonel Kiyonao Ichiki who, unfortunately for his country's cause, had acquired an arrogant contempt for her enemies following a string of successes in China. Without troubling about reconnaissance or bringing up artillery support, he marched straight to the Americans' defensive perimeter on the 'Tenaru River'[2] early on 21 August and twice made attacks across the sandbar which at that time of year blocked its mouth. Both failed with heavy losses, but Ichiki refused to retire and was duly counter-attacked over the sandbar and from the rear by an American force that had crossed further upstream. Well over 800 Japanese were killed; fifteen, all wounded, were captured, and only a handful fell back to their base at Taivu Point, where the colonel burned his regimental colours and committed 'seppuku'.

To replace these losses, the Japanese prepared a new 'Tokyo Express'. Some 800 men were loaded onto troopship *Kinryu Maru*[3], 700 more onto four old patrol boats and all set out under the care of

Destroyer Squadron 2 consisting of Tanaka's flagship, light cruiser *Jintsu*, and eight destroyers. On this occasion they would make for Guadalcanal in daylight, since Admiral Yamamoto had determined that in addition to supporting them he would make another attempt to destroy the US aircraft carriers and so gain complete command of the seas around the island. He seems, however, to have learned nothing from his misfortunes at Midway as he again dispersed his forces so widely that several of them made no contribution towards fulfilling either of his objectives.

In the Battle of Eastern Solomons, second of the six major naval actions fought out in this campaign and taking place on 24 August 1942, we need therefore only consider three groups besides Tanaka's. One was that of Vice Admiral Nagumo, now flying his flag in *Shokaku*. *Zuikaku* accompanied her as usual and between them they carried thirty-six Kates, forty-one Vals and fifty-three Zeros. Battleships *Hiei* and *Kirishima*, three heavy cruisers, one light cruiser and twelve destroyers provided the escort. Then there was the Advance Force of Vice Admiral Kondo who controlled five heavy cruisers, one light cruiser, seaplane carrier *Chitose* and six destroyers. Finally came a small group consisting only of light carrier *Ryujo* with sixteen Kates and twenty-one Zeros on board, heavy cruiser *Tone* and a further pair of destroyers.

This last formation had a task that could only have been required of a Japanese one. It was a sacrificial offering on which it was hoped the Americans would direct their assaults, leaving Nagumo's carriers untouched and their own position vulnerable. It was anticipated that *Ryujo* probably, and her escorts possibly, would be sunk but, extraordinary as it appears and despite *Ryujo*'s previous fine record, Yamamoto was fully prepared to accept this.

On the American side, *Wasp* had retired to the south to refuel but Fletcher still had seventy-four Dauntlesses, thirty Avengers and seventy-two Wildcats on *Saratoga* and *Enterprise*. These were steaming about 10 miles apart, the former protected by two US heavy cruisers, an Australian heavy and an Australian light cruiser and five destroyers; the latter by battleship *North Carolina*, one heavy and one light cruiser and six destroyers. The Americans were well aware that hostile forces were in the vicinity, for during the morning of the 24th, several Japanese reconnaissance machines were shot down by Fletcher's Wildcats and a scouting Catalina reported the presence of the *Ryujo* group. Anxious not to commit his strike aircraft prematurely, Fletcher compromised by sending out sixteen dive-bombers and seven Avengers from *Enterprise* at 1229, with orders to seek out the enemy and attack any vessels found. At 1345, thirty dive-bombers and eight torpedo-planes led by Commander Harry Felt also took off from *Saratoga*, this time with a definite target in view.

At 1300, *Ryujo* had sent a formation to raid Henderson Field. This would do little harm and cost the Japanese three Kates and two Zeros; the defenders lost four Wildcats and three pilots. Since this formation was tracked by Fletcher's radar operators, he could calculate *Ryujo*'s position; it was against her that Felt's men were directed. They sighted her at 1550, and though she evaded the bombs dropped by the first wave of Dauntlesses, Felt's own bomb struck her in almost the exact centre of her flight deck. Three more hits and four near misses reduced her to a blazing wreck and a torpedo then tore open her side and jammed her steering gear, leaving her pathetically turning in circles. She finally sank at about 2000.

For the Japanese of course, *Ryujo*'s mission had been successful; she had diverted Fletcher's strength away from Nagumo. And at 1405, a reconnaissance aircraft had given that officer the Americans' position before falling victim to the Combat Air Patrol. It seemed that the Japanese had a splendid chance to avenge Midway Island but luckily they showed little of their usual ruthless efficiency. To begin with, they did not send out a single massive raid as at Coral Sea. Instead they dispatched nine torpedo-planes, about twenty dive-bombers and twelve Zeros at 1507, but not until 1600 did they send out a second wave, and this failed to find any target. Meanwhile at 1515, Nagumo was himself attacked by two of the *Enterprise* Dauntlesses sent out on armed reconnaissance. Lieutenant Davis and Ensign Shaw scored one hit and one very near miss on *Shokaku* but, alas, the bomb that found her flight deck failed to penetrate it and achieved only minor damage.

On their part, the pilots of Nagumo's original wave never sighted the *Saratoga* group, so directed all their attention onto *Enterprise*. Rear Admiral Thomas Kinkaid who flew his flag in her took the precaution of launching his remaining strike aircraft as soon as radar detected the enemy, and he already had a strong force of Wildcats aloft. These destroyed at least three Kates and dispersed the rest. The Val dive-bombers also suffered heavily, Warrant Machinist Donald Runyan alone downing three together with at least one Zero. Those that evaded the fighters attacked at about 1640, only to meet a tremendous barrage of anti-aircraft fire, especially from *North Carolina*, at least three disintegrating in mid-air, while others crashed all around the battleship and *Enterprise*. Even after the attack, the raiders were engaged by every available American aircraft, one Val being shot down by the Avenger of *Enterprise*'s Ensign Burnett who was returning from an anti-submarine patrol when he decided to take on the role of interceptor.

Few indeed of the Japanese returned to their carriers but their courage could not be thwarted completely. Three bombs hit *Enterprise*, two of them striking close to her after elevator and penetrating to lower decks before exploding; these killed seventy-five men and started raging fires. Fortunately constant practice enabled *Enterprise*'s damage control parties to bring the flames under control and by 1749 her aircraft were again able to start landing on her. She was not yet out of danger, however, for at 1821, the ventilation system to the steering-engine compartment, switched off when the bombs hit, was re-opened. Smoke, water and fire-fighting chemicals poured into the compartment and caused an electric motor to short-circuit, jamming the rudder. For almost 40 minutes, *Enterprise* remained helpless before Chief Machinist William Smith, though twice overcome by fumes, was able to start an emergency motor and the carrier's steering control was restored.

Fletcher now withdrew both his carriers southwards – *Enterprise* ultimately to Pearl Harbour for repairs that deprived the Americans of her services for two crucial months – but not before *Saratoga*'s airmen had delivered another blow against the enemy. The Dauntlesses of Lieutenant Elder and Ensign Gordon sighted Kondo's Advance Force at about 1740 and attacked seaplane carrier *Chitose*, flatteringly identified as a battleship, scoring near misses that flooded her port engine room and forced her to retire with a heavy list. And even after the American withdrawal, *Enterprise* was able to make an important contribution towards future operations. The eleven dive-bombers that she had sent off as the enemy raid materialized were unable to return to her, so their leader, Lieutenant Turner Caldwell, took them to Henderson Field where they joined the 'Cactus Air Force' as the units there were known – after Guadalcanal's code-name – served with it for a month and all, happily, survived the perils that this entailed.

Though Japan's fleet carriers were virtually untouched, their aircraft losses had been so great that Nagumo, like Fletcher, had no wish to continue the fight, and he too withdrew. Rear Admiral Tanaka, true to his nickname, had different ideas but next morning his Reinforcement Group was attacked by aircraft from Henderson Field. His flagship *Jintsu* was badly damaged and troopship *Kinryu Maru* was brought to a halt in a sinking condition. As destroyer *Mutsuki* went alongside to rescue her passengers and crew, eight Flying Fortresses appeared. Neither side had much respect for their abilities but this time the big bombers belied their poor reputation. Three direct hits crashed into the luckless *Mutsuki*, which vanished in a cloud of steam and smoke. Soon afterwards, Tanaka received orders to retire.

It was a hard reminder that the Americans controlled the air and hence the sea during the day. The lesson was repeated on 28 August, when four destroyers attempted another daylight reinforcement mission. This too was engaged by the 'Cactus Air Force' that sank *Asagiri* and so crippled *Shirakumo* that she had to be towed back to base by one of her companions. The pattern was therefore resumed whereby the Japanese got soldiers and supplies to Guadalcanal at night, while the Americans landed their fresh troops and equipment – and also material and personnel for the 'Cactus Air Force' – by day. During the night of 13/14 September and the following day, the Americans also showed they were superior in the ground-fighting; throughout the full 24 hours, they repulsed a series of major attacks on Henderson Field by the new Japanese commander, Major General Kiyotake Kawaguchi, as decisively and almost as completely as they had those of Colonel Ichiki.

Throughout this period, Fletcher's carriers, joined on 30 August by *Hornet*, patrolled to the south-east of Guadalcanal, protecting the supply routes to the island. Here on the 31st, the unlucky *Saratoga* was hit by a torpedo from submarine *I-26* and although she did not suffer a single fatal casualty, flooding caused such damage that she had to follow *Enterprise* to Pearl Harbour, where she remained undergoing repairs for a period of six weeks. Vice Admiral Fletcher bore the blame for this mishap; he was transferred soon afterwards, to spend the rest of the war carrying out less arduous duties in the North Pacific.

On 13 September, *Wasp* recalled her exploits in the Mediterranean, flying off twenty Wildcats to join the 'Cactus Air Force'. Then both she and *Hornet* took up station to provide long-range cover for a troop convoy. At 1444 on the 15th, *Wasp* was steaming into the wind to launch and recover aircraft when submarine *I-19* fired a salvo of six torpedoes at her. Three of them found their mark and apparently two of the others ran on to threaten the *Hornet* group where they struck battleship *North Carolina* and destroyer *O'Brien*.[4] Both had to withdraw from the area for repairs and the destroyer, more seriously damaged than had been supposed, subsequently broke in half and sank.

There was no possibility of *Wasp* being repaired. As bombs and aviation fuel exploded, flames spread with terrifying speed. A huge explosion shook her at about 1500, followed by another that blew one of her elevators into the air. At 1520, 'Abandon Ship' was ordered though *Wasp* lingered on until 2100, when American torpedoes ended her agony. Of her crew, 193 died, 366 were wounded. All except one of the twenty-five aircraft that were airborne when she was hit landed safely on *Hornet*.

These losses could scarcely have been more inopportune for although the Japanese had originally considered the occupation of Guadalcanal subsidiary to the advance on Port Moresby, at the end of August they made the recapture of Henderson Field their prime objective. On 18 September, they further determined that their troops in New Guinea, now within 30 miles of Port Moresby, would go onto the defensive and begin a slow withdrawal, so that all available reinforcements could go to Guadalcanal. During early October, the 'Tokyo Express' duly brought them to the island; Lieutenant General Hyakutake personally arrived on the 9th.

It had been planned that a 'Tokyo Express' should set ashore a particularly large reinforcement of men and equipment, including heavy artillery pieces, on the night of 11/12 October. Its approach was detected and Rear Admiral Norman Scott, commanding a task force of cruisers and destroyers, some of them fitted with new, improved radar sets, attempted to intercept it, only to encounter instead an enemy covering force of similar strength to his own.

The resulting clash, known as the Battle of Cape Esperance after the north-west point of Guadalcanal, provided the delighted and relieved Americans with their first victory in a night action. The Japanese commander, Rear Admiral Aritomo Goto who had led the Port Moresby Close Support Force at Coral Sea, was killed and his flagship, heavy cruiser *Aoba*, was badly damaged. Heavy cruiser *Furutaka* and destroyer *Fubuki* were sunk and next morning, aircraft from Henderson

Field sent two more destroyers, *Murakumo* and *Natsugumo*, to the bottom. Several of Scott's vessels suffered considerable damage but only destroyer, *Duncan*, was lost.

While Scott's success dramatically lifted American spirits, however, it seemed merely a temporary irritation to Hyakutake. By 15 October, he had 22,000 men under his command, the majority of them fresh troops. The Americans could muster a thousand more but many of them were far from fresh and suffering from a variety of ailments. Hyakutake's target was Henderson Field for he rightly regarded American control of the air as a crucial factor in deciding the ownership of the island.

To assist him in attaining his aim, Hyakutake was strongly supported by the Imperial Navy. A carrier force hovered some 300 miles north of Guadalcanal to prevent any American attempt at reinforcement or evacuation and meanwhile to deliver strikes on targets of opportunity; one such on 15 October sank destroyer *Meredith* with the loss of 185 men. Japanese surface vessels were instructed to neutralize Henderson Field by bombardments. In the early hours of 14 October, the greatest of these was delivered by battleships *Kongo* and *Haruna*, while on the nights of both the 14th/15th and the 15th/16th, pairs of heavy cruisers poured their 8-inch shells onto the aerodrome.

Yet despite the damage and casualties inevitably caused, the 'Cactus Air Force' was never subdued. On 15 October, its aircraft so damaged three Japanese transports that these were forced to beach, ultimately becoming total losses. On 25 October, they repulsed another attempted bombardment, this time in daylight, and left light cruiser *Yura* crippled and on fire; her destruction was completed by Flying Fortresses. The defenders of the airfield proved equally steadfast. Starting in the afternoon of 23 October, the Japanese made a whole series of attempts to capture it. By the early hours of the 26th, the last of these had failed with immense losses. Hyakutake accepted that he must await further reinforcements before he could renew his attempts to secure Guadalcanal. Admiral Yamamoto ordered his warships to reverse course to the north.

That, sadly, was not the end of the story. On 18 October, Admiral Chester Nimitz, the Commander-in-Chief, Pacific Fleet, had replaced Vice Admiral Ghormley with Vice Admiral William Halsey, an extremely determined and pugnacious character whose nickname –

bestowed by the newspapers; no one who knew him ever called him this – was 'The Bull'. His appointment was received with delight throughout the South Pacific and gave notice to friend and foe alike that however long and hard the Guadalcanal campaign might be, the Americans would see it through to the end.

Unfortunately Halsey's virtues were weakened by one great defect: his corroding hatred of his foes often prevented him from appreciating what brave and dangerous enemies they were. So now when the Japanese had accepted that their plans had failed and their ships were interested only in retiring, he insisted on bringing about a naval battle under very disadvantageous circumstances that could well have resulted in the loss of America's only two serviceable fleet carriers.

When Halsey took up his post, he had only one carrier under his command but by 26 October, *Enterprise*, her repairs hastily completed, had returned to the South Pacific and joined forces with *Hornet* north of the Santa Cruz Islands, which in turn lay well to the east of Guadalcanal. Both of them were placed under the tactical control of Rear Admiral Kinkaid and were ordered to steam north-westward to engage the Japanese fleet. This put them outside the range of the 'Cactus Air Force' and they were further deprived of the support of a force built around battleship *Washington* that Halsey decided to retain in the vicinity of Guadalcanal to guard against another attempted bombardment. Halsey later came to appreciate his mistake, declaring that he would never again allow the Japanese to 'suck' his 'flat-tops' away to the north.

Furthermore, unlike Midway where, contrary to myth, the Americans had had larger numbers of ships and aircraft available in the actual combat-zone, at the Battle of Santa Cruz it was the Japanese who held these advantages. As usual their fleet was divided into a number of separate formations, the most important being Nagumo's Striking Force containing *Shokaku, Zuikaku*, light carrier *Zuiho*, a heavy cruiser and eight destroyers. *Junyo*, whose lack of speed made it difficult for her to operate in close company with the other Japanese carriers, was stationed to the north-west, screened by a couple of destroyers.[5] In advance of Nagumo steamed the Vanguard Group of Rear Admiral Hiroaki Abe with battleships *Hiei* and *Kirishima*, three heavy cruisers, one light cruiser and seven destroyers. The oddly entitled Advance Group – battleships *Kongo* and *Haruna*, four heavy cruisers, one light cruiser and twelve destroyers under the overall commander, Vice Admiral Kondo – in fact brought up the rear.

The ships in these various formations considerably outnumbered those with the American carriers that, as at the Eastern Solomons, formed the centres of two separate groups about 10 miles apart. *Enterprise* was guarded by battleship *South Dakota*, one heavy and one light cruiser and eight destroyers; *Hornet* by two heavy and two light cruisers and six destroyers. In aircraft, Nagumo could bring fifty-seven Kates, sixty-eight Vals and eighty-seven Zeros against Kinkaid's seventy-two Dauntlesses, twenty-nine Avengers and seventy Wildcats. In addition, *Enterprise* carried a new Air Group, the first to be formed after Pearl Harbour, the pilots of which were mostly very inexperienced, having only just completed their training. A large proportion of American aircraft losses at Santa Cruz would be the results of accidents unrelated to combat.

As so often seems to be the case, the stronger force had most of the luck. *Enterprise* at 0512 sent out sixteen Dauntlesses flying in pairs on armed reconnaissance but it was not until 0650 that two of them, flown by Lieutenant Commander Lee and Ensign Johnson, sighted Nagumo. A Japanese reconnaissance machine had discovered *Hornet* 20 minutes earlier, and though both sides prepared for action, Nagumo had the priceless advantage of being able to strike first. At 0710, a total of eighteen Kates, twenty Vals and eighteen Zeros from *Shokaku* and *Zuikaku*, plus nine Zeros from *Zuiho*, set out to strike at Kinkaid.

Nagumo then made ready for another raid, but at 0740, two more of *Enterprise*'s scouts appeared. They dived on little *Zuiho*, their bombs striking her near the stern and tearing a jagged 50-foot hole in her flight deck that prevented her from conducting any further flying operations. Though pursued for miles by the furious Combat Air Patrol, Lieutenant Strong and Ensign Irvine made good their escape, their gunners downing two Zeros for good measure. Nonetheless, Nagumo was able to get a second strike of twelve Kates, twenty Vals and twelve Zeros airborne at 0822, while *Junyo* contributed eighteen Vals and eleven Zeros soon after 0900.

Meanwhile Kinkaid was also sending out his airmen but in accordance with the then American beliefs and mindful of the need to recover lost time, they flew, as usual, in separate groups. The first of these, fifteen Dauntlesses, six Avengers armed with bombs and eight fighters, left *Hornet* at 0730, but the inexperienced Air Group on *Enterprise* could not launch its raid of three dive-bombers, eight torpedo-planes and eight fighters for another half-hour. Nine more Dauntlesses, nine bomb-carrying Avengers and seven Wildcats from *Hornet* followed at 0815.

Having taken off first, the Japanese arrived first. At 0910, their first wave hurtled down on *Hornet* in a perfectly co-ordinated assault. The Vals had already made a hit on her flight deck aft together with two very near misses, before the most spectacular incident of the raid took place. The aircraft flown by the dive-bombers' leader, Lieutenant Commander Mamoru Seki who had also led the successful attack on *Enterprise* at the Eastern Solomons, was fatally hit but, trailing a long column of flame, he deliberately dived into *Hornet*'s superstructure, then crashed on through the flight deck where two of his bombs exploded, starting a furious fire.

Immediately afterwards, two torpedoes struck *Hornet*'s starboard side, flooding the forward engine room and two boiler rooms and destroying all power and communications. Next, three more bombs found their mark, two of them penetrating deep into the carrier's hull before detonating. Finally, a blazing Kate torpedo-bomber with a doomed pilot at the controls came charging on to dash itself into *Hornet*'s bow close to the forward elevator. The raiders had lost twelve Vals and half-a-dozen Kates, including that of their commander Lieutenant Jiichiro Imajuku, to AA fire, but in ten savage minutes they had left *Hornet* dead in the water, burning from bow to stern, with 111 of her crew dead and 108 others wounded.

The American airmen continued to have ill luck, particularly those from *Enterprise*. On the way to their target they sighted and were sighted by the original Japanese strike force. The Zeros from *Zuiho* attacked out of the sun and at a cost of three of their own aircraft downed four Avengers, including that of the leader, Lieutenant Commander John Collett, and four Wildcats. The survivors attacked Abe's Vanguard Group, as did the Avengers of *Hornet*'s first wave that had lost their dive-bombers in cloud, and the whole of *Hornet*'s second wave. Heavy cruiser *Chikuma* was damaged by bombs.

Only the fifteen Dauntlesses in *Hornet*'s first wave located Nagumo – at 0930. They were engaged by some twenty Zeros that shot down one, damaged two more so badly they had to head back to their mothership, one failing to reach her, and forced the Air Group Leader, Lieutenant Commander William Widhelm to 'ditch'. He and his gunner scrambled into their life raft, from which they watched subsequent events, rather like Ensign Gay at Midway. They were rescued by a Catalina two days later.

Lieutenant James Vose, who now succeeded to the command of the remaining eleven dive-bombers, pressed on unflinchingly. Since lucky *Zuikaku*, as at Coral Sea, had found a rain squall to shelter under and Vose could see that *Zuiho* was still burning, *Shokaku* received the full weight of the Dauntlesses' attack. Four 1,000-lb bombs struck Nagumo's flagship, wrecking flight deck, hangars and elevators, starting fires, reducing her speed, causing about 100 casualties and, best of all, putting her out of action for nine months. Not one of Vose's aircraft was lost.

At this point, honours might be considered even, but the Americans had now struck all their blows, while the Japanese still had two formations airborne. Of Nagumo's second wave, one Kate had to turn back with engine trouble and one Val became separated from its fellows and attacked *Hornet* ineffectually, but the remaining warplanes targeted *Enterprise* on which by further ill fortune, all attention had been directed to a different danger. At 1002, a Wildcat pilot, Lieutenant Albert Pollock, suddenly saw a torpedo, fired by *I-21*, racing towards destroyer *Porter*. He dived down, firing, in the hope of detonating it or at least warning the destroyer, only to be shot at by her ungrateful AA gunners. It was a misunderstanding that cost *Porter* dearly. The torpedo found her boiler room and caused so much damage that the Americans had to sink her.

Consequently, when the Japanese dive-bombers plunged down at about 1015, they caught the Combat Air Patrol by surprise. The anti-aircraft fire, however, especially that from *Enterprise* and *South Dakota*, was devastating. At least fifteen Vals were destroyed and their leader, Lieutenant Sadomu Takahashi, was engaged by a Wildcat as he withdrew and subsequently 'ditched'; he and his gunner were later rescued by a Japanese tanker. Nothing, though, could prevent the Vals from scoring two direct hits and one very near miss; one bomb striking near *Enterprise*'s forward elevator that it put out of action.

Happily for *Enterprise*, Takahashi's men, in their eagerness, had not waited for their torpedo-planes. By the time eleven dark-green Kates appeared the Wildcats were ready – and annihilated them. Lieutenant Stanley Vejtasa alone was credited with having downed six, including that of the veteran Lieutenant Commander Shigeharu Murata who had led the torpedo-bombers at Pearl Harbour. It was one of his victims, however, that achieved the raid's only success; it flew on into the forecastle of destroyer *Smith*, turning this into a mass of flames. Fortunately these were mastered by her damage control personnel, aided by the initiative of Lieutenant Commander Hunter Wood who put his ship's bow close behind *South Dakota*, where the battleship's foaming wake helped to subdue the fires. At 1121, the raiders from *Junyo* also attacked. They made bomb-hits on *South Dakota* and light cruiser *San Juan* inflicting little damage, achieved only one near miss on *Enterprise*, and lost twelve Vals including their leader Lieutenant Masao Yamaguchi.

Nonetheless, *Enterprise* was still in a vulnerable position. Aircraft from both US carriers returning from their own raids had to land on her and the resulting confusion, aggravated by her inoperative elevator, made future operations very difficult. Since it was known that the Japanese still possessed two undamaged carriers, Kinkaid had little choice but to withdraw to the south-east, which he did at 1400.

Meanwhile, *Hornet*, her fires brought under control and most of her crew taken off, was being towed slowly towards safety by heavy cruiser *Northampton*. Her plight had become known to her enemies and Rear Admiral Abe's Vanguard Group was heading towards her at high speed, ready for a surface action. Yamamoto even hoped that she might be captured as reassuring evidence of the Imperial Navy's superiority. And at 1515, nine Kates and five Zeros from *Junyo* renewed the air-attacks on her. Seven of the Kates, including their leader Lieutenant Yoshiaki Irikiin, were lost but a torpedo, tearing open her starboard side, sealed *Hornet*'s fate. The remainder of her crew was ordered to leave her.

Though this decision was unquestionably correct, *Hornet* now proved embarrassingly durable. The bulk of her escorts retired but left a couple of destroyers to finish her off. They put nine more torpedoes into her but at this stage of the war American torpedoes were not famed for their effectiveness and she remained afloat. They then fired 430 5-inch shells at her, reducing her to a furnace, but she was still afloat when at 2040, the approach of Abe's ships forced them to retire.

At least there was now no question of her falling into enemy hands and at 2100, she was finally sent to the bottom by four 'Long Lances'.

It cannot be disputed that Santa Cruz was an American defeat and one that left them with only a single crippled fleet carrier ready for service. Such was their concern that, in response to urgent requests, HMS *Victorious* was sent to Pearl Harbour. Here, though, she had to re-equip with American machines and train her airmen in their use, as otherwise she would have been unable to make good any losses suffered, and by the time this had been completed, the crisis had passed.

Yet if the Americans had lost more ships, the Japanese had lost more airmen – a reversal of the situation after Midway. While seventy-four US aircraft had been destroyed most of these were the victims of accidents caused by inexperience; only twenty had fallen in combat. By contrast, sixty-nine Japanese warplanes had been shot down, twenty-three more had 'ditched' and about 140 irreplaceable veteran airmen were dead, among them, as will have been noticed, almost all the Val and Kate formation commanders. So great were the losses that *Zuikaku*, as after Coral Sea, was temporarily inoperable for lack of aircrews to man her.

It seems indeed that while the Imperial Navy in general was lifted by its victory, those concerned with its naval aviation were much less elated. Nagumo was not asked to bring his carriers into action again and like his old antagonist Fletcher, he would be found later only in less important posts.[6] Though carrier *Junyo* was still fit for action and was now joined by her sister-ship *Hiyo*, they remained well to the north-west of Guadalcanal and accordingly, unlike *Enterprise* for all her jammed elevator, they had no influence on the next, most decisive of the six savage sea-fights that were the highlights of the campaign.

This was the appropriately named Battle of Guadalcanal. It began in the early hours of 13 November and ended in the early afternoon of the 15th. The Japanese had determined on another massive effort to take Henderson Field. A series of 'Tokyo Express' missions in early November had raised Hyakutake's strength to 30,000 ground troops. Now a convoy of eleven troopships, carrying 13,500 men, escorted by eleven destroyers under Rear Admiral Tanaka and provided with long-range fighter cover by *Hiyo* and *Junyo*, was due to arrive on the 13th. To help clear the way for it, Abe, now a Vice Admiral, was to bombard the airfield with battleships *Hiei* and *Kirishima* on the previous night.

The first true aircraft carrier was HMS *Argus*. She joined the Fleet as early as September 1918 but still saw action in the Second World War and is here shown under attack while escorting the 'Harpoon' convoy to Malta in June 1942.

Most early carriers were, like *Argus*, not originally designed as such. Both USS *Lexington* (above) and IJN *Akagi* (below) were converted from battle-cruiser hulls.

British flag officers in the Mediterranean who found that possessing an aircraft carrier gave them an immense advantage. Left: Admiral Sir Andrew Cunningham, Commander-in-Chief, Mediterranean Fleet at Alexandria. Right: Vice Admiral Sir James Somerville, Commander Force H at Gibraltar.

HMS *Ark Royal* in the Mediterranean. She was the first British fleet carrier to be designed and built as a carrier from the start.

A Fulmar fighter touches down on HMS *Illustrious*. In the foreground are two Sea Gladiators. From *Illustrious* was launched the strike on Taranto that first proved the value of the aircraft carrier.

Italian battleship *Cavour* on the bottom of Taranto harbour. She was the first major warship to be sunk by aircraft from a carrier.

Swordfish on the deck of *Ark Royal*. They would bring about the destruction of the German battleship *Bismarck* by hitting her with a torpedo that jammed her rudder.

Its torpedo is fitted onto a Swordfish.

Admiral Isoroku Yamamoto, Commander-in-Chief of the Japanese Navy who planned the attack on Pearl Harbour.

Vice Admiral Chuichi Nagumo whose carrier-aircraft delivered the attack.

The attackers take off. Above: A Zero fighter from carrier *Soryu*. Below: A Val dive-bomber from carrier *Shokaku*, flown by Lieutenant Commander Kakuichi Takahashi who led the first wave of dive-bombers and was later killed in action in the Battle of the Coral Sea.

Coral Sea: 'Scratch one flat-top!' – IJN light carrier *Shoho*.

Coral Sea: The loss of 'Lady Lex'.

Japanese aircraft that fought in the early carrier battles. Top: Zero fighter. Centre: Val dive-bomber. Bottom: Kate Torpedo-bomber.

American aircraft that fought in the early carrier battles. Top: Wildcat fighters. Bottom: Dauntless dive-bombers over USS *Enterprise*. In the Battle of Midway Island, four Japanese carriers were sunk by Dauntlesses, three of them by Dauntlesses flying from *Enterprise*.

The Americans also lost a carrier at Midway. USS *Yorktown* was attacked by dive-bombers (above) and torpedo-bombers (below) all from IJN carrier *Hiryu*. She was crippled and later finished off by a Japanese submarine.

Yorktown was quickly avenged. *Hiryu*, hit by four bombs, is left abandoned and burning.

61

To the aid of Malta: Operation HURRY. On the left is HMS *Argus* with the RAF Hurricanes that will fly from her to Malta on her deck. On the right is HMS *Ark Royal* forming part of her escort. A Swordfish keeps watch above.

To the aid of Malta: Operation PEDESTAL. Sea Hurricanes on the deck of HMS *Victorious*. Behind her is HMS *Indomitable* and in the background HMS *Eagle*. This was the first time that three British fleet carriers had been included in one task group.

The Guadalcanal campaign. Above: US carrier *Wasp* sunk by a submarine. Below: US carrier *Hornet* under attack by dive-bombers and torpedo-bombers. She was crippled, abandoned and subsequently sunk by torpedoes from Japanese destroyers.

Assistance from America. Above: Martlet fighter on the deck of HMS *Indomitable*. The Martlet was the British name for the Wildcat. It was one of several American types that saw service with the Royal Navy. Below: USS *Guadalcanal*, one of the American escort carriers that helped to win the Battle of the Atlantic.

'Worthy antagonists' in the Battle of the Philippine Sea. Left: Vice Admiral Marc Mitscher, Commander of Task Force 58, the Fast Carrier Force of the US Fifth Fleet. Right: Vice Admiral Jisaburo Ozawa, Commander of the Japanese First Mobile Fleet.

Hellcat fighter on the deck of USS *Lexington* (the second vessel to bear this name). In the background is USS *Enterprise*. During the Battle of the Philippine Sea, the new Hellcats and their highly-trained pilots inflicted terrible losses on the Japanese.

IJN carrier *Zuikaku* under attack in the Battle of the Philippine Sea. In the foreground are two of her escorting destroyers. Though severely damaged, *Zuikaku* survived, only to be sunk by US carrier-aircraft just over four months later in the Battle of Leyte Gulf.

Another victim of the US airmen in the Battle of Leyte Gulf was light carrier *Zuiho* seen here in action during that battle.

US carriers also suffered at Leyte Gulf. Above: Light carrier *Princeton*, sunk by a lone enemy dive-bomber. Below: Escort carrier *Gambier Bay*, sunk by gunfire from enemy heavy cruisers.

US escort carrier *St Lo*, first but far from last warship to be sunk by Kamikaze attack.

The Royal Navy in the Pacific: Seafires over HMS *Indomitable*.

Luckily for the Americans, their code-breakers had revealed the enemy's intentions and so enabled them to take counter-measures. On 11 November, *Enterprise*, although her wrecked elevator had still not been repaired, proceeded to a position south-east of Guadalcanal. Reinforcements brought the 'Cactus Air Force' to a strength of over 100 operational aeroplanes. And on the 11th and 12th, two convoys, protected by Rear Admiral Norman Scott, the victor of Cape Esperance, and Rear Admiral Daniel Callaghan respectively, unloaded men and supplies for the US ground troops. A heavy air raid was beaten off at the cost of minor damage to Callaghan's flagship, heavy cruiser *San Francisco*, rammed by a crippled Betty bomber, and the two groups then combined under Callaghan's command to engage a more formidable foe.

On Friday 13 November, Callaghan and Scott with thirteen warships met Abe's battleships in a night action. By morning, both were dead and Scott's flagship, light cruiser *Atlanta*, was so damaged she had to be scuttled. Destroyers *Cushing*, *Laffey*, *Barton* and *Monssen* had been sunk; *San Francisco*, heavy cruiser *Portland*, light cruiser *Juneau* and two more destroyers had been badly damaged; and a torpedo from submarine *I-26* finished off the wretched *Juneau* next morning. On the Japanese side, only destroyers *Akatsuki* and *Yudachi* had gone down, but battleship *Hiei* had been crippled and left limping away slowly to the north.

Enterprise now made her most important contribution to the battle. Kinkaid had adopted a policy that would later be called 'shuttle-bombing'; he sent out nine Avengers and four Wildcats under instructions to attack any targets found and then proceed to Henderson Field. At about 1020, these sighted *Hiei* and, ignoring a salvo from her 14-inch guns, put two torpedoes into her. They then flew on to Guadalcanal where they refuelled and rearmed and at 1430, were back to strike *Hiei* – which had meanwhile been hit three times by Dauntlesses of the 'Cactus Air Force' – with two more torpedoes that left her dead in the water. She sank at about 1900, taking 450 officers and men down with her.

Yamamoto did not let her loss end the operation. Tanaka's transports retired temporarily but would resume their advance on the 14th, and on the night of the 13th/14th, a strong force of cruisers and destroyers bombarded Henderson Field, wrecking a number of aircraft but failing to make the aerodrome inoperable. Next morning, its pilots damaged several of the bombardment vessels; after which *Enterprise* once more took a hand. Lieutenant Gibson and Ensign Buchanan on an armed reconnaissance mission attacked the retreating enemy at 0915, and both scored bomb hits on heavy cruiser *Kinugasa*. An hour later, seventeen Dauntlesses and ten Wildcats from *Enterprise* finished her off.

Thereafter the American airmen concentrated on the Japanese troop transports. During the day, the 'Cactus Air Force' destroyed four of them and so damaged a fifth that she had to turn back. Kinkaid sent off another 'shuttle-bombing' raid from *Enterprise*: its eight Dauntlesses and twelve Wildcats sank two more transports, then continued on to Henderson Field. This left Kinkaid with only eighteen fighters, so he now retired, but not before detaching from his screen battleships *Washington* and *South Dakota* and four destroyers under Rear Admiral Willis Lee, with orders to proceed to Guadalcanal so as to oppose any further bombardment missions.

It was just as well, for Vice Admiral Kondo had been instructed to deliver a really effective blow at Henderson Field. He originally commanded two heavy cruisers, one light cruiser and five destroyers, but to them he added battleship *Kirishima*, another light cruiser and four destroyers from Abe's force. Shortly before midnight on the 14th/15th, Lee and Kondo clashed.

At first the Japanese had much the better of it, losing destroyer *Ayanami* but sinking three US destroyers, *Benham*, *Preston* and *Walke*, and badly damaging *South Dakota* and the fourth destroyer, *Gwin*. Mercifully, Lee's flagship *Washington* was equipped with the very latest radar, the aid of which enabled him to direct a devastating barrage onto *Kirishima* that left her in flames, her steering gear wrecked and two turrets out of action. Though she was still capable of withdrawing, it was clear that she could never do so in time to escape the same fate as *Hiei* at the hands of the 'Cactus Air Force' and, the Japanese incorrectly believed, of *Enterprise*. To save pointless loss of life, her survivors were taken off, her sea valves were opened and she joined her sister-ship on the floor of Ironbottom Sound.

It was perhaps the ultimate tribute to the effectiveness of air attacks on surface warships. That this was a wise decision was shown in the last phase of the battle. The indomitable Tanaka, in an attempt to get as many men and supplies ashore as possible, beached his last four transports near to the Japanese base at Tassafaronga that night, then hastily took his destroyers to safety. During the morning of the 15th, the 'Cactus Air Force' systematically demolished the stranded vessels and slaughtered their crews, their passengers and the men trying to unload them. Just 2,000 demoralized soldiers, 260 cases of ammunition and 1,500 bags of rice reached Hyakutake. The Americans had shattered the last Japanese attempt to reinforce Guadalcanal.

The remainder of the campaign may be dealt with briefly. The Japanese thereafter did no more than keep their existing troops supplied, thus allowing the Americans to take the offensive and slowly but surely drive back a stubborn enemy. Not that they had everything their own way. Indeed on 30 November, another clash at night, the Battle of Tassafaronga, proved not only the last of the six major naval actions but, for the Americans, the most humiliating.

Shortly before midnight, a US Task Force of four heavy cruisers, one light cruiser and six destroyers, warned by their code-breakers, ambushed a 'Tokyo Express' of eight destroyers led by the redoubtable Rear Admiral Tanaka. Seven of the Japanese vessels formed a column with the other one stationed some 2,000 yards to port, nearest to the Americans. This luckless ship, *Takanami*, drew almost all the American fire and was duly sunk, but her sacrifice enabled Tanaka's other destroyers to counter-attack, not with guns but with their 'Long Lances'. All four of the US heavy cruisers were struck and had it not been for improved damage control procedures set in place after Savo Island, every one of them would have been lost. As it was, *Northampton*, her side torn open by two torpedoes from *Oyashio*, capsized and sank; *Minneapolis*, *New Orleans* and *Pensacola* were put out of action for nine months or more; and some 400 American seamen lost their lives.

Clearly the Japanese could still be deadly in a night-action and in future they were harried after dark only by PT-boats, the American equivalent of the British Motor Torpedo Boats. On the night of 11/12 December, these gained an important success by sinking destroyer *Terutsuki* on which Tanaka was then flying his flag. Even he began to query whether the retention of Guadalcanal was worth the dangers involved. His superiors agreed and on 31 December, the Emperor gave his formal permission for the garrison there to be withdrawn. Preparations for this were concealed from the Americans by a fortuitous change in the main Japanese naval code and by Japanese land-based bombers making attacks on US warships in the vicinity of the island. On 29 and 30 January 1943, a series of raids by torpedo-carrying Bettys sank heavy cruiser *Chicago*[7], while on 1 February, dive-bombers sank destroyer *DeHaven*.

Meanwhile on the night of 14/15 January, the Japanese had at last landed more men – 600 of them – on Guadalcanal. This, though, was to provide fresh troops to act as a rearguard for their intended evacuation. On the night of 1/2 February, twenty destroyers successfully carried out the first part of this, though one of them, *Makigumo*, was so damaged by a mine that she had to be scuttled. On the 4th, most of the remaining Japanese garrison, including Hyakutake, were rescued. On the 7th, the rest were taken off. In all, 11,000 men were evacuated safely. The Americans only found out two days later.

The six month struggle for Guadalcanal had cost the US Navy twenty-four major warships: *Wasp*, *Hornet*, six heavy cruisers (if we may include *Canberra*), two light cruisers and fourteen destroyers. The Japanese losses were smaller and on balance less important: *Ryujo*, two battleships, three heavy cruisers, one light cruiser and eleven destroyers – eighteen in all. Yet their sunken ships would prove impossible to replace, whereas the amazing industrial capacity of the United States, then just getting into its stride, would soon make good American losses and thereafter increase their Fleet to a size that neither Japan nor any other country could hope to match.

Moreover as a result of the Guadalcanal campaign the American seamen had become qualified to make the best possible use of their material superiority. At its start, the Japanese had worked out their tactics and were well trained in the use of them. The US ships, by contrast, contained a high proportion of new recruits who had entered the service after the commencement of hostilities, received limited training and knew little of the problems they were likely to encounter. By the time the campaign ended, their experiences had taught them almost all the necessary lessons. As Tanaka, no mean judge, declared: they 'grew wise'.

Strategically, the capture of Guadalcanal was of immense importance. When the Japanese lost their airfield, the threat to the Australian supply lines was lifted; whereas the Americans had secured an advance base from which they could take the offensive, first against the northern Solomons, then on into the heart of Japan's newly won conquests. On 18 April 1943, they gave a dramatic illustration of this when sixteen Lockheed Lightnings from Henderson Field, acting on information from their code-breakers, appeared over the southern tip of Bougainville Island. Here, at the cost of one of their number, they intercepted and shot down two Bettys and three of their escorting Zeros. Among the Japanese who were killed was the Commander-in-Chief of their Navy.

Perhaps for Admiral Yamamoto death was not wholly unwelcome. In the volume of his Official History describing *The Struggle for Guadalcanal August 1942 – February 1943*, Professor Morison refers to a captured Japanese Intelligence Summary declaring that the ultimate ownership of Guadalcanal would mark 'the fork in the road which leads to victory for them or for us'. As Morison records with justifiable satisfaction, henceforward 'the war followed the right fork' – for the Americans. 'It was rough, tough and uncharted, but it led to Tokyo.'

And before that other roads would lead to Rome and to Berlin.

Notes

1 *Canberra* was only one of a number of losses suffered by the Australians in the early part of the Pacific War. Britain therefore arranged the transfer of heavy cruiser HMS *Shropshire* to the Royal Australian Navy, with which she later served with distinction.

2 This was what it was called by its defenders and the Marine Corps still gives this name to the battle that was to come. In reality, though, the river was the Ilu, having been wrongly identified on the Americans' inadequate maps.

3 The word 'maru' included in the name of Japanese merchant vessels was one added to the names of aristocrats' sons during Japan's feudal age. To give it to a ship implies a personality, in the same way as Europeans or Americans call a vessel not 'it' but 'she'.

4 Another enemy submarine, *I-15*, was in the vicinity but it seems that she made no attack. Japanese torpedoes had an amazingly long range.

5 Carrier *Hiyo*, which like *Junyo* had been converted from a passenger liner, had originally formed part of this group but had been forced to retire with engine trouble.

6 In mid-1944, Nagumo was in charge of Japanese forces in the Mariana Islands when the Americans invaded Saipan where he had his headquarters. On 6 July, with its loss clearly imminent, he committed suicide. By a strange coincidence, Vice Admiral Takagi who had led the Carrier Striking Force at Coral Sea was also in Saipan at this time, in command of the submarines in the area, and was killed in action.

7 This episode has been dignified by the Americans as the Battle of Rennell Island.

Chapter 7

Convoy Cover

As the Americans fought their way across the Pacific towards Tokyo, they met resolute opposition on land, at sea and in the air; but at least they had few worries about the security of their supply-lines, since the Japanese submarines concentrated on attacking warships, not merchantmen. On the contrary, it was the Japanese supply-lines that were menaced by undersea assaults and once early deficiencies in the torpedoes of America's submarines had been rectified, they made a mockery of Japan's early conquests by preventing an ever-increasing proportion of her newly-acquired raw materials from reaching the Japanese homeland. In the European theatre it was a very different story, with the materials that Britain and Russia needed to wage war, and in the case of Britain even the food to sustain her population, coming under relentless threat from Germany's U-boat fleet, the 'Wolf Pack'.

In the early days of the Second World War, the U-boats' activities were limited by a shortage of numbers, problems with torpedoes and restrictions imposed by Hitler for diplomatic reasons, much to the disgust of his naval chiefs. By mid-1940, however, the numbers had been increased, the problems rectified and the restrictions lifted, leading to a period that the U-boat crews called 'The Happy Time'. It was made still more happy by their having gained an important ally, though one that would in turn hasten the entry of aircraft carriers into that longest and grimmest of the war's great struggles, the Battle of the Atlantic.

As from August 1940, British merchant vessels also had to face not only the U-boats but the Focke-Wulf Fw 200C Condors. These were huge four-engined bombers whose range of 2,210 miles at a cruising speed of 180 mph enabled them to fly from their base at Bordeaux, strike at shipping well to the west of the British Isles and far beyond the reach of shore-based fighters, and then continue on to land in Norway. By March 1941, they had sunk eighty-five vessels including five in one day on 9 February and they added to their deadly effectiveness by acting as scouts for the U-boats. They would circle a convoy for hours, safely out of the range of any AA guns, sending out a constant stream of information – indeed there is an amusing if improbable story of a Convoy Commodore signalling a request to the Focke-Wulf to fly the other way round as he was getting giddy watching it.

To combat the Focke-Wulf menace it was essential that convoys be given fighter cover. In his memoirs, *Afternoon Light*, Sir Robert Menzies, the then Prime Minister of Australia who was in England at this time, describes how Churchill related his plan that, in the absence of aircraft carriers, 'ships in convoy should each carry a fighter aircraft, with a catapult mechanism'. When Menzies asked 'what the fighter-pilot was to do after his attack aloft, Winston's reply was that he would ditch his plane as near as possible to a ship and hope to be rescued.' When this proposal was put to the First Sea Lord, Admiral of the Fleet, Sir Dudley Pound, he told Churchill bluntly that it was 'nonsense' – but that did not conclude the incident, as Menzies believed.

Churchill, in fact, was not to be dissuaded and two different types of vessel would in due course be employed on this hazardous duty. Fighter Catapult ships were converted naval auxiliaries, flying the white ensign and manned by naval personnel. It was originally intended that the fighters they would carry would be Fulmars but these lacked the necessary speed and rate of climb to be effective, and HMS *Maplin*, formerly the fast banana-boat *Erin*, was therefore given first two, later three adapted Hurricanes. She sailed on convoy protection duties from May 1941 to June 1942 and on 3 August 1941, her senior pilot, Lieutenant Robert Everett, earned a DSO by shooting down a Condor 450 miles from Land's End; he then 'ditched' his Hurricane and was picked up safely.

Only Hurricanes were allocated to the other type of vessel to carry catapult-fighters. There were thirty-five of these CAM-ships, the initials standing for Catapult Aircraft Merchantmen[1], and they served from May 1941 to as late as July 1943 in both the Atlantic and the Arctic. Their pilots shot down six enemy aircraft including three Condors, damaged others and drove off several more; their value as a deterrent was immense; and despite all the dangers they faced, only one pilot lost his life and that not through any fault of man or machine, but because a parachute did not open sufficiently.

Yet while the CAM-ships and Fighter Catapult ships had certainly carried aircraft, they had no flight decks and so could not retrieve them. They therefore cannot be classed as true aircraft carriers. Nonetheless, quite apart from their own achievements they paved the way for the auxiliary or escort carrier, the first of which would follow hard on their heels. In February 1940, a German blockade runner, the 5,600-ton *Hannover*, had been intercepted. Her crew attempted to destroy her by starting fires but these were eventually extinguished and the vessel towed into port. In June 1941, she reappeared, fitted with a flight deck 420 feet long by 60 feet wide (but no hangar or elevator), renamed as HMS *Audacity*. Her new career would be short but so revealing that by the time it ended, the Allies would be demanding that more escort carriers be produced as fast as possible, and the Germans were regarding their destruction as a matter of primary importance.

Audacity's first operation came on 13 September 1941, when she set out to cover a convoy bound for Gibraltar, whence its ships would proceed to ports in West Africa or round the Cape of Good Hope to the Middle East. The route lay dangerously close to the Condors' base at Bordeaux and *Audacity*'s main role was to provide fighter protection against them; she therefore carried Martlets of 802 Squadron though, since she lacked a hangar, she could only operate half-a-dozen of these.[2] As they could land back on her, however, it was possible for them to fly patrols and these quickly proved a valuable weapon against the U-boats also. On the evening of the 15th, a pair of Martlets sighted a submarine just over the horizon from the convoy. Racing up, they forced it into a hasty dive that caused it to lose contact, thereby causing a lengthy postponement of the threatened attack.

It was not until 20 September, in fact, that another U-boat sighted the convoy. This also was forced to dive by the Martlets but it had already sent out its report and that night two merchantmen were torpedoed and went down, while others lost touch in the confusion, one of them being sunk later. Early on the 21st, a Focke-Wulf Condor joined in the fight, bombing and sinking another freighter. It quickly paid for its success, as a couple of Martlets pounced on it and shot it into the sea.

At Gibraltar, *Audacity* joined the escort of a large homeward-bound convoy but this time her voyage was without incident except that one of her fighters made a poor landing and went over the side. Happily, the pilot was rescued. Another 'Gibraltar run' in November proved more demanding, with *Audacity*'s Martlets again engaging prowling Condors. They shot down two of these but the CO of 802 Squadron, Lieutenant Commander Wintour, was killed by return fire from a Condor's gunners. This convoy, though, was little more than a practice for the passage of Convoy HG 76 that left Gibraltar on 14 December 1941.

Intelligence reports had indicated that a large concentration of U-boats had gathered across the route of HG 76 and heavy attacks on it were certain to take place. A strong covering group was therefore provided, led by Commander Frederick John Walker, who had given his team intensive training in anti-submarine tactics and was destined to become the most successful of U-boat 'killers'. On this occasion, he had the further advantage that his escort group had received an important reinforcement: *Audacity*.

The little auxiliary carrier first proved her worth early on 17 December, when her patrolling aircraft discovered *U-131* shadowing the convoy. Walker at once sent a detachment of ships to the scene and they depth-charged the submarine, forcing her to the surface. At first she offered resistance, shooting down a Martlet that strafed her bridge, killing the pilot. As shells from Walker's destroyers began to fall around her, however, her captain accepted that his position was hopeless and scuttled her; he and his crew being taken aboard by their attackers.

This success prevented further assaults until 18 December, but from then until the early hours of the 22nd, there was a continuous struggle between the convoy and the 'Wolf Pack', that saw the destruction of three more U-boats, and the loss of two merchantmen and destroyer *Stanley*. *Audacity* continued to give warning of submarines and direct destroyers against them, as well as attending to scouting Condors. Two of these were damaged and driven off by her Martlets on the 18th, while on the following day, the interceptors downed two more Focke-Wulfs and damaged yet another.

Sadly, though, the U-boats were destined to achieve one final success. The practice had been adopted on this and previous operations of detaching *Audacity* at dusk and keeping her clear of the convoy until morning. As darkness fell on 21 December, she therefore withdrew and was thus steaming alone when *U-751*, cautiously approaching on the surface, sighted her. Soon after 2000, a torpedo struck her port side, flooding her engine room and bringing her to a halt. The submarine then closed in to point-blank range to put at least two more torpedoes into her. She sank at 2035, with heavy loss of life, including that of her skipper, Commander Mackendrick.

Her achievements were not forgotten. The United States had now entered the war and American shipyards were starting to produce escort carriers, originally as conversions from freighters or tankers but later purpose-built. They also supplied such ships to the Royal Navy. The first of these was HMS *Archer*, quickly followed by *Avenger*, *Biter* and *Dasher*, and since *Archer* was constantly troubled with mechanical defects, it was *Avenger* that first saw service. She would earn a reputation to rival that of *Audacity* as a convoy protector, though on a very different route – through the icy waters of the Arctic Ocean to the Russian ports of Murmansk and Archangel.

Not that *Avenger* was the only, or even the first carrier to participate in convoys to Russia. From the moment of the German invasion, Churchill had promised the Russians every possible help and the famous PQ convoys, as they were called after the letters with which their code-names began – returning convoys bore the letters QP – would soon be delivering tanks, motor transport, aircraft, ammunition, fuel, raw materials and medical supplies to Britain's new ally. Unfortunately, Germany had also gained a new ally, for Finland had sought revenge for a brutal Russian attack on her in 1939, and the enemy thus had bases within close range of the ports to which the Arctic convoys were directed. It seemed only sensible therefore to provide fighter cover for the merchantmen while their precious cargoes were being unloaded.

Accordingly when the very first Russian convoy, prior even to the first of the 'PQs', assembled at Iceland at the end of August 1941, its seven merchantmen not only enjoyed the distant protection of a naval force that contained *Victorious*, but was accompanied by *Argus* with twenty-four RAF Hurricanes on board. On 7 September, these flew from her to Vaenga airfield near Murmansk. The merchantmen continued to Archangel where they discharged their main cargo of munitions and also put ashore fifteen more Hurricanes in crates. These later joined the ones already at Vaenga to form two RAF squadrons that served with distinction until the approach of winter put an end to operations – at which point they handed over their machines to Russian pilots whom they had previously taught to fly the Hurricanes, and returned home.

'General Winter' – a long standing nickname for the incredibly harsh Russian winters – also aided the Russians with shattering effect and this had a profound influence on the German outlook with regard to the PQ convoys. While they believed that they would knock out Russia within six months, the supplies being sent from Britain appeared little more than a nuisance. But when their power of movement was brought to an end, they were driven back from the outskirts of Moscow, and perhaps only Hitler's stubborn resolve not to yield an inch of ground without a struggle prevented a retreat more catastrophic than that of Napoleon: then their attitude changed completely.

In January 1942, German aircraft, submarines and surface warships began to congregate in Norway, not only to strike at the Russian convoys but to guard against a possible British invasion which Hitler had become convinced would be attempted and for which, interestingly enough, Churchill tells us he 'always hankered' and 'fought hard' throughout most of 1942. On 16 January, *Bismarck*'s sister-ship *Tirpitz* arrived at Trondheim and on 12 February, *Scharnhorst*, *Gneisenau* and *Prinz Eugen* broke out of Brest and through the English Channel with the ultimate aim of joining her – a great humiliation for the British, partly redeemed by the courage of the inadequate forces sent against them.[3] Fortunately for the PQ convoys, both the battle-cruisers were heavily damaged by mines and Bomber Command hit *Gneisenau* while she was under repair in dry dock, putting her out of action for the rest of the war. Only *Prinz Eugen* reached Norwegian waters – just in time to be crippled by a submarine's torpedo.

That, though, still left the most lethal threat to the ships supplying Russia: *Tirpitz*. On 6 March, accompanied by four destroyers and flying the flag of Vice Admiral Otto Ciliax who had commanded the battle-cruisers during their 'Channel Dash', she set out to attack the two convoys then at sea: PQ 12 on its way to Russia and the returning QP 8. Both of these had been revealed to the Germans by intercepted and decoded wireless signals, and in the case of the former, by a scouting Condor as well.

For their part, the British were kept well informed of the build-up of German naval and aerial strength in Norway, and Admiral Tovey's Home Fleet, which included two battleships, a battle-cruiser and carrier *Victorious*, was also on hand. Tovey's task was not an easy one, since he had to guard two separate convoys, he was faced with a formidable opponent and his movements were restricted by Admiralty orders to remain out of range of German shore-based bombers and torpedo-planes and to keep his vessels concentrated so that they could all be protected by his carrier's Fulmars. Soon after midnight on 6/7 March, he received a report from submarine *Seawolf* patrolling off Trondheim that 'a large enemy warship' was heading northwards at high speed. Tovey at once steered to close the convoys, due to pass each other at midday on the 7th, and ordered *Victorious* to send out an air search at dawn.

It was never launched. Dawn brought vile weather: fog, clouds and heavy snow-squalls. Tovey could not locate *Tirpitz*, while Ciliax, after detaching his destroyers so as to search over a wider front, could still find neither convoy, though the destroyers came so close to QP 8 that they sank a Russian ship that had straggled behind it. Throughout that day and for most of the following one, both sides groped about ineffectively until finally at 1800 on 8 March, Ciliax abandoned his mission and set a course for Trondheim.

Tirpitz was now no longer the hunter but the hunted. Intercepted signals notified the Admiralty, and hence Admiral Tovey, of the battleship's intentions and the Home Fleet which was then about 200 miles to the west, turned south-eastwards to cut her off. Once more Tovey warned *Victorious* to make ready for operations at daybreak and, in improving weather, she sent out six Albacores to search for their target at 0640, and a strike force of twelve more armed with torpedoes at 0730. They were spurred on by a signal from Tovey, telling them they had 'a wonderful chance which may achieve most valuable results'.

It was not to be. At about 0800, one of the scouting Albacores sighted *Tirpitz* but since she was herself seen as well, Ciliax appreciated that an attack by carrier aircraft would almost certainly follow. He therefore changed course to eastward to make for Narvik. *Tirpitz* was now steaming into a strong wind and this combined with her speed to ensure that when the torpedo-armed Albacores appeared at 0842, they could only overhaul her very slowly. They climbed into cloud cover, intending to pass ahead of her but just as they were about to fly over her, the clouds parted, ending any hope of their achieving surprise. They therefore split into four sub-flights of three aircraft each and attacked from both sides.

As the Germans would later confirm, the assault was made with 'determination and dash', regardless of a tremendous barrage of AA fire that brought down two Albacores; but it was not well co-ordinated by pilots who had only recently been brought together and who lacked intensive training and experience. *Tirpitz* was able to evade all their torpedoes and reached Narvik safely that evening. The only consolation for *Victorious* was that an attack on her by three Junkers Ju 88 bombers in the afternoon made no hits either.

Neither Hitler nor Raeder was happy about the lack of results achieved by this sortie and both were alarmed at what they considered was a narrow escape for *Tirpitz*. The value of the aircraft carrier was again emphasized and the Germans now resumed work on their own carrier, the *Graf Zeppelin*, and planned to convert heavy cruiser *Seydlitz* and three liners, *Europa*, *Potsdam* and (another) *Gneisenau*, into carriers as well. It was really too late for such steps, however, and Germany's ever-increasing requirements in other fields soon led to the abandonment of the intended conversions, while even the work on *Graf Zeppelin* was given little priority and was again halted in 1943. Still uncompleted, she was scuttled at Stettin on the River Oder on 24 April 1945. The wreck was later refloated by the Russians but capsized under tow, supposedly because she had become top-heavy through having been overloaded with loot.

German respect for carriers also contributed to a reluctance to commit their giant battleship against the Arctic convoys as long as she faced the possibility of attack by naval aircraft. It may be, though, that a shortage of fuel was an equal consideration, for when *Tirpitz* was next directed against a convoy, *Victorious* again formed part of the distant covering force. *Tirpitz* left harbour on the afternoon of 5 July 1942, only to turn back in the evening. By that time, in any case, her presence was no longer needed, since her intended target, convoy PQ 17, was already disintegrating.

Evidence obtained by the 'Ultra' Intelligence had revealed that a strong enemy surface force including *Tirpitz* had assembled ready for an attack on the convoy but by the evening of 4 July had given no indication as to whether this had in fact sailed or not. Nonetheless Admiral Pound, despite the contrary opinions of his Intelligence staff, was convinced it had. He therefore directed the convoy to scatter and its escorts to be prepared to engage an enemy that never materialized. Proceeding individually, robbed of their protection against U–boats and deprived of the concentrated AA fire that had previously defied air attacks, the merchantmen were decimated. Eleven only reached Archangel. Twenty-three freighters, a tanker and a rescue ship were lost, as were the 430 tanks, 210 aircraft and 3,350 vehicles that formed part of their cargo.

For political reasons it was essential that a new large convoy be sent to Russia quickly but commitments elsewhere meant that PQ 18 had to be postponed until September. Moreover, German Intelligence had again been active and obtained detailed information of Allied plans. Extensive preparations were made to engage the convoy with submarines and aircraft, particularly the latter because the Luftwaffe had mistakenly believed that the dispersal of PQ 17 had been achieved by air attacks. Reichsmarschall Göring personally urged his men to make a 'special effort' against PQ 18, and they had ninety-two torpedo-planes – Heinkel He 111s and Junkers Ju 88s – and 133 long-range bombers with which to do so.

To protect the forty merchantmen – flying the flags of Britain, the United States, Russia and Panama – that comprised PQ 18, the commander of the escorting forces, Rear Admiral Robert Burnett, was given the anti-aircraft cruiser *Scylla*, eighteen destroyers and, most important, one escort carrier. It was now that HMS *Avenger* made her appearance and she alone was responsible for providing fighter cover, as *Victorious* had left Arctic waters to serve on the 'Malta Run', and later to assist the Americans in the Pacific as related elsewhere in this narrative.

Avenger was not really very well suited for her immensely important task. Of some 8,200 tons displacement, she had originally been built as the merchantman *Rio Hudson*, to which the US shipyards had added a 440 foot long flight deck with a small hangar under its after end. So hastily had she been converted that 'teething troubles' were inevitable, not least with her engines that at their best enabled her to make no more than 17 knots. Her aircraft strength was limited to three Swordfish, now armed with depth charges for anti-submarine duties, and eighteen Sea

Hurricanes, six each from 802 and 883 Squadrons and a further six kept dismantled in her hangar as reserves. This was a prudent precaution because apart from the likelihood of combat casualties, one fighter was lost overboard in rough weather while *Avenger* was proceeding to her rendezvous with the convoy.

Well suited or not, *Avenger* and her airmen were to be in the centre of the action, to experience dangers and disappointments, and ultimately to triumph over heavy odds. The first action came at 1304 on 12 September, when four Hurricanes were sent off against a three-engined Blohm & Voss BV 138 flying-boat that was shadowing the convoy. So did the first disappointment. The Hurricanes drove this away but it escaped, partly because of extensive cloud cover but partly because the fighters were adaptations of Hurricane Mark Is, armed only with eight machine guns. These had inflicted great losses earlier in the war but were much less effective now that enemy aircraft had been provided with far more protective armour.[4]

Avenger's Swordfish made their first contribution at 1955, when one of them sighted a U-boat with its conning tower awash ahead of the convoy. Destroyers summoned to the scene dropped depth charges and the submarine, though undamaged, was at least prevented from making any attack. About an hour later, another submarine, *U-88*, was detected, this time by the escort vessels, and was sunk.

On 13 September, the battle for PQ 18 began in earnest. At 0815, one of *Avenger*'s Swordfish spotted a submarine on the surface, tracking the convoy and signalling details of its composition, course and speed to the rest of the 'Wolf Pack'. It hastily submerged when the Swordfish appeared but its reports had done their work and some 40 minutes later, two merchantmen were torpedoed almost simultaneously, both going down. During the rest of the day, U-boats repeatedly attempted to reach another attacking position but were as repeatedly thwarted by the escorts, greatly assisted by the Swordfish that either directed their attacks on the U-boats or themselves dropped depth charges, though without result – at least not on the 13th.

Avenger's Sea Hurricanes were handled much less efficiently. The convoy was shadowed by at least five enemy aircraft but these were able to avoid the interceptors by skilful use of cloud cover. Then at 1500, half-a-dozen Junkers Ju 88s attacked. Five of the Hurricanes helped to disrupt the raid and all the bombs went wide, but it was a feint only.

While *Avenger*'s fighters were thus engaged or were back on the carrier refuelling after their ineffectual pursuits of the aerial scouts, a terrifying formation of over forty Heinkel He 111s and Junkers Ju 88s, each carrying two torpedoes, swept towards the convoy only some 35 feet above the sea, resembling, it was said, 'A huge flight of nightmare locusts coming over the horizon.'

On the Convoy Commodore's flagship, a signal was raised ordering a turn towards the attackers, thereby reducing the target offered, but it seems that many of the merchantmen did not see this or were so horrified at the threat confronting them, that they reacted far too late. The torpedo-planes dropped their deadly 'fish' simultaneously and no less than eight of the convoy were struck and sunk; an ammunition ship, the *Empire Stevenson*, disappearing in a horrific explosion. Five enemy aircraft were shot down but all by anti-aircraft guns since not one of *Avenger*'s interceptors was able to engage them. To complete the fighter pilots' misery, that evening four Sea Hurricanes attacked a Heinkel He 115 float-plane that not only got away but shot down one of them in flames, killing Lieutenant Taylor, 802 Squadron's CO.

Fortunately, the spirit of the convoy's defenders was such that, far from being crushed by the misfortunes of the 13th, they were determined to learn from their mistakes and so ensure that the rest of the story would be very different. In the early hours of 14 September, the U-boats claimed another victim, but for the remainder of the day the escorts were to hold the upper hand. *Avenger*'s Swordfish again co-operated with them splendidly and were, indeed, about to record their most conclusive contribution.

At 0940, *U-589* had surfaced to recharge her depleted batteries some 6 miles on the convoy's starboard bow and safely out of sight – or so her captain must have thought. The Swordfish, however, were patrolling out beyond the convoy and one of them now spotted the submarine, forcing her to dive. Dropping a smoke flare to mark her position, the Swordfish called for assistance and circled the area until attacked and driven away by a Junkers Ju 88. Even this contributed to the U-boat's doom, for when nothing was visible through her periscope, she resurfaced to continue replenishing her batteries and was sighted by destroyer *Onslow*, racing up in answer to the Swordfish's report. Though the submarine again submerged, *Onslow* was relentless and after a series of depth charge attacks a large underwater explosion, a mass of floating wreckage and a great pool of oil confirmed the destruction of *U-589*.

The inevitable air attacks did not begin until 1235 and found *Avenger* well prepared to meet them. Her skipper, Commander Colthurst, had decided to maintain a continuous Combat Air Patrol over the convoy, with the Sea Hurricanes landing to refuel in strict rotation. He was also determined not to divert precious fighters against reconnaissance machines or even against small bombing raids, reserving them for use against really large formations. Paradoxically, his task was made easier by Göring, who had ordered his men to make *Avenger* herself their priority target, partly for the prestige to be gained by sinking a carrier, partly because air strikes would be much easier if the opposition of the defending fighters could be removed.

Accordingly this first raid, by some twenty Junkers Ju 88s armed with torpedoes, was directed against the little 'flat-top'. Half-a-dozen of her Hurricanes defended her with particular fervour, shooting down two of the Junkers, damaging several more beyond repair, and so disrupting their formation that all the torpedoes missed. Another group of Ju 88s, this time carrying bombs, followed hard on the heels of the torpedo-planes, but it too was met by Hurricanes and *Avenger* again escaped unharmed.

A further bombing raid began at 1340, but this was rightly suspected to be a diversion and so was opposed only by the convoy's gunners. The real attack commenced at 1410, when twenty-two Heinkel He 111 torpedo-planes made another attempt on *Avenger*. Unfortunately for the raiders, *Avenger* had steamed out in front of the convoy when meeting the previous attacks and the Heinkels had assumed she would still be there. When they belatedly spotted her, they could only reach her by flying low over the convoy, presenting tempting targets for its AA gunners. To add to their difficulties, they were attacked from astern by *Avenger*'s Hurricanes which, with a reckless determination that no one who saw it ever forgot, followed their enemies into the full fury of the barrage.

Though *Avenger* was again untouched, one torpedo found its mark in the convoy, where the ammunition ship *Mary Luckenbach* disintegrated into 'a vast column of fire and smoke many thousands of feet high'. Three of the gallant Hurricanes were also lost, all victims of their own side's gunfire, but in each case a destroyer was on the scene with exemplary and reassuring promptness and all the pilots were rescued safely. Five of the Heinkels had been shot down; nine others returned to their base so badly damaged that they never flew again.

Sporadic raids continued throughout the rest of the day and the whole of the next day, but, harried by flak and fighters, they did no damage. On the day following, in increasingly bad weather, all air attacks died away. Enemy submarines continued their attempts to get at the merchantmen but the escorting warships prevented all of these from succeeding and, in the early hours of the 16th, sank *U-457*.

In the afternoon of the 16th, a large portion of the escort, including *Avenger*, left PQ 18 to cover a returning convoy, QP 14. As has been described, *Avenger* had lost four Hurricanes in combat and one earlier in bad weather. Yet her splendid hangar crews not only rectified the damage suffered by seven other Hurricanes in action or in accidents but assembled and made serviceable the six reserve aircraft, so that by the 17th, the carrier controlled thirteen Hurricanes ready for combat, one more than she had had originally. Perhaps disappointingly they saw no further action in defence of QP 14 but the three Swordfish, all of which had also had to have damage repaired, would again be found spotting U-boats, attacking them with depth charges – though without result – and performing other duties such as helping to search for stragglers.

It had correctly been concluded that PQ 18 would not be troubled by air attacks on 17 September, as it would then be at the limit of the Luftwaffe's range but these would be resumed on the 18th, when the convoy was on its last lap. An early raid did sink one more merchantman but when fifteen torpedo-carrying Heinkel He 111s appeared at 1150, the Hurricane of Flying Officer Burr, who had waited patiently for a chance to see action through all the preceding drama, was catapulted off the CAM-ship *Empire Morn*, effectively disrupted this formation and shot down one of them. Burr then flew almost 240 miles to the airfield of Keg Ostrov near Archangel where he landed safely.

Twenty-seven of PQ 18's forty merchantmen also reached Archangel carrying, as Luftwaffe records sadly acknowledge, 'hundreds of modern tanks and aircraft, thousands of road vehicles and a mass of other war and industrial materials – enough to equip a whole new army for the front'. The records also reveal that thirty-three torpedo-planes, six bombers and two reconnaissance aircraft had been destroyed or damaged beyond repair. It was too high a price to pay and the Germans accepted this. The bulk of their torpedo-bombers were transferred to the Mediterranean where, if they had to 'ditch', their crews had a fair chance of survival instead of quickly freezing to death. Never again would an Arctic convoy face anything like the same weight of attack from the skies.

While the majority of the hostile aircraft destroyed had fallen to the AA gunners, *Avenger*'s Hurricanes had certainly downed three Heinkels and two Junkers and damaged at least seventeen other machines. How many of these, unable to manoeuvre properly, fell easy victims to AA fire or returned to base only to be 'written off' will never be known. Nor is it particularly important, for all accounts agree that the carrier-fighters' greatest contribution had lain in breaking up the enemy formations. The devastation caused by the attack on 13 September, engaged only by gunfire, contrasts sharply with the almost complete failure of later assaults opposed by both flak and fighters. Once again the presence of a carrier had proved invaluable.

Although escort carriers would sail with later Arctic convoys, to the advantage of their merchantmen and the discomfiture of their enemies, their service was now in the main diverted, first to the North African theatre in a different role to be discussed later, then to the Atlantic and the perennial struggle there with the U-boats. Since all were agreed that the continuous cover that escort carriers could provide would almost certainly prove decisive, it is easy to understand American complaints about the long delays before those which they had supplied to the Royal Navy in fact entered service. The British retorted that the vessels in question had a number of defects, as the problems with *Archer*, and, to a lesser extent, *Avenger* demonstrated, and it was necessary to incorporate modifications, particularly if they were to be fit to operate in the extreme weather conditions to be found in the Arctic. No doubt these arguments were valid but in early March 1943, events took an unpleasant turn that gave every point to the American attitude.

During the first three weeks of that month, 107 ships were lost in the North Atlantic and for a ghastly moment it appeared that the convoy system that had defeated the U-boats in the First World War would be unable to do so in the present conflict. Fortunately it transpired that the situation had been caused by a whole number of factors coming together: an exceptionally large mass of shipping congregating in mid-Atlantic beyond the range of Allied aircraft and facing an unusually high number of U-boats; some brilliant interceptions by the German code-breakers; and a corresponding failure of the 'Ultra' Intelligence owing to a change in the enemy's cypher. These circumstances would not be repeated. On the contrary, new factors quickly restored the Allies' advantage: improved radar; a ship-borne High Frequency Direction Finder – alias H/F D/F or Huff-Duff – that could detect a submarine's signals; an increase in the number of long-range Liberators based in Iceland from ten to thirty, enabling about thirteen to be operational at any one time; and the presence of the escort carrier.

First of her type to arrive on convoy duty in late March was USS *Bogue*. She was accompanied by five destroyers, with which her twelve Avenger aircraft co-operated in the way pioneered by their namesake, HMS *Avenger*, during the passage of PQ 18, reporting U-boats and forcing them to submerge. The first British support group came into operation in April. It was formed around escort carrier *Biter*, controlling nine Swordfish and three Martlets. These again acted in effect as lookouts, sighting submarines and calling on *Biter*'s escorts to deal with them – activities that resulted in the destruction of *U-203* on 25 April and of *U-89* on 12 May.

Nor was it long before aircraft from escort carriers began to sink enemy submarines without the assistance of surface vessels. On 22 May, an Avenger from USS *Bogue* sank *U-569*. The convoy *Bogue* was protecting was also guarded by HMS *Archer* and next day one of her Swordfish, newly fitted with rocket projectiles, sank *U-572*. On the day following, the Germans admitted defeat and withdrew their submarines from the North Atlantic routes to areas where they hoped to find easier targets.

Also in May 1943, carriers of an entirely new type made their appearance. These were Merchant Aircraft Carriers or MAC-ships and they were created by the addition of a flight deck some 400 feet long by 60 feet wide to either 8,000-ton grain ships or 11,000-ton tankers. Like the CAM-ships before them, they carried their usual cargo as well as aircraft, in their case three or four of the hardy Swordfish that were probably the only aeroplanes that could have operated successfully from vessels with a short deck, limited facilities and a speed rarely exceeding 12 knots; even the staid Captain Roskill allows a diversion from more weighty matters to comment on the 'little short of miraculous' way in which Swordfish could land on a MAC-ship in 'absolutely dense fog'.

The first MAC-ship was the *Empire MacAlpine* and she first provided cover for a convoy on 29 May 1943. Within a year there were nineteen of her type on duty in the North Atlantic and they continued to serve for many months thereafter; it was from the MAC-ship *Empire MacKay* that the Fleet Air Arm's beloved Swordfish made its last operational flight as late as 27 June 1945. In addition to their value as a deterrent, their aircraft made at least twelve attacks on U-boats with rockets or depth charges and it is rather sad to have to record that despite all their efforts, no 'kills' resulted.

It was very different in the case of the escort carriers. Of course there were so many more of them. In July 1943, the escort carrier USS *Casablanca* was commissioned, the first to be built as such from the start. She was of 9,570 tons displacement, had a flight deck 512 feet long, with a small starboard island, could make over 19 knots and could operate thirty-five to forty aircraft. So awesome was the industrial strength of the United States that in exactly one year fifty vessels of the *Casablanca*-class were built. In all, the US Navy possessed seventy-seven escort carriers during the war, though not all of them saw active service, and also supplied thirty-eight others to the Royal Navy. It may be mentioned that the purpose-built escort carriers had lifts wide enough to accommodate aircraft like Sea Hurricanes that lacked folding wings. Perhaps the finest escort carriers, however, were four built in Britain – *Activity, Nairana, Vindex* and *Campania* – with enclosed hangars and steel flight decks.

These numbers were such that the Americans not only prepared escort carriers for the British but, despite the claims of the Pacific, could send several of their own ships to join *Bogue*. Having withdrawn from the North Atlantic, the U-boats directed special attention to the waters south and south-west of the Azores. It was to this area that *Bogue*, now equipped with Wildcats as well as Avengers, was ordered and she and her escorting destroyers formed a Hunter-Killer Group, not restricted to operations in close proximity to convoys like the MAC-ships but free to track down submarines reported for instance by 'Huff-Duff'. Her task and that of her successors was, in one sense, made easier because the U-boats were being equipped with increased and improved anti-aircraft guns and ordered to fight aircraft on the surface rather than diving.

It was not a wise decision. In June 1943, *Bogue*'s warplanes sank two

U-boats, one being a submarine-tanker or 'Milch Cow' as they were called, the duty of which was to refuel and resupply the U-boats engaged on offensive operations. They sank a third submarine in July, but by that time other US Hunter-Killer Groups built around escort carriers had arrived as reinforcements, their Avengers equipped with a new weapon, an anti-submarine homing torpedo, called with rather grim humour 'Fido'. During July and August, aircraft from *Santee* sank three U-boats, one a 'Milch Cow'; those from *Core* sank four, one a 'Milch Cow'; those from *Card* sank four, three of them 'Milch Cows'. And for all the Germans' 'fight-back' tactics, the Americans lost only two Wildcats and their pilots and one Avenger, the crew of which survived.

September saw a slight lull but in October the clashes between escort carrier aircraft and U-boats were resumed, this time mainly on the 'Gibraltar run' or in the seas west of Africa. USS *Card* once more proved a champion U-boat 'killer', her pilots destroying four of them, including two 'Milch Cows', while those from *Core* and *Block Island* added one each, the latter another 'Milch Cow'. Appropriately enough, though, it was *Bogue* that ended 1943 in style, her aircraft in the last two months of the year sinking two submarines and crippling a third that was finished off by her accompanying destroyers. To complete her exploits, it may be mentioned here that she sank another U-boat in March 1944 and finally on 20 August, her pilots were responsible for the destruction of *U-1229*, engaged not on operations against convoys, but on a secret mission to land German agents on the coast of the United States.

It will have been noticed that in 1943 all the 'kills' since May were achieved by American escort carriers, but the British escort carriers had also been a valuable deterrent and in 1944, their veteran Swordfish would again be responsible for a share of the enemy's losses in the Atlantic. On 10 February, those from *Fencer* sank *U-666* and on 15 March, those from *Vindex* assisted in the sinking of *U-653*. *Vindex* was again prominent on 6 May, in a slightly different role. Usually in a shared 'kill' the escort carrier's aircraft sighted or crippled the submarine and her escorting warships finished the job. On this occasion, it was a pair of frigates whose attacks brought *U-765* foaming to the surface but before they could engage her, a Swordfish flown by Lieutenant Commander Sheffield, CO of 825 Squadron, roared down to drop depth charges that sent the submarine sliding stern-first to the bottom.

Another escort carrier that appeared on the 'Gibraltar run' in early 1944 was HMS *Pursuer*, embarking no strike aircraft but only twenty Martlets – or rather Wildcats, for they had now resumed their US Navy name – for fighter cover. On 12 February, these intercepted a formation of long-range Heinkel He 177s armed with glider-bombs. They shot down two of them, drove away the rest and prevented any damage to the convoy they were protecting. It was also on the 'Gibraltar run' that the Sea Hurricanes that had played such a decisive part in the great PEDESTAL and PQ 18 convoys gained their final victories when Sub-Lieutenants Burgham and Mearns, flying from escort carrier *Nairana*, each shot down a Junkers Ju 290 transport on 26 May.

Mention of PQ 18 serves as a reminder that in 1944, British escort carriers were following in the wake of *Avenger*, guarding convoys to Russia against both submarines and aircraft. First to do so in both February and early March was HMS *Chaser* equipped with eleven anti-submarine Swordfish and eleven Wildcat fighters. The old Swordfish in particular again performed wonders for although the freezing conditions were such that when they had landed their crews often had to be lifted out of their cockpits, they destroyed three U-boats in the three days of 4 to 6 March.

The later days of March found two escort carriers, *Activity* with Swordfish and Wildcats, and *Tracker* with Avengers and Wildcats, escorting another Arctic convoy. In four days from 30 March to 2 April, fighters from the two carriers shot down, without loss, three Condors, a BV 138 and two Junkers Ju 88s. The strike aircraft did have casualties, an Avenger crashing on *Tracker* and exploding into flames, and a Swordfish (and a Wildcat) being shot down by the AA guns of submarines. In return, on 1 April, an Avenger from *Tracker* made a rocket attack on *U-355*, so damaging her that she was easily disposed of by the destroyer *Beagle* and on the 2nd, a Swordfish from *Activity* and an Avenger and a Wildcat from *Tracker* joined forces to sink *U-288*. In early May, escort carrier *Fencer* proved even more effective against the U-boats on a further Arctic convoy, her Swordfish destroying a total of three of them.

No American escort carriers took part in these Russian convoys but they continued with their almost equally dangerous task of covering those in the Atlantic. On 19 March 1944, Lieutenant Dowry from *Block Island* bombed and sank *U-1059* but at the cost of his own life. Three days earlier, *Block Island*'s airmen had helped to sink *U-801*. In early May, they located *U-66* which was destroyed by the escorts. But on 29 May, *U-549*, evading the little carrier's screen, sank her with a couple of torpedoes. It was a sad end to a useful career and little consolation that *U-549* was herself detected and sunk immediately afterwards.

USS *Guadalcanal*'s exploits had a more fitting culmination. During the first three months of 1944, her aircraft destroyed three U-boats and on 4 June, attacks from her escorting warships, with some assistance from her Avengers, damaged *U-505*. It appears that some of the submarine's crew rushed to the conning tower shouting that she was sinking and she therefore hurriedly surfaced. In reality, her injuries were not as serious as supposed and as her crew abandoned her, an American boarding party, specifically trained for the task, poured onto her, disconnected scuttling charges, checked flooding and captured her intact. She was towed to Bermuda in triumph and yielded valuable Intelligence information including codebooks and a cypher machine. This was not the first time a U-boat had been taken[5] but the timing of it made it especially significant. Two days later, British, American and Canadian soldiers stormed ashore on the beaches of Normandy.

It was the final evidence that the U-boat campaign had failed. Not only had they been unable to starve Britain into surrender, but they had not prevented the build-up of men and material needed to deliver the massive assault that would result in the liberation of Western Europe. Not that even now did the submarines cease their savage depredations or the escort carriers their relentless pursuits. During the rest of the year, US escort carriers' airmen participated in the destruction of four U-boats in the Atlantic – one each being claimed by the experienced *Card* and three newcomers, *Croatan*, *Solomons* and *Wake Island* – as well as that of *U-1229* by *Bogue* as already recounted. In the Arctic, aircraft from the British escort carrier *Vindex* helped to sink three German submarines, and *Campania* two more. And their continuous patrols and searches ended only when, to again quote the Official History[6], 'the last U-boat had raised its evil, dripping hull to the surface and hoisted the black flag of surrender'.

Notes

1 A number of accounts declare that the initials stood for 'Catapult Armed Merchantmen' but they were not armed with a catapult; they were armed – if this expression may properly be used – with a fighter aircraft on a catapult. That the 'A' stood for 'Aircraft' is confirmed in Admiralty records, in Captain Roskill's Official History and in Ralph Barker's detailed account of the CAM-ships' exploits, neatly entitled *The Hurricats*.

2 The first American escort carrier, the 10,000-ton *Long Island*, converted from the merchantman *Mormacmail* and commissioned in August 1941, did have a hangar, connected to her 360-foot-long flight deck by a single elevator, enabling her to operate fifteen to twenty aircraft.

3 An example of 'extreme determination' acknowledged even by the Germans was the attack made by six Swordfish of 825 Squadron. All of these were lost; a posthumous Victoria Cross, the Fleet Air Arm's first, being awarded to their leader, Lieutenant Commander Eugene Esmonde who had once led the Swordfish from *Victorious* against *Bismarck*. On this occasion, though, 825 was not flying from a carrier but was based at Manston airfield in Kent.

4 The pilots of 802 and 883 Squadrons were well aware of this and had long pleaded to be given adaptations of Hurricane Mark IIs armed with four 20mm cannon – but in vain. By a rather cruel irony, a large number of cannon-armed Hurricanes did sail with Convoy PQ 18, but only in crates on merchantmen for delivery to the Red Air Force.

5 On 9 May 1941, *U-110* was captured by a boarding party from destroyer *Bulldog* after her scuttling charges had failed to explode. She sank next day under tow but had already given up her secrets, including in her case also a cypher machine. On 27 August 1941, *U-570* on her first patrol was depth charged by a Hudson of 269 Squadron RAF flown by Squadron Leader Thompson. She was forced to the surface and surrendered. British warships brought her to Iceland where details of her construction were carefully studied. Later she would serve her new masters under the name of HMS *Graph*.

6 The Epilogue to Captain S.W. Roskill's *The War at Sea 1939-1945 Volume III 'The Offensive'*, Part II '1st June 1944-14th August 1945'. A black flag was used to indicate surrender because a white one could be mistaken for a battle ensign at a distance. As a matter of interest, though, when *U-570* surrendered, as mentioned above, her crew did wave 'a white article' that turned out to be a shirt.

Chapter 8

Support and Protect

L ong before the Allies landed in Normandy, carriers had helped
to ensure the success of other amphibious operations in all parts
of the globe. The first of these, at Guadalcanal, has already been
described, but it is a tribute to American determination and American
industrial capability that almost exactly three months later, American
and British–manned but American–built escort carriers would be
present at the first major landings in the western theatre of war.

These together comprised an Allied invasion of Vichy French North
Africa, collectively code-named Operation TORCH. There was
considerable concern over the amount of French resistance to be
expected and the possibility that the landing forces might be cut off by
Hitler persuading Spain to seize Gibraltar or at least render its harbour
and airfield unusable by artillery fire. It was correctly predicted,
however, that the scale of the former and the likelihood of the latter
would depend very much on whether Eighth Army had previously won
a decisive victory at El Alamein. General Alexander, as Commander-in-
Chief, Middle East, therefore chose 8 November 1942 as the date for the
assault so that there would be enough time for Montgomery to achieve
success but not enough for the enemy to send out substantial
reinforcements.

There were three main landing areas for the TORCH formations.
Furthest to the east, a combined British and American force would be
put ashore at Algiers; carrier *Argus* and escort carrier *Avenger* of PQ 18
fame were among its supporting units. To the west of this, American
ground troops who had been based in Britain were to land at Oran,
escorted by Royal Navy ships, including *Furious* and escort carriers
Biter and *Dasher*. Both these operations would enjoy the distant cover
provided by Vice Admiral Syfret's Force H, which had *Victorious* and
Formidable as part of its composition. On 6 November, the 'flat-tops'

gained their first success when a Martlet from *Formidable* piloted by Lieutenant Dennis Jerram, who had previously made four 'kills' flying Hurricanes when 'on loan' to the RAF in the Battle of Britain, downed a scouting Bloch MB 174.

Finally, an all-American task force would sail direct from the United States, heading for the Atlantic coast of French Morocco, from which an alternative line of communications could be provided in case the one through the Straits of Gibraltar was severed. It was divided into three sections. The largest, including carrier *Ranger* and escort carrier *Suwanee*, would set its troops ashore at Fedala, just north-east of Casablanca. Escort carrier *Santee* would be part of the force supporting a subsidiary attack some 150 miles south-west of Casablanca at Safi. And a further group would make for Mehdia, north of Fedala, with its ultimate objective the capture of a crucial aerodrome at Port Lyautey. Two more escort carriers accompanied this group: *Sangamon* with Dauntlesses, Avengers and Wildcats, and *Chenango* with seventy-six Curtiss Warhawks that would fly to Port Lyautey once it had been captured.

It was during Operation TORCH that a new British warplane made its debut. The Supermarine Seafires, squadrons of which served on *Victorious*, *Formidable*, *Furious* and *Argus*, were naval variants of the Spitfire. They were admirable as interceptors: highly manoeuvrable, well armed – two 20mm cannon and four 0.303-inch machine guns – with a good rate of climb and a top speed of about 340 mph. Unfortunately they also had a singularly limited range and worse still a weak undercarriage, politely described as 'too genteel' for landing on a heaving flight deck. Twelve of them would be lost during TORCH, many of these as the result of accidents and during their period of service, more Seafires would be destroyed when attempting deck landings than through all other causes put together.

Their first combats, however, were encouraging. At 0616 on 8 November, a Seafire from *Formidable* flown by Sub-Lieutenant Long attacked a reconnaissance Douglas DB7 over Algiers Bay. It subsequently crashed on the coast but since this was not seen by Long, its crew were killed and the French believed it had been hit by anti-aircraft fire, it was never claimed as the first Seafire victory. That honour would therefore be accorded to Sub-Lieutenant Baldwin, a pilot from *Furious*, who downed a Dewoitine D520 fighter over Oran later that morning.

Carrier aircraft rendered various services in support of the ground troops at Algiers, among them reconnaissance missions by Fulmars from *Victorious* and bombing raids on French batteries by Albacores from both *Victorious* and *Formidable*. By way of retaliation, a formation of Junkers Ju 88s attacked Force H that evening, but succeeded only in causing minor damage to *Formidable*. There were no other aerial combats after the destruction of the DB7 mentioned earlier, and by 1900, all resistance had ceased. This was partly because both airfields at Algiers were secured quickly. American troops captured Maison Blanche and at about 0900, eighteen Hurricanes from Gibraltar landed there and were rapidly made ready to repel enemy air-raids. The aerodrome at Blida was strafed by Martlets from *Victorious* and at about 0830, the Fleet Air Arm pilots observed white handkerchiefs being waved by airfield personnel. While three other Martlets remained on watch overhead, the leader of the flight, Lieutenant Nation, landed and accepted the surrender of the base on behalf of the Allies. When the soldiers arrived shortly afterwards, they found him cheerfully drinking coffee with the airfield authorities.

It was a very different picture elsewhere on 8 November. At Oran, the day opened with a raid by eight Albacores from *Furious*, escorted by twelve Sea Hurricanes, six each from *Biter* and *Dasher*, on the airfield at La Senia. The leading Albacore was shot down in flames by AA fire but the others pressed on to bomb hangars, destroying them and the twenty-five aircraft in them, while the Hurricanes strafed machines out in the open; twenty-two of these were later found abandoned, though some had already been unserviceable before this attack. The Albacores were pounced upon by twelve Dewoitine D520s before they could gain height and three had to force-land, their crews being taken prisoner. The Hurricanes from *Biter* then attacked the French fighters, downing five of them without loss. The pilots from *Dasher*, short of experience, took no part in the air battle and then failed to find their way back to their carrier. One baled out, while the others crash-landed on a racecourse near the coast. None of the airmen were hurt but all aircraft except one were 'written off'.

Much more fighting would be recorded by the US carriers in the Morocco landings, even though many of the American airmen had had minimal experience and training. This was especially the case with *Santee*. Ironically, the landing at Safi that she supported achieved quick success on 8 November and subsequently the main task of her pilots was strafing enemy aircraft on the ground and enemy transport vehicles – though not very effectively. Yet four of her nine Dauntlesses, seven of her eight Avengers and ten of her fourteen Wildcats were lost – all except possibly one Wildcat through causes other than enemy action.

In the main landing at Fedala and the nearby one at Mehdia, the American airmen showed much more of their true potential. Escort carriers *Suwanee* and *Sangamon* took care of the Combat Air Patrol and scouted for enemy submarines. Offensive actions were mainly conducted by Dauntlesses and Wildcats from *Ranger*. The former bombed harbour installations at Casablanca; the latter, in many cases themselves carrying bombs, concentrated on airfields, destroying twenty-eight warplanes on the ground and shooting down four bombers that had just taken off. A number of French fighters also got airborne, but in a series of savage clashes, lost six Curtiss Hawk 75As and three Dewoitine D520s, with one more Dewoitine crashing on take-off. Three Wildcats were shot down as well; another was hit by flak and forced to 'ditch'.

French warships from Casablanca also gallantly tried to disrupt the landings but American surface vessels sank four destroyers and compelled two more to beach. Light cruiser *Primaguet* leading the sortie was attacked by Dauntlesses and strafing Wildcats. These, for the loss of two dive-bombers, hit her four times and drove her ashore, heavily damaged and on fire.

Fighting continued throughout 9 November, but by the morning of the 10th, Oran, Casablanca and Port Lyautey had still not been taken. Fortunately the victory at El Alamein now had its anticipated effect. Admiral Jean Darlan, heir-apparent to the aged Marshal Pétain as Vichy's head of state, was in Algiers visiting a son dangerously ill with polio. Since his aversion to the British was notorious and his first reaction to TORCH was to arrest Mr Robert Murphy, the US Consul-General in Algiers, he was scarcely a loyal supporter of the Allied cause. On the other hand, he was much more realistic than many of his compatriots. At 1120 on 10 November, he ordered all French troops in North Africa to end their resistance.[1]

Unhappily, in Casablanca this news was not confirmed until late that evening and in the meantime the fighting continued. At 1420, nine Dauntlesses with an escort of Wildcats from *Ranger* were directed against the French battleship *Jean Bart*. She was immobilized and incomplete but she did have a turret of four 15-inch guns operative, with which she had been firing on American warships from long range. Two 1,000-lb bombs tore her open and she settled on the mud of Casablanca harbour with her decks awash. Rumours of the cease-fire had already reached Port Lyautey where the airfield was occupied without resistance by midday. The first Warhawks from escort carrier *Chenango* were duly sent there, the operation being completed by the 12th. All but two reached Port Lyautey but it had been badly damaged by bombing and strafing, and a considerable number suffered landing accidents – as did four of the thirty-five Warhawks from the newly-arrived HMS *Archer* which flew off to join them on the 13th.

Meanwhile on 9 November, the first German troops had arrived in Tunisia where the campaign would not end for another six months. Late on the 10th, Junkers Ju 88s attacked the old *Argus*, causing only minor damage that did not prevent her from covering another invasion at the little port of Bougie east of Algiers early next morning. Escort carrier *Avenger* had also been detailed to protect this landing but she had had to seek refuge in Algiers harbour to rectify engine defects. Having done so, she set out for home but sadly, on 15 November, she was struck by a single torpedo from *U-155* and blew up with the loss of almost her entire crew.[2]

Aircraft carriers of various types would be present at several later Allied landings in the Mediterranean. *Formidable* and *Indomitable* helped cover those on Sicily in July 1943. In September, *Formidable* was back to help cover the main invasion of Italy at Salerno and was joined by *Illustrious*, by *Unicorn* which was technically an aircraft repair ship but had a flight deck and so could double as a light carrier, and by escort carriers *Attacker*, *Battler*, *Hunter* and *Stalker* to provide close support.

This, though, was less effective than usual, for the Seafires, now embarked on escort carriers as well as their larger sisters, with their short range and weak undercarriages again proved unsuitable for carrier duties. They shot down only two hostile aircraft and lost ten of their own number, with thirty-two more damaged beyond repair, mainly as the result of crashes when attempting to land. Finally in August 1944, nine British or American escort carriers took part in the landings in the south of France, though again the Fleet Air Arm suffered heavily, losing forty-three machines, chiefly from landing accidents or having to 'ditch'.

Operation DRAGOON, as the invasion of southern France was code-named, had met comparatively little resistance because it coincided with the culmination of the campaign in Normandy where huge numbers of German troops had been trapped in what would be called the 'Falaise Pocket'. The Normandy campaign in turn had commenced with the greatest of all amphibious operations on 6 June 1944. Operation OVERLORD was not supported by any carriers, though naval aircraft flying from land bases took part, but carriers had participated in previous missions that had played a big part in ensuring its success.

If OVERLORD was to succeed at all, the supplies needed for both the initial landings and the subsequent fighting in Normandy, not to mention the soldiers from the United States and Canada who were to take part, had to be brought to Britain over secure supply lines. The contribution made by escort carriers in particular to quelling the threat to these posed by the U-boats has already been recounted, but there was a further daunting possibility: that German capital ships might be sent to disrupt them. Battle-cruiser *Scharnhorst*, her sortie against an Arctic convoy betrayed by the 'Ultra' code-breakers, had been sunk on 26 December 1943, after an old-style gun-duel with the British battleship *Duke of York*, but there still remained *Tirpitz* and in March 1944, 'Ultra' gave warning that she had recovered from damage inflicted by midget submarines in September 1943 and was carrying out sea-trials.

It is true that Hitler was normally most reluctant to risk his giant battleship but he had made exceptions in the past as the survivors of Convoy PQ 17 could testify. And if ever the Germans were prepared to take a desperate gamble it would be in an attempt to wreck the invasion of North-West Europe that they and the Allies both acknowledged would be the final decisive moment in the war in the Western Hemisphere.

Since *Tirpitz* was based at Alten Fjord in the north of Norway beyond the range of British heavy bombers, it was clear that an assault on her could only be delivered from aircraft carriers. Accordingly, the Royal Navy prepared Operation TUNGSTEN, an attack on *Tirpitz* by Fairey Barracudas, a type that had first appeared at the Salerno landings and could carry either torpedoes or, as on this occasion, bombs, flying from *Victorious* and *Furious*. They were accompanied by escort carriers *Emperor*, *Searcher*, *Pursuer* and *Fencer*, the last-named conducting anti-submarine patrols with her old Swordfish, while the first three provided additional fighter protection. In the early hours of 3 April 1944, all these vessels reached a position about 120 miles north-west of Alten Fjord, and at 0415, the first wave of attackers, twenty-one Barracudas and forty fighters, took off.

Tirpitz was just weighing anchor when at 0525, the naval airmen began their assault. There was no time for her crew to make ready to meet it or for a smokescreen to be put up. She shot down one Barracuda but they struck her with nine armour-piercing or high-explosive bombs; though these did less damage than had been hoped because they did not in fact penetrate her main armour belt, partly, ironically enough, as a result of the pilots coming in at too low a level in order to make certain of scoring a hit.

At about the same time that the first wave attacked, a further twenty Barracudas and forty fighters were leaving their carriers. One of the bombers crashed into the sea just after take-off, killing its crew, but the remainder reached Alten Fjord at about 0630, and although the smoke-screen was now more effective, they hit *Tirpitz* with five more bombs, one of which unfortunately did not explode. Again just one Barracuda was lost. By 0800, all the surviving aircraft had returned to their carriers, which retired from the area without further excitement.

Though *Tirpitz* had sustained no vital harm, her superstructure had been extensively damaged and 122 of her crew were dead as well as 316 more wounded. Better still, her injuries kept her out of action for three months and by the time they were repaired the great invasion of Normandy had already been launched. That later carrier-attacks on the battleship in July and August were unsuccessful and on 22 August during one of them escort carrier *Nabob* was torpedoed by *U-354* and put out of action for the rest of the war, was of comparatively little consequence. It was a pity, though, that the Fleet Air Arm was not responsible for the final destruction of *Tirpitz*. On 15 September, Lancaster heavy bombers flying from bases in Russia damaged her so badly that she had to be sent south to Tromso to effect repairs. Here she was within range of British airfields and on 12 November, a raid by thirty-two Lancasters hit her with three 12,000-lb bombs that tore open her port side and caused her to capsize.

Her elimination did not end offensive actions by carriers in northern waters, chiefly against enemy shipping; the last of these was executed as late as 4 May 1945, by escort carriers *Queen*, *Searcher* and *Trumpeter*. All three were equipped with American aircraft, Avengers and Wildcats. For that matter, at the time of Operation TUNGSTEN, all the fighters that accompanied the Barracudas on their strikes had been American. They included Chance-Vought Corsairs; despite a top speed of 405 mph, fine manoeuvrability and an armament of six 0.5-inch machine guns, this type was not used on board American carriers until early 1945 because of poor deck-landing qualities; but the British were less choosy in their eagerness for any aircraft that had been designed for use on carriers rather than adapted, like the Seafires, from land-based warplanes.

The majority of American naval aircraft of course were serving in the Pacific. During the summer and early autumn of 1943, the US South Pacific forces under Halsey had been methodically capturing the Japanese-occupied islands in the northern Solomons, while General Douglas MacArthur's South-West Pacific forces had been securing bases in the Papuan Peninsula and the Huon Peninsula to its north-west. It had been discouragingly calculated that at this rate of progress, it would take ten years before the Americans would reach the Japanese homeland – but in July and August, decisions had been taken that would dramatically revise this estimate.

One of these was that although the objective of the Halsey and MacArthur advances had been the capture of the main Japanese base at Rabaul, this would not now be attempted; instead Rabaul would be surrounded and left to 'wither on the vine'. Its isolation was completed in late February 1944, when MacArthur's troops invaded the Admiralty Islands north-west of Rabaul, securing them by early April. Next, MacArthur planned to leap 400 miles westward to Hollandia in northern New Guinea, a move wryly code-named Operation RECKLESS, but minor when compared with the other advance decided upon in mid-1943 – one to be made across the immense distances of the Central Pacific Ocean.

Nothing like this had ever been attempted previously and it was only made possible by the incredible industrial strength of the United States. The Central Pacific Fleet – Fifth Fleet it would be re-entitled in early 1944 – under the overall command of Vice Admiral Raymond Ames

Spruance contained an Amphibious Force, a Support Force that incorporated a growing number of escort carriers and a Service Force to keep it supplied. Its spearhead, however, was its Fast Carrier Force and this was improving, steadily and far from slowly, in both size and calibre.

On 31 December 1942, the aircraft carrier *Essex* was commissioned. Of 27,100 tons, with a speed of 33 knots, and capable of operating up to 110 aircraft, she was the first of fourteen of her class to see service with the US Navy during the Second World War. Among these, for the confusion of posterity, were a new *Lexington*, *Yorktown*, *Wasp* and *Hornet* and by autumn 1943, the first two of these, together with *Essex* herself and *Bunker Hill*, were among the warships commanded by Spruance. On 14 January 1943, light carrier *Independence* – 11,000 tons, 32 knots speed and a complement of over thirty aircraft – was commissioned, having been adapted from the hull of a light cruiser. She and four sister-ships, *Princeton*, *Belleau Wood*, *Monterey* and *Cowpens*, were also on hand when the great drive across the Central Pacific began.

To equip these new carriers and the veteran *Enterprise* and *Saratoga*, also included in Spruance's command, came new carrier-aircraft. The Curtiss Helldivers, two-seater dive-bombers that gradually replaced the much-loved Dauntlesses, were somewhat disappointing despite a top speed of 295 mph, an armament of two 20mm cannon plus two 0.300-inch machine guns for the observer, a long range and the ability to carry 2,000-lb of bombs. The trouble was that they were structurally not as sound as the Dauntlesses and could never be dived as steeply for fear of losing their wings. Even so, they would play a large part in the American triumphs that were to come.

There could have been no reservations about the Grumman Hellcats that more rapidly replaced the gallant Wildcats, at least on US 'flat-tops'. They had a maximum speed of 367 mph, a long range, an armament of six 0.5-inch machine guns, superb visibility, a fine rate of climb and the same rugged reliability as the Wildcats. Hellcats were capable of carrying bombs or rockets, but their true role was that of interceptors. Their design had been heavily influenced by the expressed views of experienced pilots and specifically intended to make them superior to the Zeros – as indeed they were. Hellcat pilots would shoot down 5,156 enemy aircraft during the war; 4,947 of them when flying from US carriers of various types. Their Fleet Air Arm colleagues might well have envied them.

How effective were the new fighters was demonstrated on 1 September 1943, when Hellcats from light carriers *Princeton* and *Belleau Wood* shot down three scouting flying-boats in succession so swiftly that none of them were able to get off a sighting report and the remaining ones at their base were grounded in the belief that they must have some defect that had caused these mysterious losses. On the previous day, other Hellcats had escorted dive-bombers and torpedo-planes from *Essex*, *Yorktown* and light carrier *Independence* in a strike on Marcus Island.

During September, October and November, the US carriers in various combinations made eight more raids on Marcus Island, attacked the Gilbert Islands, Wake Island and Rabaul and covered American landings on Bougainville. The raids on Rabaul were especially effective. On 5 November, the strike aircraft from *Saratoga* and light carrier *Princeton* badly damaged four heavy and two light cruisers and two destroyers. On the 11th, those from *Essex*, *Bunker Hill*, *Saratoga*, *Princeton* and *Independence* – including twenty-three Helldivers, in action for the first time – sank destroyer *Suzunami* and four merchantmen. In addition, during the two raids and while repelling counter-attacks on the 11th, the Americans so decimated the Air Groups of *Shokaku*, *Zuikaku* and *Zuiho*, with which the enemy had attempted to stiffen Rabaul's defences, that of the 173 naval aircraft the Japanese carriers had sent there, only fifty-two survived to return to them.

All these operations were designed to lead up to the first step in Spruance's push across the Central Pacific. This began in earnest on 20 November, with invasions of Tarawa and Makin in the Gilbert Islands. All Spruance's six fleet and five light carriers were present, striking at defences on the targets or at airfields on neighbouring islands from which counter-attacks might be delivered. Close support and fighter protection were provided by escort carriers *Coral Sea*, *Corregidor* and *Liscombe Bay* at Makin and *Sangamon*, *Suwanee* and *Chenango* (that a year earlier had all taken part in the landings in Morocco) at Tarawa. Two other escort carriers, *Barnes* and *Nassau*, were also involved, ferrying a total of forty-four Hellcats, scheduled to land on Tarawa's airfield once it was secured.

They met ferocious resistance. The capture of Tarawa cost the Americans 3,000 casualties, one-third of them fatal. Of the 3,000 Japanese combat troops, just seventeen surrendered. There were only 300 Japanese combat troops on Makin, but they held out against overwhelming odds for four days; one solitary prisoner was taken. Late on 20 November, a raid by land-based torpedo-bombers lost eight Bettys but scored a hit on light carrier *Independence* that put her out of action for several months. A number of attacks were also delivered at night, but without results and on the 26th, the US carriers achieved their first 'kill' after dark when a Betty was shot down by Lieutenant Commander Phillips from *Enterprise*, flying, surprisingly enough, an Avenger, not a fighter. On the same night, though, Commander 'Butch' O'Hare, the Americans' first naval-air 'ace' was shot down in flames.

An equally tragic but more serious loss had already occurred two days earlier. The only enemy resistance at sea came from submarines, but one of these, *I-175*, was able to put a torpedo into escort carrier *Liscombe Bay* off Makin, detonating her store of bombs and tearing her apart in a spectacular sheet of flame. Of her crew of some 900, 644 lost their lives, including Rear Admiral Mullinnix and Captain Wiltsie.

Fifth Fleet moved on to assault Kwajalein in the Marshall Islands on 1 February 1944. It was secured by the afternoon of the 4th, though fleet carrier *Lexington* was hit by a torpedo-bomber and put out of action for three months. On 17 February, Fifth Fleet covered the invasion of Eniwetok – it was secured by the afternoon of the 21st – and Spruance then detached eight escort carriers to provide close support for General MacArthur's landings at Hollandia and Aitape in New Guinea on 22 April.

Meanwhile, again on 17 February, Fifth Fleet's carrier pilots had begun a series of raids on Truk, Japan's main base in the Caroline Islands which was to be bypassed and isolated as Rabaul had been. They sank light cruiser *Naka*, destroyers *Fumitsuki*, *Oite* and *Tachikaze*, nineteen merchantmen and five tankers, and destroyed 110 Japanese warplanes on the ground, damaging some seventy others. Over fifty more enemy aircraft were shot down for the loss of only four Hellcats. The Japanese were able to mount only one counter-attack, during which a Kate torpedoed and badly damaged carrier *Intrepid*.

None of these operations had been threatened by the First Mobile

Fleet, as the Japanese now called the main body of their Navy. The Americans rightly considered, however, that their next move, the invasion of Saipan in the Mariana Islands, planned for 15 June 1944, was almost bound to be opposed by Japanese warships, because the capture of the Marianas would give them airfields from which heavy bombers could strike at the Japanese homeland. And indeed when Admiral Soemu Toyoda who had recently become the Imperial Navy's Commander-in-Chief[3], learned of the Saipan landings, he immediately ordered his Fleet into action.

The Americans were kept well informed of the approach of their enemy, not by their code-breakers as at Midway but by scouting submarines – and were ready for it. The Saipan invasion was backed by eight escort carriers embarking a total of eighty-two Avengers and 114 Wildcats. Five more escort carriers were in reserve at Eniwetok, detailed to guard a follow-up assault on the most southerly of the Marianas, Guam. And Task Force 58, the carrier component of Fifth Fleet, led by Vice Admiral Marc Mitscher, to whom Spruance had delegated tactical control, was stationed west of the southern Marianas by noon of 18 June. Here it could engage the Japanese Fleet and still cover the Saipan bridgehead. In all, Mitscher commanded seven fleet carriers, his flagship *Enterprise, Lexington, Yorktown, Hornet, Wasp, Bunker Hill* and *Essex*, and eight light carriers, *Belleau Wood, Bataan, Monterey, Cabot, San Jacinto, Princeton, Langley* and *Cowpens*.

These vessels and their close escort – Spruance's flagship, heavy cruiser *Indianapolis*, three other heavy cruisers, thirteen light cruisers and fifty-three destroyers – were divided into four Task Groups some 12 miles apart. A fifth Task Group of seven battleships, four heavy cruisers and fourteen destroyers was stationed about 15 miles west of the carriers on the enemy's probable line of advance, with a pair of picket destroyers still further to the west. Commanded by Vice Admiral Lee of Guadalcanal fame, this formation was prepared for a surface action, but in practice, as at Coral Sea and Midway, the battle would be fought only by the warplanes on each side. With these Mitscher was liberally supplied: besides over sixty float-planes on the battleships and cruisers, he controlled 174 Helldivers, 59 Dauntlesses, 192 Avengers and 467 Hellcats.

While the number of American carriers had grown steadily throughout 1943 and early 1944, the Japanese carrier strength, despite desperate efforts, had fallen ever further behind. Five passenger ships had been converted to escort carriers but one of these, *Chuyo*, had been sunk by submarine *Sailfish* on 4 December 1943, and in any case they proved very unsuitable and justified their designation as carriers mainly because they ferried aircraft to various island bases. They were also used as transports of other kinds and, by a tragic irony, when *Chuyo* was lost she took down with her twenty captured American submariners who were being taken to prisoner of war camps in Japan.[4]

Rather more successful were the conversions to light carriers of seaplane carriers *Chitose* (which we met in the Battle of the Eastern Solomons) and *Chiyoda* and of submarine tender *Ryuho*. The Japanese also planned to build a number of fleet carriers of various sizes and at the time of the Saipan landings, the 29,300-ton *Taiho* was also in service. She carried some sixty aircraft, was provided with an impressive anti-aircraft armament and despite having a flight deck protected by 3-inch armour, she was a fast ship, capable of at least 33 knots. In sharp contrast to the massive American shipbuilding programmes, however, these four ships were the only ones to have joined Japan's Carrier Task Force since the Guadalcanal campaign.

New Japanese carrier-aircraft were appearing as well. The best that could be managed in the way of fighters were later versions of the Zero, but the Vals were being replaced by the Yokosuka Judys and the Kates by the Nakajima Jills. The former were two-seaters with a top speed of 360 mph, capable of carrying 1,100lb of bombs. Like the Helldivers, however, they were less structurally sound than their predecessors and so could not dive as steeply. The Jills were really Kates with a more powerful engine that gave them a top speed of about 300 mph and a longer range. Like the Kates, they could carry either a torpedo or bombs and they were highly respected by their opponents for their potentially lethal qualities.

Admiral Toyoda had decided not to put to sea himself as Yamamoto had done at Midway, but to remain at Naval Headquarters in Tokyo where he would have the advantage of better communications. He delegated tactical command to the head of the Mobile Fleet, Vice Admiral Jisaburo Ozawa, a staunch supporter of naval air-power from before the war and an imposing figure, unusually tall for a Japanese man, whose dignified bearing would later earn the respect even of his former enemies, some of whom would later become his friends. Among these was Professor Morison, who pays Ozawa the high compliment of ranking him as a 'worthy antagonist' to Spruance and Mitscher.

As usual with the Japanese, the Mobile Fleet approached in widely separated formations, though this time with more logic. Its main body, under Ozawa's direct command, consisted of two Task Groups containing in all five fleet carriers, Ozawa's flagship *Taiho*, *Shokaku*, *Zuikaku*, *Hiyo* and *Junyo*, light carrier *Ryuho*, battleship *Nagato*, three heavy cruisers, one light cruiser and nineteen destroyers. The other three light carriers, *Zuiho*, *Chiyoda* and *Chitose*, were part of Vice Admiral Takeo Kurita's Van Force, steaming 100 miles ahead of Ozawa. This would be the first formation encountered by US aircraft and it was hoped it would become their main target, leaving a clear field for the larger Japanese 'flat-tops'. For this reason Kurita was given the bulk of Mobile Fleet's heavy surface warships with a massive array of anti-aircraft guns: giant battleship *Yamato* that had been Yamamoto's flagship at Midway, her younger sister *Musashi*, two smaller battleships, four heavy cruisers and nine destroyers.

It can be seen at a glance that the Japanese were much the weaker in numbers of carriers and of warships generally. In naval aircraft their position was still worse because here their inferiority was in quality as well as quantity. The speedy Judy had too long a take-off run to be used on the light carriers, and *Chiyoda* and *Chitose* could not operate the Jill either. In consequence, while Mobile Fleet contained almost a hundred Judys, it also had twenty-seven of the older Vals; eighteen Kates as well as eighty-one Jills. Its Zeros, of which it controlled about 230, were also no longer the formidable opponents of the past, being outclassed by the Hellcats, and some seventy of them were intended for use as fighter-bombers in order to make good the shortages of strike aircraft. Even in float-planes, of which they had forty-three, the Japanese were weaker.

As if these obvious disadvantages were not enough, the Japanese laboured under further difficulties that would become only too apparent when action was joined. The Americans had not just created new types of warplanes, they had also designed a new anti-aircraft shell. This had a miniature radar set in its nose reflecting signals off solid objects such as aircraft. When the intervals between the outward and returning signals became very short, indicating that the shell was in close proximity to its target, it detonated automatically: there was no longer any need to score a direct hit.

Worse still, as we have seen, most of Japan's experienced naval airmen had been sacrificed during the battles over or around Rabaul. Shortage of time and shortage of petrol as a result of the operations of US submarines had meant that their successors were inevitably of poor quality. Whereas by this stage of the war, American carrier pilots had received up to two years' training and over 300 hours' flying time before they saw combat, Ozawa's airmen were compelled to go into action after training at most for six months and in many cases for only two or three months, with minimal knowledge of the tactics they would have to employ and, because of the lack of petrol, with hardly any recent flying hours behind them. And the shortage of fuel had had one further disadvantageous effect. The tankers supplying the Mobile Fleet had been forced to take on oil from wells in Borneo that was so pure that it could be used by ships without having to be processed. Unfortunately it was dangerously – and as would be proved, lethally – volatile.

Against all these adverse factors, the unlucky Ozawa could set only one real advantage. Their lack of armour plating, and of such benefits as self-sealing fuel tanks, made Japanese warplanes very vulnerable but it did give them a much longer range than American machines. Ozawa had correctly assessed Spruance as a cautious officer who would remain close to the Marianas so as to protect the Saipan landings. The Japanese could therefore stay outside the reach of US carrier aircraft and 'shuttle-bomb' their enemies, with their own aircraft landing on Guam after making their attacks and then, refuelled and rearmed, returning to the Mobile Fleet, attacking the Americans again on the way.

Ozawa also believed he had a further advantage. He hoped that aircraft from Guam and other Japanese bases in the vicinity would assist him with attacks of their own, and indeed would have considerably reduced the American numbers before Mobile Fleet went into action. In reality, Japanese attacks had been largely futile, though on the 17th, a Judy bomber hit escort carrier *Fanshaw Bay* and damaged her sufficiently to cause her withdrawal from the combat-zone. A series of American raids on Guam, by contrast, had eliminated about 150 Japanese aircraft and caused a great deal of damage to their landing-grounds; and on the 19th, a final sweep by Hellcats destroyed about forty more. Yet the Japanese commanders on Guam consistently misled

Ozawa by making exaggerated claims of success, while at the same time concealing their own losses from him.

By the afternoon of 18 June, Ozawa had reached a position from which he could send out his aerial scouts to search for his enemies and these duly detected three of the US Task Groups. By that time, though, night was beginning to fall and in view of his airmen's inexperience, Ozawa delayed further action until next day. The Japanese were still out of range of American aircraft and Mitscher accordingly urged that Task Force 58 steam westward to reduce the distance between the rival fleets. Spruance, however, refused; he feared that the Japanese might outflank him and fall on the vulnerable Saipan invasion forces, the protection of which he rightly regarded as his primary duty.

The great clash between carriers that would become known as the Battle of the Philippine Sea was therefore postponed to 19 June. Its first shots were fired at 0530, when a reconnaissance Judy from Guam again sighted the American fleet. It was promptly shot down by the Combat Air Patrol from light carrier *Monterey* but not before reporting its sighting to Ozawa. At 0830, Vice Admiral Kurita's Van Force launched eight Jills from *Zuiho*, the only vessel under Kurita's command that could operate them, and a total of sixty-one Zeros, forty-five of them fighter-bombers, from all three of his light carriers. Half-an-hour later, twenty-seven Jill torpedo-planes, fifty-three Judy dive-bombers and forty-eight Zeros from *Taiho*, *Shokaku* and *Zuikaku* followed them.

On the Japanese carriers, all eyes were fixed on their inexperienced but eager airmen as they climbed skywards. No one noticed a periscope that broke surface on the starboard bow of Ozawa's flagship *Taiho*. It belonged to US submarine *Albacore* that had skilfully evaded the destroyer screen to reach a perfect firing position. At 0909, a salvo of torpedoes sped towards their target.

At this moment there occurred a sublime example of that instinctive selfless courage that was the hallmark of the naval aviators on both sides. Warrant Officer Sakio Komatsu had just taken off from *Taiho*'s deck when he suddenly noticed a torpedo on the point of striking his ship. Without hesitation, he dashed his Zero fighter onto it; torpedo, aircraft and pilot vanishing in a mighty explosion. For a moment it seemed that his sacrifice had saved *Taiho*. Only one torpedo hit her and, no doubt much to the disappointment of those on *Albacore*, she steamed on, apparently unaffected.[5] Yet the blow had cracked a tank containing aviation fuel and the deadly fumes began to spread through the ship, made worse by a vain attempt to clear them by turning on her ventilation system.

Though he had been attacked by a submarine, Ozawa could still congratulate himself that his tactics had prevented any immediate likelihood of an assault by the aircraft of the US carriers, while he had been able to launch strikes at them. He would have been much less satisfied if he could have seen how badly the men making those strikes were faring.

American radar spotted the first Japanese wave at 0959 when it was 150 miles away. At a range of 75 miles, to the astonishment of all on Mitscher's carriers, the enemy aircraft began to orbit while the crews received instructions on the tactics they were to adopt. This gave eight Hellcats from *Essex* a chance to engage them and they were quickly followed by fighters from *Bunker Hill* and light carriers *Princeton* and *Cowpens*. At least twenty-five Japanese warplanes were destroyed without getting near their targets, while the sole US loss was a Hellcat from *Bunker Hill* whose pilot, Lieutenant Commander Hoel, was forced to bale out after downing three enemy machines. The remaining attackers were unable to get through to the American carriers, suffered further losses to fighters and the new proximity-fuze AA shells and scored only one hit on battleship *South Dakota* that did little damage. Of the raid's sixty-nine aircraft, only twenty-four got back to their motherships.

Ozawa's second raid was equally unsuccessful. It was detected by radar at 1107, engaged by Hellcats from *Essex* at 1139 when 60 miles from its targets, and thereafter harried by a growing number of interceptors. Only a few Japanese reached the American carriers; Judy bombers causing slight damage to *Wasp* and *Bunker Hill* with near misses. Others attacked Lee's battleship group and a torpedo-carrying Jill deliberately crashed into *Indiana*, its weapon fortunately failing to explode. This time just thirty-one Japanese aircraft returned to the Mobile Fleet.

A third strike of seven Jills and forty Zeros, twenty-five of them fighter-bombers, took off from *Hiyo*, *Junyo* and *Ryuho* at about 1015, but was directed well away from Mitscher's true position by a false sighting report. Only a few aircraft found their targets at about 1300, inflicted no damage and lost one Jill and six Zeros to Hellcats from

Yorktown and *Hornet*. A final wave of thirty-six Judys, two Jills and forty-four Zeros from *Zuikaku*, *Junyo* and *Ryuho* set out at about 1130. It too was misdirected and only a handful of bombers discovered the American carriers at 1423, most of them being downed by AA fire. The greater part of this wave, twenty-seven Judys, the two Jills and twenty Zeros, made for Guam but were intercepted by fighters from *Essex*, *Hornet* and *Cowpens* and all were shot down, damaged beyond repair or crashed while attempting to land on Guam's ravaged airfields. Eleven of this final raid regained their carriers.

These were by then in a sorry condition. At 1222, three torpedoes from submarine *Cavalla* had crashed into the starboard side of *Shokaku*, igniting the crude Borneo fuel in a spectacular mass of flames. Her very experienced damage control parties fought heroically to save her, but this time her situation was beyond recall. At about 1500, the fires reached *Shokaku*'s magazines. A final huge explosion rocked the doomed carrier and she sank almost instantly.

Twenty minutes later came another colossal explosion. A spark had ignited the fumes seeping through *Taiho*. The blast blew out the sides of her hangar, smashed holes in her bottom, killed everyone in her engine room, reduced her flight deck to a mass of twisted steel and started fires raging throughout her entire length. A reluctant Ozawa, his staff and the Emperor's portrait were transferred to heavy cruiser *Haguro* where, by a further misfortune for the Japanese, it was difficult for Ozawa to exercise effective command since her communications facilities were strictly limited. There was little time to rescue other survivors. At 1532, a second vast explosion rent *Taiho* and she capsized and sank, taking 1,650 of her crew with her.

Thirteen aircraft also went down with *Taiho*, nine more had been lost with *Shokaku*, and the Mobile Fleet's naval air strength was now reduced to a total of just 100. The Americans had lost twenty-three Hellcats in action, plus six more operationally. Sadly, though, the day that saw the fighters' greatest achievement ended with a final clash in which Zeros from Guam shot down and killed Commander Brewer, the *Essex* Air Group Leader who had been the first to engage the Mobile Fleet's initial raid.

A day of violent action was followed by a surprisingly quiet night. At 2000 on the 19th, Mitscher at last persuaded Spruance that it was now safe to take the offensive and Task Force 58 headed westward towards the enemy, leaving only *Essex* and light carriers *Langley* and *Cowpens* to guard the Saipan landings. Mitscher did not, however, send out aircraft on night reconnaissance, feeling that his airmen, after battling all day, must have a period of rest. Not until 0530 on 20 June did he order a search to be made and this found nothing.

Nor did the Japanese send out scouts during the hours of darkness, the decision in their case arising partly from their heavy losses and partly from a knowledge of their pilots' inexperience. Float-planes set out on the 20th, coincidentally also at 0530, but saw no enemy ships, though at 0715, they did report seeing US carrier-aircraft. Vice Admiral Kurita, whose ingrained pessimism would rob Japan of her greatest opportunity since Pearl Harbour a few months later, urged immediate flight, but Ozawa would not hear of this. Since he needed to refuel his ships, he recalled Kurita's Van Force and prepared to rendezvous with a six-strong group of tankers. Shortly after this was made, he managed to transfer his flag to *Zuikaku*, where he at last learned the extent of the Mobile Fleet's aircraft losses. Yet having received false assurances from the Japanese commanders in the southern Marianas that many of his warplanes had successfully landed, he believed he could resume the battle with their help on the 21st. He has been accused of gullibility but surely he had a right not to expect that his own colleagues would deliberately mislead him.

In any case it perhaps made little difference. At 1605, Lieutenant Nelson, the pilot of an Avenger from *Enterprise*, sighted the Mobile Fleet. His report was intercepted by the Japanese and Ozawa, realizing that his Fleet was no longer outside the range of the American carrier-aircraft, finally accepted defeat and set off north-westward at high speed. He may well have hoped to avoid further damage, for any American strike would have to be made at extreme range; a strong head-wind would face the attackers on their return journey; and when they reached their carriers they would have to make night-landings, for which a large proportion of them were untrained.

Any such hopes were not fulfilled. Mitscher, who had been longing for a chance to take the offensive all day, was prepared to ignore all risks. Just after 1630, seventy-seven Helldivers, fifty-four Avengers, many carrying bombs not torpedoes, and eighty-five Hellcats set out towards the enemy. At 1840, they spotted the first hostile formation – the oil tankers. Some of the Helldivers attacked them, crippling two that had to be scuttled later. Most of the raiders pressed on to engage the Japanese warships, sighted some 30 miles further to the north-west. In the face of desperate resistance by the Zeros of the Combat Air Patrol, through a spectacular display of anti-aircraft fire, the Americans hurled themselves against the Mobile Fleet.

Among the attackers was a torpedo-carrying Avenger from *Belleau Wood*, flown by Lieutenant George Brown who had vowed that he would sink a carrier no matter what happened. His aircraft was badly damaged, his two crewmen were forced to bale out, and he was himself wounded but he led two other Avengers from his flight, piloted by Lieutenants Benjamin Tate and Warren Omark, in an attack on carrier *Hiyo*. Two torpedoes struck her, bringing her to a halt, blazing furiously; she sank two hours later. Tate and Omark tried to guide Brown back to their carrier but their little group flew into a cloud and when it emerged, Brown had vanished, never to be seen again.

Aircraft from *Yorktown*, *Enterprise*, *San Jacinto* and *Belleau Wood* all attacked *Zuikaku*, scoring numerous bomb hits. She too burst into flames and at one point it seemed she would have to be abandoned, but her gallant damage control personnel mastered the fires just in time. Light carrier *Chiyoda* took two bombs that started a fire and badly damaged her flight deck. Light carrier *Ryuho*, battleship *Haruna* and heavy cruiser *Maya* were all hit but suffered lesser damage. The Japanese also had sixty-five aircraft destroyed – lost with *Hiyo*, wrecked on the decks of the vessels that were bombed, shot down in combat or crashed on landing – leaving Mobile Fleet with only thirty-five. Fortunately for the Japanese, the speed of none of their damaged vessels was reduced and all made good their escape. The Americans lost ten Helldivers, four Avengers and six Hellcats in the course of their attack.

That attack marked the end of the Battle of the Philippine Sea, but not of the American airmen's ordeal. They still had to get back to their carriers. Mitscher did everything he could to help. Ignoring the possibility of Japanese submarines being in the vicinity, he ordered his ships to switch on navigation lights, flight deck lights and searchlights, and for star shells to be fired. Even so, many an aircraft, damaged or short of fuel, 'ditched' on the way back or in the vicinity of Task Force 58. One aircraft crashed on *Lexington*, two others on *Bunker Hill* but, incredibly, a bomber and a fighter touched down on *Enterprise* at the same time, both safely. There were even some amusing moments: one treasures the story of a pilot from one of the light carriers who felt he would never be able to land on her short flight deck, flew to what he thought was the biggest 'flat-top' in sight, landed safely – and found he was on his own ship after all! Nonetheless, eighty aircraft were lost, though rescue operations later saved all but sixteen of their pilots and thirty-three of their crewmen.

With the repulse of the Mobile Fleet, the conquest of Saipan was assured, and it was quickly followed by the capture of the other main islands in the southern Marianas, Tinian and Guam. On 18 July, the same day that the fall of Saipan was announced, the government of General Tojo fell as well. It was the first indisputable evidence that in the Pacific as in Europe the end of the war might not lie too far in the future.

Notes

1 Darlan would gain no personal benefit from his cynical change of front. On Christmas Eve, he was shot dead by a youthful anti-Vichy fanatic named Bonnier de la Chapelle, who in turn was hastily court-martialled and shot two days later.

2 Another escort carrier that took part in Operation TORCH suffered an even more unhappy fate not long afterwards. On 27 March 1943, HMS *Dasher* was destroyed by an internal petrol explosion while carrying out exercises in the Firth of Clyde. British sources consider this an example of the lack of safety precautions in the early American-built escort carriers. The Americans blame British lack of experience. No doubt there were faults on both sides but it may be noted that new recruits who came to serve on the US Navy's own escort carriers were told by the old hands that their official naval abbreviation of CVE – for fleet carriers it was CV; for light carriers CVL stood for 'Combustible, Vulnerable, Expendable'.

3 Yamamoto's immediate successor had been Admiral Mineichi Koga but on the night of 31 March/1 April 1944, his aircraft had disappeared in a storm over the Philippines. Toyoda seems to have been a better strategist as well as a much more determined and aggressive opponent.

4 Three more of these escort carriers were to be sunk by US submarines before the year was out: *Taiyo* on 18 August by *Rasher*; *Unyo* on 16 September by *Barb*; *Shinyo* on 17 November by *Spadefish*.

5 A sad footnote, this one: *Albacore* was sunk off the coast of Japan on her next patrol in November 1944, so her crew never learned of their great achievement.

Chapter 9

The Biggest Battle

For the leading figures in the Imperial Japanese Navy, the immediate question was not how long the war would last but how long their warships would be able to play any meaningful part in it. The depressing answer given by their Intelligence services was: only as long as they could prevent the Americans from recapturing the Philippines. With the Philippines lost, Japan's supply lines to oil, rubber and other essential raw materials in Malaya and the Dutch East Indies, already under pressure from US submarines, would be severed completely. This in turn would neutralize the Imperial Navy, because if it was based in the south it would be unable to receive ammunition from Japan and if it remained in home waters it would be unable to receive fuel from Japan's newly-conquered territories.

It must therefore have caused acute anxiety that Japanese Intelligence also reported that the Americans planned to assault Leyte Island in the Central Philippines, bypassing Mindanao, the main island in the south of the group. This was indeed the next American objective and the target date for it had been set at 20 October 1944.

To prepare the way for the Leyte landing, Vice Admiral Mitscher's fast carriers, now designated Task Force 38 in Admiral William Halsey's Third Fleet[1], made a series of strikes on enemy bases from which reinforcements could be sent. On 10 October, they raided Okinawa, where they arrived on the heels of a convenient typhoon, achieved complete surprise and inflicted heavy damage. On the 11th, they attacked Luzon in the Northern Philippines and finally, on the 12th, Formosa (modern-day Taiwan).

This last strike had been anticipated by Admiral Toyoda and met strong opposition. This began late that evening, when pilots from light carrier *Independence*, who had been specially trained to operate at night, shot down five Bettys; it was followed by a whole series of daylight raids. On the 13th, a Betty, already on fire, crashed onto the flight deck of carrier *Franklin*, slid across it and went over the side into the sea. Heavy cruiser *Canberra*, named in honour of HMAS *Canberra* that had perished fighting alongside US ships at Savo Island, was hit by a torpedo-bomber and so damaged that she had to be towed out of the danger-zone. Next day, light cruiser *Houston* was also struck by a torpedo, and she took a second one two days later, but she too was towed to safety.

During the Formosa operation, the Americans lost seventy-six aircraft in action, thirteen more on operations, and sixty-four aircrew. Yet they destroyed almost 500 Japanese naval warplanes in the air or on the ground. Among these losses were some 150 aircraft transferred by Toyoda from carriers to land bases – though since their pilots were at best half-trained and probably incapable of operating from their motherships at sea, this was perhaps not as great a mistake as has been maintained.

While the US Third Fleet was striking at Formosa, the US Seventh Fleet was carrying General MacArthur, Lieutenant General Walter Krueger and Krueger's Sixth US Army towards Leyte. It was commanded by Vice Admiral Thomas Kinkaid who had given MacArthur loyal service since November 1943 and won his trust and confidence. Seventh Fleet contained 738 ships in all, including eighteen escort carriers and six battleships, and its task was to land the soldiers in Leyte Gulf, which lies between the eastern coast of that island and the southern coast of the larger but less strategically important island of Samar.

On 20 October 1944, after preliminary strikes by aircraft from the escort carriers and a bombardment by the battleships, the landing was duly made and achieved complete success. On the 21st, Tacloban and Dulag airfields were captured, though both were so badly flooded that they were scarcely fit for use. By the 23rd, 132,400 men and 200,000 tons of supplies were ashore. On the 24th, Krueger set up his command post on Leyte and MacArthur did the same on the following day.

Seventh Fleet suffered only minor casualties as the price for its success. On 19 October, destroyer *Ross* hit two mines but proved to be the only destroyer to survive such a dual misfortune in the whole war. On the afternoon of the 20th, a torpedo-bomber badly damaged light cruiser *Honolulu*. Early on the 21st, a bomber crashed, apparently deliberately, into HMAS *Australia*, a heavy cruiser that was a veteran of Seventh Fleet operations and she, like *Honolulu*, had to retire from the combat-zone. Two of the escort carriers withdrew on the 24th to collect replacement aircraft. None of these events, however, had any real effect on Seventh Fleet's ability to cover and support the landing forces.

Seventh Fleet in turn received cover and support from Halsey's mighty Third Fleet, which had taken station east of the Philippines. This would not be quite as strong as it had been during the strikes on Formosa, for on the evening of 22 October, Halsey had detached one of his four Task Groups for rest and reprovisioning. Unfortunately, the Group that he chose was that of Vice Admiral John McCain which was the strongest of the four, including fleet carriers *Wasp*, *Hornet* and *Hancock* and light carriers *Monterey* and *Cowpens*, and he did not recall it when the first reports of Japanese movements were received.

Even without McCain's Group, Third Fleet could boast fleet carriers *Lexington* (Mitscher's flagship), *Essex*, *Intrepid*, *Franklin* and the veteran *Enterprise*, light carriers *Princeton*, *Langley*, *Independence*, *Cabot*, *San Jacinto* and *Belleau Wood*, six battleships, two heavy cruisers, seven light cruisers and forty-four destroyers. Although the number of warplanes varied on every ship, on average the five large carriers contained thirty Helldivers, eighteen Avengers and forty-two Hellcats each, and the six light carriers, nine Avengers and twenty-two Hellcats each. These resources were quite sufficient to enable Halsey alone to cope with any fleet the Japanese might send into battle.

Yet in practice, the Americans' situation was not as satisfactory as it appeared. The chain of command had a fundamental weakness in that while Kinkaid was under MacArthur, Halsey took his orders from Admiral Nimitz in Pearl Harbour. The result was a lack of liaison between Third and Seventh Fleets. Worse still, as it transpired, Halsey's instructions told him not only to protect the beachhead but to destroy any enemy force that appeared. Aggressive by nature and dangerously contemptuous of his enemies, he believed this implied that he could regard the protection of the beachhead as subsidiary, and persisted in his view despite clear statements to the contrary from both Nimitz and MacArthur.

Halsey's eagerness for action had one further adverse effect. He issued orders directly to his Task Group Commanders, bypassing his chief subordinate Vice Admiral Mitscher, who, as Professor Morison states in his volume on the battle, *Leyte June 1944 - January 1945* became 'little better than a passenger in his beloved Fast Carrier Forces, Pacific Fleet'. This was most unfortunate because Mitscher's much greater combat experience would probably have prevented most if not all of the errors that would bedevil the Americans throughout the coming conflict.

Any American difficulties, however, were minor compared with the anxieties faced by Admiral Toyoda. The chief of these was that Vice Admiral Ozawa's carrier force, now based in home waters, was desperately weak. Since the Battle of the Philippine Sea it had been joined by three fleet carriers of some 17,000 tons, *Amagi*, *Unryu* and *Katsuragi*, but unfortunately they were all valueless, because there were no trained pilots to man their aircraft. The Japanese had also adapted two battleships, *Hyuga* and *Ise*, replacing their after guns with a flight deck, hangar and lift. It was intended each should house twenty-two seaplanes that would be launched by catapults and subsequently land in the sea and be hoisted aboard by cranes. None of the special seaplanes needed ever became available, however, and there would have been no pilots for them even if they had done.

Nonetheless, there was never any possibility that the Imperial Navy would not take part in the fight for Leyte. As Toyoda bluntly put it: 'There would be no sense in saving the fleet at the expense of the loss of the Philippines.' Since his carriers could not hope to save Leyte, the essence of Toyoda's plan, optimistically named Operation SHO – the word means 'victory' – was to attack Leyte Gulf with his Fleet's heavy gunnery units, particularly the great battleships *Yamato* and *Musashi*. These had a standard displacement of over 64,000 tons, were of almost 72,000 tons when fully laden and mounted the largest naval guns in existence, nine of 18.1-inch calibre set in three triple turrets, two forward and one aft. These vessels and indeed most of Japan's surface warships under Vice Admiral Kurita had been stationed near Singapore so as to be close to their fuel supplies but on 18 October, they proceeded to Brunei Bay, Borneo. Here they were refuelled and at 0800 on 22 October, Kurita, with the bulk of his ships, set out again – for Leyte Gulf.

This group that for simplicity's sake may be called the Japanese Central Force consisted of *Yamato*, *Musashi*, three smaller battleships,

Nagato, *Kongo* and *Haruna*, ten heavy cruisers, two light cruisers and fifteen destroyers. Kurita's mission was to steam west of Palawan, itself the most westerly of the Philippines, then turn east to pass south of Mindoro, cross the Sibuyan Sea, move through the San Bernardino Strait between Luzon and Samar and finally head south along Samar's eastern coast to attack Leyte Gulf from the north.

Seven hours after Kurita's departure, Vice Admiral Shoji Nishimura, who had a shorter distance to cover, also left Brunei. The Van of the Southern Force, as the Americans named it, contained battleships *Yamashiro* and *Fuso*, heavy cruiser *Mogami* and four destroyers. It was to pass south of Palawan into the Sulu Sea, proceed north of Mindanao and then, turning sharply north, enter the Surigao Strait between Leyte and the small island of Dinagat to attack Leyte Gulf from the south.

To reinforce Nishimura, the Rear of the Southern Force, heavy cruisers *Nachi* and *Ashigara*, light cruiser *Abukuma* and four more destroyers, set out from Okinawa, steaming west of Luzon and Mindoro before entering the Sulu Sea. However, Shima had only been detailed to support Nishimura at the last minute and knew nothing of his colleague's plans. He did not, therefore, wish to join the Van Force, when as the senior officer, he would have had to take command; instead he followed it at a distance of at least 40 miles.

Had even a fair proportion of these vessels reached Leyte Gulf, the Americans would have suffered a major disaster. Though the bulk of the transports had left by 25 October when the Japanese ships were planned to arrive, the landing beaches, piled high with food, ammunition and other equipment, would have presented a wonderful target for the Japanese big guns. So would the temporary headquarters of the Army commanders, including that of MacArthur; all, like the supplies, within easy range of ships in the Gulf. If the beaches were shelled, the US Sixth Army would have been deprived of its food, its ammunition and its leaders. It would also have been deprived of its air support.

Ironically, the Japanese did not know of the existence of Seventh Fleet's escort carriers but they lay right in Kurita's path. Should they be annihilated, then, declares Professor Morison, 'General MacArthur's Army would have been cut off like that of Athens at Syracuse in 413 BC. Third Fleet alone could not have maintained its communications'; –

a fact that was admitted by Halsey in a signal to MacArthur on 26 October. Such a disaster, particularly coming after a long series of American successes, might have had immense repercussions.

It seems that this prospect was suddenly realized by the Japanese Army for it belatedly decided to dispatch reinforcements to Leyte. These were to be landed at Ormoc Bay on the west of the island by two transport groups: the larger under Vice Admiral Naomasa Sakonju consisting of one heavy cruiser, one light cruiser, one destroyer and four transports; the other under Commander Hisashi Ishii containing only three destroyers.

But how was Kurita to deal with the mighty Third Fleet that blocked his path to Seventh Fleet and the landing beaches? Operation SHO decreed that he would do so by evading it. It would be lured northward during Kurita's approach, and after causing havoc in Leyte Gulf, he would again elude it by retiring through Surigao Strait, by then already penetrated by Nishimura and Shima.

The unhappy task of providing the lure was given to Vice Admiral Ozawa's Northern Force. The Japanese had for some time considered using the battleship-carriers *Hyuga* and *Ise* as sacrificial decoys in the same way as *Ryujo* had been used at the Eastern Solomons – a scheme of which, incidentally, the Americans were aware from Intelligence reports. To sweeten the bait, Toyoda now decided to add to them fleet carrier *Zuikaku*, light carriers *Zuiho*, *Chiyoda* and *Chitose*, three light cruisers and ten destroyers. On board the carriers were just twenty-five Jills, four Kates used as high-level bombers, seven Judys and eighty Zeros, twenty-eight of them fighter-bombers. The standard of their airmen was so low that Ozawa felt it advisable to fly several off to shore bases – but it scarcely mattered for both Toyoda and Ozawa were grimly aware that if the Northern Force succeeded in its mission, this might well be at the cost of its own destruction.

To support their surface warships in the absence of carrier aircraft, the Japanese land-based naval aircraft in the Philippines were ordered to attack Third Fleet as from 24 October, and Vice Admiral Takijiro Onishi decided that as Japan's sailors were risking all in the coming battle, her airmen should make similar sacrifices: to be certain of a hit, they should be prepared to crash deliberately into American carriers. On 20 and 21 October, he formed the first units of a 'Special Attack Corps' to do just that. It was given the name 'Kamikaze' meaning

'Divine Wind', after a typhoon that had destroyed a Mongol invasion fleet in 1281. And already on the 15th, a subordinate commander, Rear Admiral Masafumi Arima, had set out with the express intention of ramming an American carrier. Though shot down at a safe distance, he had 'lit the fuse of the ardent wishes of his men.'[2]

The Battle of Leyte Gulf that followed, fought across an area of almost 500,000 square miles, lasting for several days and involving warships slightly more in numbers and considerably more in tonnage than did even Jutland, was the biggest naval action in history. Nor does such a comparison take account of the involvement of aircraft – just five seaplanes at Jutland but in hundreds at Leyte Gulf – or of submarines, that did no harm at Jutland but considerable damage at Leyte Gulf.

Indeed it was submarines that opened the battle. In the early hours of 23 October, USS *Bream* sighted Sakonju's Transport Unit and torpedoed heavy cruiser *Aoba*, putting her out of action. Shortly afterwards, submarines *Darter* and *Dace* made a brilliantly successful attack on Kurita's Central Force. *Darter* put four torpedoes into the flagship, heavy cruiser *Atago*, which sank 18 minutes later with the loss of some 360 officers and men. Kurita himself was ignominiously pulled out of the water by a destroyer and subsequently taken on board *Yamato*. *Darter* also hit heavy cruiser *Takao* with two torpedoes, so damaging her that she had to return to Brunei escorted by a pair of destroyers. *Dace* then hit heavy cruiser *Maya* with four torpedoes, igniting her magazines; she sank four minutes later. That *Darter* subsequently ran aground while trying to get into position for another attack on *Takao* and became a total loss, detracted little from this achievement, especially as all her crew were rescued by *Dace*. Kurita now had five less ships with which to engage Seventh Fleet.

If 23 October was a day of triumph for America's submarines, the 24th demonstrated the skills of her naval airmen. First to shine were her aerial scouts. At 0746, Lieutenant Max Adams, pilot of a Helldiver from *Intrepid*, sighted the Central Force south of Mindoro. Then both Transport Units were spotted – and attacked; the larger one by aircraft from *Intrepid* that hit light cruiser *Kinu* on the bow with a 1,000-lb bomb, though inflicting only minor damage; the smaller one by aircraft from *Franklin* that sank destroyer *Wakaba*, among those lost being the unit's leader Commander Ishii. Her two companions rescued survivors and returned to their base at Manila.

At about 0900, Lieutenant Raymond Moore from the veteran *Enterprise* discovered the Van of the Southern Force. He was joined by other *Enterprise* aircraft engaged on armed reconnaissance missions; they attacked, hitting but not seriously harming battleship *Fuso* and destroyer *Shigure*. One Hellcat was forced to 'ditch' but its pilot, Commander Fred Bukatis, was later rescued by an American submarine.

Admiral Halsey was not too interested in Nishimura, or in Shima who was also located shortly before midday. At 0827, he belatedly ordered McCain's Task Group to rejoin him – though since it was then some 600 miles to the east, it could not possibly see action until the 25th – and instructed his other three Task Groups to rendezvous east of San Bernardino Strait. He intended to concentrate the full weight of Third Fleet against Kurita, leaving the Southern Forces for Kinkaid to deal with. He did not, however, inform his fellow commander of this decision – an indication of the lack of co-ordination between them.

Before Halsey could deliver his planned blows at Kurita, Japanese land-based aircraft were already racing towards his own ships. Fortunately, the position of only one of his Task Groups was known to the enemy and it was against its carriers, *Lexington*, *Essex*, *Princeton* and *Langley*, that three raids in quick succession were delivered. Fortunately also, radar gave early warning of the attackers shortly after 0800, and most of them were intercepted while still some distance from their targets.

In the resulting air-combats the Japanese suffered such losses that their orthodox land-based warplanes could play no effective part in the rest of the battle. The Hellcats from light carrier *Princeton* alone claimed thirty-four 'kills'. It was the Hellcats from *Essex*, though, that recorded the highest scores by individual pilots. Lieutenant Rushing personally destroyed six Zeros, while Commander David McCampbell, who had shot down seven enemy aircraft during the Battle of the Philippine Sea, destroyed nine more on this occasion, an achievement that led to the award of a Congressional Medal of Honour. He would end the war with a total of thirty-five victories, the highest by a US naval pilot.

At 0938, the carriers' triumph seemed assured. Not one of them had been touched and all organized raids had been broken. Yet that triumph would be grieviously marred by a single brave, capable Japanese airman. As the carriers turned into the wind to recover their fighters, a solitary Judy dive-bomber burst out of the cloud-cover where it had skilfully avoided detection. Ignoring a formidable amount of anti-aircraft fire, it made a perfect approach run on *Princeton*, dropped its 550-lb bomb with uncanny accuracy, passed astern still apparently unharmed – and was shot into the sea by a fighter from *Langley*.

Too late! The bomb crashed through *Princeton*'s flight deck to explode deep in her hull. The blast ignited six Avengers in her hangar and the torpedoes with which they had been fitted in readiness for a strike on Kurita began to detonate one after the other. Flames spread rapidly and a huge column of smoke towered a thousand feet into the sky. At about 1000, a series of violent explosions brought *Princeton* almost to a halt, split open her flight deck, blew the forward elevator high into the air, after which it fell back into the pit, and hurled the after elevator onto the flight deck upside down. All her crew except fire-fighting parties, some 240 strong, were ordered to leave her.

Around the wounded carrier a number of her escorting vessels gathered, to rescue survivors and to help hose water onto the flames. An increasingly rough sea meant that several of them were banged against *Princeton*. Light cruiser *Birmingham* and destroyer *Irwin* sustained damage, while destroyer *Morrison* was temporarily jammed under *Princeton*'s overhanging side and among other misfortunes had a jeep and an electric aeroplane tractor slide off the carrier to crash onto her bridge, whence they bounced onto her main deck.

In the middle of this frantic activity, two more waves of enemy aircraft were detected. These came from Ozawa's Northern Force and contained in all eight Jills, seven Judys and sixty-one Zeros, twenty-one of them fighter-bombers. Most of these were again intercepted at a safe distance and their inexperienced crews were quite outclassed by the Hellcat pilots. They did not lack courage, however. The Judys – from *Zuikaku*, the only vessel with Ozawa capable of handling them – burst past the fighter screen and, rightly ignoring *Princeton*, plunged down on the other three carriers with such ferocious determination that some Americans later believed, erroneously, that this had been a suicide attack. Three were shot down. The others scored two near misses on *Langley* and one each on *Lexington* and *Essex*, but these caused only minor damage.

This assault had ended before 1400 and attention again turned to the attempts to save *Princeton*. An hour later, it seemed she might well be saved, for all fires had been quenched except one. This was still very dangerous because it was near a compartment containing a number of bombs, but it was thought that if these were going to explode they would have done so already. It was decided to take *Princeton* in tow and at 1523 *Birmingham* had closed to within 50 feet in order to do so. Her decks were crowded with fire-fighting and rescue personnel, men handling the tow lines, medical officers and orderlies, anti-aircraft gunners, officers of the watch and no doubt anyone not otherwise immediately employed, eager to see what was happening.

At this moment the bombs detonated, tearing off *Princeton*'s stern and flight deck and hurling savage pieces of steel, including broken gun barrels, beams from the carrier's deck and huge metal plates onto *Birmingham*. Literally in a flash she became, in the words of Captain Inglis, 'a veritable charnel house' with 229 dead and 420, including Inglis, wounded. On *Princeton* the blast decimated the fire-fighters, leaving scarcely a man uninjured.

Even now *Princeton* appeared seaworthy but her fires had sprung up again, threatening her fuel tanks and main magazine, so reluctantly her damage control parties were ordered to abandon her and destroyer *Irwin* to finish her off. Unfortunately *Irwin*'s torpedo director had been rendered useless by her earlier knocks against *Princeton*. Of the six torpedoes she fired, one hit well forward and did no damage, three missed and two, unbelievably, turned round and came back at the destroyer which narrowly evaded them. Light cruiser *Reno* then fired two torpedoes that detonated *Princeton*'s forward fuel tanks. She disintegrated in one final vast explosion. Thanks to the rescue efforts of her escorts, she lost only 108 killed and 190 wounded, less than half the casualties of poor *Birmingham*.

During the Japanese raids the American airmen had destroyed 120 enemy warplanes, losing only ten of their own aircraft, plus thirty-one more that went down with *Princeton*. They would lose eighteen more to AA fire in a series of attacks on Kurita's Central Force in the Sibuyan Sea. There were six of these in all, starting at 1020 and continuing all afternoon, three delivered by aircraft from *Intrepid* and *Cabot*, two by aircraft from *Lexington* and *Essex* and one by aircraft from *Enterprise* and *Franklin*. Spectacular reports poured in from the American pilots, suggesting that the majority of Kurita's vessels had been severely damaged at the very least.

In reality while heavy cruiser *Myoko* was hit by a torpedo and forced to return to Brunei, it seems clear that the airmen concentrated on Kurita's battleships and on one of them in particular. *Yamato* took four bombs and *Nagato* two but their thick armour saved them from serious harm. It was a different story with *Musashi*. In the first three raids she was hit by a total of nine torpedoes and seven bombs. Her forecastle sank so much that the sea came right over it, to break against her huge forward turrets, and her speed dropped to only 12 knots. Accompanied only by heavy cruiser *Tone*, she fell behind her companions. It was while she was thus crippled that the Avengers and Helldivers from *Enterprise* and *Franklin* found her. At least four torpedoes and six bombs struck her – indeed even reliable Japanese officers have estimated that the true figure may have been as high as ten of each.

It was too much even for a titan like *Musashi*. She was now unmanageable, listing relentlessly ever more to port, with flooding uncontrolled. At 1935, she finally rolled over and sank, taking with her Rear Admiral Toshihei Inoguchi, thirty-eight other officers and 984 men. Her survivors were taken aboard a pair of destroyers and these then retired from the scene.

Meanwhile, Admiral Halsey had been receiving other welcome news. He was desperately anxious to locate the Japanese carriers which, he was certain, must be participating in the present operation. Ironically, of course, his enemies wanted him to do so and Ozawa's flagship *Zuikaku* had therefore deliberately broken radio silence on various frequencies, though an undetected fault in her transmitter meant that her temptations passed unnoticed. The logical place for the carriers to be was north-east of the Philippines, heading straight for Leyte Gulf from the Japanese homeland. Halsey, inexplicably, had ordered no early searches in this direction, and when he attempted to retrieve his error, he was delayed by the air-attacks on Third Fleet. Not until 1405 did Helldivers from *Lexington* set out to find the elusive 'flat-tops'.

At 1540, Lieutenant Walters spotted an enemy force, built around *Hyuga* and *Ise*, that Ozawa had sent ahead in a somewhat desperate attempt to divert attention away from Kurita by bringing about a surface battle. Next, two big destroyers, detached as pickets, were sighted, and finally, at 1640, Lieutenant Crapser located Northern

Force's carriers. Ozawa was delighted. He recalled the Advance Force, sent the picket destroyers home and, since he wished to pull Third Fleet as far north of the San Bernardino Strait as possible, he spent the night of 24/25 October steering various courses while remaining roughly 200 miles from Luzon's north-eastern cape. To this, by a weird quirk of fate, a sixteenth-century Spanish navigator, for reasons unknown, had given the name of Engano: Cape Deception.

Admiral Halsey was certainly deceived – and beyond the most optimistic hopes of Toyoda or Ozawa. He knew that enemy forces were approaching from three different directions but as he had left Nishimura and Shima to Kinkaid, he was concerned only with Kurita and Ozawa. Of these, the former was reported to be retiring but the Japanese were notoriously stubborn and there was always the possibility that Central Force's retirement was only temporary, as indeed Kurita intended it should be. Unfortunately, Halsey had accepted at face value the vastly exaggerated claims made by his pilots and so felt that even if a few undamaged vessels should 'plod through San Bernardino Strait' they 'could no longer be considered a serious menace to Seventh Fleet'.

At 1512, that is before any part of the Northern Force had been sighted, Halsey had stated that a new group, to be called Task Force 34, consisting of four battleships and supporting vessels under the command of Vice Admiral Willis Lee, 'will be formed' to deal with Kurita if he sortied from San Bernardino. Halsey had intended this as merely an indication of future intentions, but it was taken as an order by Nimitz, by Mitscher and, most important, by Kinkaid, all of whom thought the new Task Force had actually come into existence.

Having located the Japanese carriers, Halsey could have formed Task Force 34 and left it to guard San Bernardino Strait while the rest of Third Fleet attacked the Northern Force. Or if he felt that Task Force 34 would need fighter protection – though Lee would have been happy to dispense with this in view of the decline in Japan's air power and in the skill of her airmen – he could have left one of his Task Groups to support it. Or, indeed, he could have massed his whole strength off San Bernardino, destroyed any of Kurita's ships that emerged from it, which they would have had to do in single file, and turned on Ozawa later.

Unfortunately, acting defensively was never to Halsey's taste.

Moreover, he had again unquestioningly accepted exaggerated reports from his pilots and so believed the Northern Force was considerably stronger than was in fact the case.³ He therefore determined he would bring against it every gun and every aircraft he possessed. At 2022, without leaving even a picket destroyer to send warning of the approach of Central Force, the whole of Third Fleet raced after Ozawa – exactly as the Japanese had wanted.

Having once made his decision, Halsey refused to allow anything to alter it. The night-fliers from light carrier *Independence* had been keeping track of Kurita. They had to be recalled as *Independence* accompanied the rest of Third Fleet, but their latest reports revealed that Kurita was now heading for San Bernardino; his vessels included several battleships, one being of the *Yamato*-class – it was of course *Yamato* herself – and far from 'plodding' they were making more than 20 knots. Yet despite these warnings and protests from Lee and Rear Admiral Gerald Bogan who commanded the Task Group containing *Independence*, Halsey continued to head northwards. Behind him, at 0035 on 25 October, Central Force passed through the Strait and, astonished to find nothing to oppose it, steamed south towards Leyte Gulf.

As a crowning misfortune, when Halsey gave notice of his actions, he stated that he was 'proceeding north with three Groups', thus giving the unfortunate impression that this meant with part only of his command. Having heard the previous message about Task Force 34, Nimitz, Kinkaid and at first Mitscher, all thought that this was being left behind to guard San Bernardino. The result was that not only had Halsey given Kurita an unobstructed passage to Seventh Fleet, but Seventh Fleet was quite unaware of this.

Accordingly, Kinkaid believed he had only Nishimura and Shima to worry about. He ordered his subordinate, Rear Admiral Jesse Oldendorf, to block the 12-mile-wide stretch of water where Surigao Strait enters Leyte Gulf and destroy the Southern Forces as they tried to break through. With a strength of six admittedly elderly battleships – five of them, indeed, restored after injuries received at Pearl Harbour – four heavy cruisers including HMAS *Shropshire*, four light cruisers and twenty-eight destroyers including HMAS *Arunta*, Oldendorf could easily have matched both his enemies even had they joined forces, which they did not. He planned first a series of torpedo attacks by his destroyers, then a barrage at close range from his battle line.

The resulting night action shows the damage that might have been inflicted on Central Force had Halsey defended San Bernardino. At the cost of one destroyer, *Albert W. Grant*, severely damaged by shells from both sides but later repaired, Oldendorf all but annihilated the Van of the Southern Force, killing Nishimura and sinking battleship *Yamashiro*, battleship *Fuso* and destroyers *Yamagumo*, *Asagumo* and *Michishio*. Only heavy cruiser *Mogami* and destroyer *Shigure* were able to withdraw southwards, the former badly damaged and not fully under control.

At this inauspicious moment, the Rear of the Southern Force appeared, and *Mogami*, which it will be remembered had rammed her sister-ship *Mikuma* at Midway, now rammed Shima's flagship, heavy cruiser *Nachi*. Light cruiser *Abukuma*, hit by a PT-boat's torpedo, had already had to retire, and Shima now sensibly decided his position was impossible and ordered all his ships to withdraw. This, though, did not end the ordeal of the Southern Forces. Early on 25 October, Avengers from Kinkaid's escort carriers put two torpedoes into *Mogami*. These finally brought her to a halt, but she still remained afloat until all her survivors had been taken off and even then it needed another torpedo from a Japanese destroyer to send her down. The other cripple, *Abukuma*, was sunk early on the following day, the 26th, by US Army Liberator and Mitchell bombers. The southern arm of the Japanese pincers had been irretrievably broken.

Dawn on 25 October found another Japanese force apparently facing total destruction. Losses in action or operationally had left Ozawa's Northern Force with just four Jills, a solitary Judy, nineteen Zero fighters and five Zero fighter-bombers – twenty-nine in all; whereas Vice Admiral Mitscher, to whom Halsey had at last delegated tactical command, controlled 214 Helldivers, 171 Avengers and 404 Hellcats, three of them survivors from *Princeton*. Shortly before 0600, a seemingly endless succession of aircraft began to leave the US carriers' decks: first the Combat Air Patrol, next search-planes from *Lexington*, finally sixty-five Helldivers, fifty-five Avengers and sixty Hellcats coming from all three Task Groups with the record-breaking Commander David McCampbell acting as target co-ordinator.

At 0710, the scouts sighted the Japanese ships 145 miles distant heading northward and at about 0830, the first attack began. As the raiders appeared, *Zuiho* pulled out of formation to launch fifteen Zeros that gallantly rushed into action, downing one Avenger and damaging others before they were overwhelmed by the Hellcats. Nine Zeros were shot down; presumably the rest perished when their fuel was exhausted. The Americans met no further opposition in the air, though they were faced by a daunting barrage of AA fire that, rather surprisingly, claimed only ten victims during the course of the day. It seems, however, that it did help to spoil the attackers' aim.

This first raid, though, achieved considerable success. The Helldivers from *Lexington* and *Essex* scored numerous bomb hits on light carrier *Chitose* that staggered to a halt, burning and listing, to sink at 0937. The Helldivers from *Intrepid* scored one hit on *Zuiho* but this did only minor damage. *Intrepid*'s torpedo-planes attacked *Zuikaku*, as did those from light carrier *San Jacinto*. She was hit aft, her speed reduced to 18 knots, her steering control so damaged that she had to be steered by hand, and her communications system wrecked, forcing Ozawa to transfer his flag to light cruiser *Oyodo* so that he could continue to exercise his command. A torpedo also hit destroyer *Akitsuki* which blew up and sank instantly.[4]

Even as this assault was ending at about 1000, a second small raid began. Light cruiser *Tama*, struck by a torpedo, fell out of formation with her speed reduced to about 10 knots. Helldivers – they came from *Lexington* and *Franklin* – concentrated on light carrier *Chiyoda*, scoring three hits that left her dead in the water and on fire, while *Hyuga*, light cruiser *Isuzu* and two destroyers hovered round her trying to help. The Americans had now finally formed Task Force 34 under Lee, containing all six battleships, and sent it ahead of their carriers specifically to dispose of any cripples: the group around *Chiyoda* made splendid potential victims.

But Vice Admiral Lee would never get the opportunity to engage them. At 0822, as the first American formations were preparing to attack the Northern Force, a signal was received on Halsey's flagship, battleship *New Jersey*. It had been sent off by Kinkaid an hour and a quarter earlier, its urgency was made clear by its being not in code but in plain English and its contents were horrifying: Japanese capital ships, confirmed in later signals as including four battleships and eight cruisers, were firing on Seventh Fleet's escort carriers and threatening to penetrate to the vital beachhead in Leyte Gulf.

A whole series of appeals for aid followed from Kinkaid and the

Seventh Fleet units under fire. Halsey ignored them. He did order McCain's Group to help Seventh Fleet but McCain was further away than Halsey. Only at 1000, when he received a signal from Nimitz, demanding to know the whereabouts of Task Force 34 which Nimitz thought had been left to guard San Bernardino, did Halsey falter. After mulling over the situation for about an hour, he finally ordered Task Force 34 to go to the aid of Seventh Fleet. To give Lee air cover, he added Bogan's Task Group – *Intrepid*, *Cabot* and *Independence* – to his strength.

Ironically enough, Halsey had now divided his command in the very manner that Lee and Bogan had wished him to do when the Northern Force was first discovered. He then split it up still further by forming a new Task Group consisting of his two fastest battleships, *Iowa* and his own *New Jersey*, with a small escort and sending this well ahead – ultimately 40 miles ahead – of Lee's remaining four battleships and Bogan's carriers. Third Fleet, with a fire-power greater than that of the entire Japanese Navy, was now outgunned by Ozawa in the north and outgunned by Kurita in the south.

Third Fleet's overwhelming superiority in carrier-aircraft, by contrast, was employed by Mitscher with cool efficiency. Shortly before 1200, he launched the day's third raid on Northern Force: some 200 warplanes from both his remaining Task Groups with Commander Hugh Winters from *Lexington* as target co-ordinator. On the way, some of *Franklin*'s aircraft attacked *Hyuga* and her escorts, doing no damage but persuading them to rejoin Ozawa. *Chiyoda* was left alone with her crew still on board – probably at their own request.

Reaching the main part of Northern Force at about 1310, Winters directed his men to attack in two waves. In the first, Helldivers from *Essex* and *Langley* scored several hits on *Zuiho*, starting fires that were, however, brought under control. The airmen from *Lexington*, together with a few from *Langley*, assaulted *Zuikaku*. She too was hit by bombs and in her case also by three torpedoes that struck her almost simultaneously, bringing her to a halt, burning and listing heavily. Winters then sent the aircraft from *Enterprise*, *Franklin* and *San Jacinto* against *Zuiho*. They scored more bomb hits, reducing her speed and causing her fires to spring up again, but she doggedly continued limping northward.

Zuikaku, though, had reached the end of her remarkable career. At

1414, quietly and without any explosion, the last of the carriers that had attacked Pearl Harbour rolled over and sank. Commander Winters, watching with triumph, not unmixed with a strange sense of regret, reported that she flew to the end 'a battle flag of tremendous size, perhaps fifty feet square' that her crew had hoisted to the masthead as a last defiant gesture.

Three more raids followed during the course of the afternoon. A small one from *Lexington* and *Langley* attacked at 1445, most of its pilots concentrating on *Zuiho*. They hit her with two more bombs and at last two torpedoes found their mark. The gallant little light carrier had also used up all her luck; she went down at 1526. The later attacks between them scored seven near misses on *Hyuga* and one hit and an astonishing thirty-four near misses on *Ise*, but both suffered only slight injuries.

Yet the Northern Force would still suffer further casualties. At 1625, a cruiser-destroyer force detached by Mitscher opened fire on *Chiyoda*. She promptly burst into a mass of flames and a towering column of smoke. At 1650, she capsized, sinking almost at once. The Americans continued their pursuit after dark and engaged three Japanese destroyers that had been searching for survivors; they sank the 2,700-ton *Hatsutsuki*. Also after dark damaged light cruiser *Tama*, limping home alone, was sunk with all hands by US submarine *Jallao*. Even so, despite the odds against them, ten of Ozawa's ships made good their escape.

The decoys had carried out their difficult and dangerous task at less cost than either Toyoda or Ozawa had anticipated. It remained to be seen whether their unselfish valour had won the Battle of Leyte Gulf for the Japanese. This would depend upon sixteen small, slow, unarmoured escort carriers divided into three groups, known from their voice-radio call-signs as 'Taffy 1', '2' and '3', each of them guarded by three destroyers and four of the smaller, slower destroyer-escorts which were designed simply for anti-submarine warfare. 'Taffy 1' under the overall commander, Rear Admiral Thomas Sprague, contained four escort carriers, *Sangamon*, *Suwanee*, *Santee* and *Petrof Bay*, and was stationed 90 miles south-east of the entrance to Leyte Gulf. Opposite to this entrance was Rear Admiral Felix Stump's 'Taffy 2' – *Natoma Bay*, *Manila Bay*, *Kadashan Bay*, *Ommaney Bay*, *Marcus Island* and *Savo Island* – while 'Taffy 3' under Rear Admiral Clifton Albert Frederick

Sprague (no relation to his namesake) was steaming north some 60 miles east of Central Samar.

'Taffy 3' therefore would be the first to encounter Kurita. It was composed of escort carriers *Fanshaw Bay* (flagship), *Kitkun Bay*, *Kalinin Bay*, *Gambier Bay*, *White Plains* and *St Lo*, destroyers *Hoel*, *Heermann* and *Johnston* and destroyer-escorts *Dennis*, *Raymond*, *John C. Butler* and *Samuel B. Roberts*. Its escort carriers between them contained ninety-seven Avengers and seventy-two Wildcats – in Seventh Fleet only *Sangamon* and *Suwanee* had the latest Hellcats. All three groups were there not to fight naval battles but to provide anti-submarine patrols and fighter cover over the beachhead, plus various odd jobs: early on 25 October for instance, *Marcus Island* sent off ten Avengers with water and rations for the troops ashore.

At about 0645, Ensign Hans Jensen from *Kadashan Bay* on anti-submarine patrol made a radar contact that on investigation proved considerably more threatening. While officers in 'Taffy 3' were still querying his report of four Japanese battleships, eight cruisers and numerous destroyers; masts and superstructures began to appear over the northern horizon. One of Kurita's lynx-eyed lookouts had spotted the escort carriers' masts even earlier. On both sides surprise was complete.

It seemed that the Japanese had every advantage, but Kurita mishandled the situation from the start. His experiences in the Battle of the Philippine Sea, and earlier in the present battle, where he had watched the magnificent *Musashi* being battered to death, had inspired a profound fear of carrier aircraft. Desperate to engage his enemies before their warplanes were able to take off, he ordered 'General Attack', thereby permitting every ship's captain to choose his own tactics. All control vanished as each unit rushed forward independently and Kurita, to his cost, would never regain it.

By contrast, Rear Admiral Clifton Sprague who had every cause for panic, remained calm. Sending out immediate calls for aid, he ordered all his ships to make smoke, increased speed to $17^{1}/_{2}$ knots, the most his escort carriers could manage, turned due east into the wind and began to launch his aircraft as rapidly as possible. Forty-four Avengers and sixty-five Wildcats got airborne from 'Taffy 3' but they were armed only with whatever happened to be on board at the time. *Gambier Bay* for instance sent up nine Avengers. Of these, only two carried torpedoes and one of them was so short of fuel it had to 'ditch' within a few minutes, three carried bombs, two just depth charges and the last two no weapons at all.

As they hurtled down the flight decks, great columns of water, red, blue, green, yellow, purple, pink and white, sprang up all around them: the Japanese shells were marked with different dyes to assist in spotting fall of shot. *White Plains* was the first target. Several salvoes in quick succession straddled her, shaking her so savagely that men were thrown off their feet. Electric power and steering control were temporarily lost. Luckily the Japanese were deceived by the very closeness of their near misses. Smoke was now pouring from *White Plains* as she endeavoured to cover herself and they believed she was on fire. They shifted their attention to *St Lo*. She also was straddled, so closely that water was flung over her flight deck and shrapnel caused several casualties.

Mercifully, a heavy rain squall now suddenly swept over 'Taffy 3', dramatically reducing visibility. This and the smokescreen caused Japanese accuracy to fall away rapidly. And in addition, Sprague's airmen were now attacking. A bomb struck heavy cruiser *Suzuya*, reducing her speed to 20 knots. Battleship *Kongo* had her main range-finder put out of action by machine gun fire. Fighters out of ammunition and bombers with no bombs or torpedoes made 'dummy runs' to divert or slow down the enemy; Lieutenant Commander Edward Huxtable, the Air Group Commander of *Gambier Bay*, made mock attacks for two hours without a weapon of any kind in his Avenger.

Aircraft that were damaged or out of fuel sought safety at Tacloban airfield on Leyte, repaired just sufficiently to receive them by Army engineers. Some crashed on landing but the majority got down safely and later returned to strike at Kurita once more. Other aircraft landed on the escort carriers of 'Taffy 2'; at one point *Manila Bay* had machines from *Sangamon* (of 'Taffy 1'), *White Plains*, *Kitkun Bay* and *Gambier Bay* all on her flight deck at the same time.

Rear Admiral Stump was also preparing to send his own aircraft against Central Force, but they had first to be armed and made ready and then there might be delays in locating the enemy. Rear Admiral Thomas Sprague was still less able to assist, having sent his aircraft to attack the remains of the Southern Forces. Kinkaid ordered Oldendorf to help but Seventh Fleet's older, slower battleships would be no match for Kurita's, their accompanying light cruisers were short of ammunition, their destroyers had used all their torpedoes, and in any case Oldendorf could not possibly arrive in time to save 'Taffy 3'.

Only Clifton Sprague's own destroyers and destroyer-escorts could aid their carriers immediately. Their principal opponents were the Japanese heavy cruisers. Aggressively led by Vice Admiral Kazutaka Shiraishi, these were attempting to out-flank the little 'flat-tops' and turn them back into the guns of their battleships. At 0727, destroyer *Johnston* scored a torpedo hit on Shiraishi's flagship *Kumano*, reducing her speed to 16 knots and effectively putting her out of the chase. *Suzuya* dropped out as well, in order to pick up Shiraishi and his staff.

That still left four heavy cruisers, *Tone*, *Chikuma*, *Chokai* and *Haguro*, closing in on the escort carriers, forcing them onto a south-westerly course towards Leyte Gulf – the way the Japanese wanted them to go. The American screening vessels gallantly interposed themselves, launching their torpedoes and pouring their 5-inch shells into the enemy ships.

A high price was paid for this gallantry. First destroyer *Hoel*, then destroyer-escort *Samuel B. Roberts* and finally destroyer *Johnston* were sunk and most of the others were damaged.[5] Nor, although they frequently distracted attention from the escort carriers, could they hope to prevent the heavy cruisers from scoring some hits on them.

First to suffer was *Kalinin Bay*. She took her first 8-inch shell at 0750, her second at 0805. *Gambier Bay* was first struck at 0810, then a near miss, exploding very near the forward engine room, blew a hole about four feet square below the water line. Flooding was so rapid that within five minutes the engine room had to be abandoned and *Gambier Bay*, slowing to 11 knots, fell astern of her colleagues. Shells continued to crash into her. Badly on fire, with the tanks of aircraft in her hangar exploding and her steering controls knocked out, she finally came to a halt when a shell hit her after engine room. At 0850, 'Abandon Ship' was ordered. At 0907, *Gambier Bay* capsized and sank.

As their tormentors came ever closer, the remaining escort carriers opened fire on them with the only weapon available: a single 5-inch gun astern. *Fanshaw Bay*, *Kalinin Bay* and *White Plains* all scored hits on the heavy cruisers. But as usual, the decisive damage was inflicted by carrier-aircraft. Rear Admiral Stump was only able to launch the first of a whole series of strikes at about 0745, but thereafter his airmen, aided by some from 'Taffy 3', attacked with a desperate determination.

Again the dangerous Japanese heavy cruisers became the main targets. At about 0845, *Suzuya*, now on her own striving to catch up with the pursuit, was hit and brought to a halt – and she may have received further hits in later raids. At 0902, *Chikuma* was struck by two torpedoes, probably dropped by Avengers from Stump's flagship *Natoma Bay*, and reeled out of the line on fire. At 0905, *Chokai* was taken by surprise by four Avengers from *Kitkun Bay* led by Commander Richard Fowler; their 500-lb bombs made two very near misses, one direct hit astern, three direct hits on her bow and five more amidships and she also swung away, shaken by explosions. All three later sank, though *Suzuya* lingered on until 1322. *Haguro* had one of her turrets knocked out by a bomb. Light cruiser *Yahagi* and two destroyers were damaged by strafing.

Yet despite these casualties, Kurita still had every chance of winning the Battle of Leyte Gulf. His remaining vessels were still firing on Clifton Sprague's escort carriers. *White Plains* was struck by a 6-inch salvo from light cruiser *Noshiro*. *Fanshaw Bay* took four hits, one below the water line, plus two very near misses. *Kalinin Bay*, already hit by two 8-inch shells, received eleven more and one 14-incher. Her main steering gear was knocked out, necessitating steering by hand. One shell, plunging through the flight deck, hit the forward elevator where it exploded, completely wrecking the elevator platform. She probably only survived because most of the shells went clean through her thin hull without exploding.

Kalinin Bay was also threatened by torpedoes from enemy destroyers. Lieutenant Leonard Waldrop from *St Lo* sighted one heading towards the carrier, strafed and exploded it. This warned *Kalinin Bay* and depressing her 5-inch gun as far as possible, she began firing at another torpedo coming perilously close. A shell burst 10 feet ahead of it and it veered away. No damage was done in this attack but all Japanese destroyers (and cruisers) carried reloads of torpedoes and only four destroyers had taken part in it anyway; there would be plenty of opportunity for further attempts.

Beyond 'Taffy 3', Stump's escort carriers were now threatened as well. They had been steaming on a converging course in order to fly off their aircraft and the running battle had drawn dangerously near. At one point battleship *Kongo* opened fire on Stump's destroyers guarding the rear of 'Taffy 2'. She was attacked in turn by a solitary Avenger from *Ommaney Bay* flown by Lieutenant Clark Miller. His torpedo missed but she turned away and ceased firing on 'Taffy 2'.

Nonetheless, it seemed only a matter of time before 'Taffy 3' would be annihilated and 'Taffy 2' overtaken. And only 45 miles away now was Leyte Gulf with its vulnerable beachhead, the destruction of which had been Kurita's main objective. Then, at 0925, *Tone* and *Haguro*, now within 10,000 yards of Clifton Sprague's carriers, suddenly swung to port and broke off the action. The whole Central Force, on a signal from Kurita, reversed course. The unsung, unglamourous little escort carriers and their few screening vessels had repulsed the most powerful Japanese surface fleet ever to engage an American formation.

Kurita had at first intended his withdrawal to be only temporary. His ships had become widely scattered; *Yamato*, a frequent target for the torpedoes of aircraft and destroyers and so forced to take constant evasive action, lagging at the rear of the chase. He had had no idea that *Tone* and *Haguro* had closed to almost point-blank range. His original plan was to reunite his force, re-establish control and then proceed with his mission to assault the bridgehead in Leyte Gulf.

Yet once he had had time in which to reflect, this prospect became ever less attractive to him. Now that he had given the escort carriers a respite, they would be ready for him if he resumed his advance. Since he believed their strength was far greater than it really was, it seemed to him that he would be faced with a series of increasingly heavy assaults from the air. For three hours his ships milled around in much the same area, making no further move southward, until at 1236, he made up his mind. He signalled to Toyoda that he was abandoning his planned 'penetration of Leyte anchorage'. Operation SHO had failed.

Central Force now steamed northward at full speed, harried by naval aircraft. Stump's pilots were approaching exhaustion but they still made bomb hits on battleship *Nagato* and heavy cruiser *Tone*, though neither was seriously damaged. Vice Admiral McCain's Task Group also made its first contribution to the battle, attacking from long range – too long for some of its aircraft that ran out of fuel – but its only achievement was to strike *Tone* with a bomb that did not explode.

Had Halsey steamed south at full speed with all six of Lee's battleships when he had first received news of Kurita's attack on

Sprague, he would have been in a position to block the escape of Central Force through the San Bernardino Strait. As it was, a cruiser-destroyer force sent in advance to catch any stragglers, did find one unlucky destroyer, *Nowake*, that had been standing by *Chikuma* to rescue survivors, and sank her in the early hours of 26 October. The rest of Kurita's ships had already passed through the Strait and made good time crossing the Sibuyan Sea during the night.

Next morning, aircraft from the Task Groups of McCain and Bogan, which had rendezvoused north-east of San Bernardino at 0500, set out after them. A series of attacks proved somewhat disappointing but did hit *Yamato* with two bombs, though without inflicting much harm, and heavy cruiser *Kumano* with one, badly damaging her. Two torpedoes and one bomb sank light cruiser *Noshiro*. Another bomb sank destroyer *Hayashimo*.

The indefatigable pilots of 'Taffy 2' also refused to be left out of the action. During the previous night, the vessels of Vice Admiral Sakonju's Transport Force had landed 2,000 men in Ormoc Bay on the western side of Leyte. They then retired; but on the morning of the 26th, they were sighted by Seventh Fleet's reconnaissance aircraft. Twenty-nine Avengers and twenty-three Wildcats from Stump's escort carriers set out to engage them. They carried only small bombs or rockets but from noon onwards, they persistently bombed and strafed their targets, sinking first destroyer *Uranami*, then light cruiser *Kinu*.

Seventh Fleet's aggressive attitude was the more commendable because as well as facing Kurita, on both 25 and 26 October it had the dubious honour of becoming the target of a new and terrifying form of aerial assault. At 0740 on the 25th, while 'Taffy 3' was engaged with Central Force, four Zero fighter-bombers burst out of low cloud above Rear Admiral Thomas Sprague's 'Taffy 1'. The first, achieving complete surprise, deliberately crashed into the flight deck of escort carrier *Santee*, plunging through this into the hangar. Its bomb exploded as it struck, blowing a hole 30 feet long by 15 feet wide in the flight deck and starting fires that were spread by fuel from the Zero's tanks and those of some of *Santee*'s own aircraft.

Two other Zeros attacked immediately afterwards but whereas *Santee* had not had time to fire a single shot in her own defence, both of these were hit by Sprague's anti-aircraft gunners and crashed near

Sangamon and *Petrof Bay* respectively, causing little damage. Even on *Santee*, the fires were brought under control within eleven minutes – but sixteen dead men and twenty-seven wounded, plus one more unlucky seaman killed by splinters on *Sangamon*, marked the first success of the Kamikazes.

Next, at 0756, *Santee* was torpedoed amidships by Japanese submarine *I-56*. Flooding caused a slight list but the little carrier escaped surprisingly lightly. Unfortunately this incident distracted attention from the fourth Kamikaze and two minutes after the torpedo hit, this dived onto *Suwanee*, bursting through her flight deck into the hangar where its bomb exploded starting fires, temporarily wrecking her steering control and jamming the after elevator. Again the damage control parties quickly quenched the flames, and within two hours they had also repaired the flight deck sufficiently to enable aircraft to land on it once more.

Worse, though, was soon to follow. At 1049, Clifton Sprague's 'Taffy 3', now beginning to reorganize after its running battle with Kurita, became the target of a Kamikaze attack by five bomb-carrying Zeros. 'Taffy 3' was not caught by surprise and opened fire with every gun that could be brought to bear. Two of the attackers, attempting to get at *Fanshaw Bay*, were brought down in flames at a safe distance. Another was blown up immediately over *White Plains*, scattering debris as well as gruesome remains of the pilot over her flight deck. A fourth struck *Kitkun Bay* a glancing blow and bounced off into the sea, though its bomb exploded as it hit, causing some damage.

And one Zero made a perfect approach run on *St Lo*. Flown according to Japanese records by the formation commander, Lieutenant Yukio Seki, it struck the flight deck squarely and smashed through it into the hangar. There its bomb exploded, hurling burning fuel in all directions. Bombs and torpedoes on the hangar deck started to detonate: first a minor explosion that sent up clouds of smoke, then a bigger one that split open the flight deck, then a really huge one that blew the forward elevator high in the air, to land upside down on the flight deck.

As flames spread throughout the whole of the vessel's length and other explosions began to fling parts of the flight deck and entire aircraft hundreds of feet into the air, it became apparent that *St Lo* was doomed. 'Abandon Ship' was ordered as early as 1100. Despite further detonations, one of which seems to have torn out a large section of the hull since the carrier shifted from a list to port to a steeper list to starboard, the evacuation of the crew, including that of seventy-five stretcher cases, was carried out successfully, just in time. At 1125, *St Lo*, that had defied the great guns of *Yamato*, sank by the stern. Up above, three more Zeros that had provided the fighter escort for the attackers returned to base to describe the first, but very far from the last sinking achieved by the Kamikazes.

St Lo was still afloat when at about 1110, fifteen Judy bombers appeared. The Combat Air Patrol intercepted most of these but inevitably a few got through. One, attempting to crash into *Kitkun Bay*, was shot down short of its target; minor damage was caused by shrapnel. Four other Kamikazes attacked *Kalinin Bay*, already hit so frequently by Kurita's heavy cruisers. Two were brought down at a safe distance but the others kept coming: the first crashed into the port side of the flight deck, the second into the after part of the superstructure. Yet *Kalinin Bay* remained in formation and her fires were quenched in less than five minutes. By this time her damage control parties must have thought they could cope with anything.

There would be one more suicide raid in the battle. This came at noon on 26 October, the target being 'Taffy 1'. Six Zeros were sighted but the Combat Air Patrol downed three of them – unfortunately it seems that these were the fighter escort. Of the three Kamikazes, two were shot down astern of *Petrof Bay*, one by an Avenger returning from its anti-submarine patrol, the other by the carrier's AA gunners. The third Zero was also damaged but it was not to be stopped and crashed into *Suwanee* right on top of an Avenger that had just landed. Both aircraft and the Zero's bomb exploded, wrecking the forward elevator and setting fire to seven fighters and two more Avengers on the flight deck.

For several hours the fires raged. A number of officers and men were trapped on the bridge and only rescued after the navigator, Lieutenant Premo, had fought his way through the flames to get help – but he was badly burned in the process and died a few hours afterwards. Chief Ship's Fitter William Brooks was wounded and knocked unconscious, but on recovering he crawled under the aircraft in the hangar to turn on its sprinkler system, thus preventing them from catching fire. His action may well have saved the ship. As it was, she survived, though this and the previous Kamikaze attack cost her 143 killed and 102 injured, some of whom died later.

The Kamikaze attacks brought Seventh Fleet's casualties for 25 and 26 October to 1,130 dead and 913 wounded. They also added another vessel to those lost by the Americans in the battle: light carrier *Princeton* together with escort carriers *Gambier Bay* and *St Lo* and the two destroyers and one destroyer-escort sunk in the fight with Central Force. These were almost insignificant compared with the Japanese losses: *Zuikaku*, *Zuiho*, *Chiyoda*, *Chitose*, three battleships including *Musashi*, six heavy cruisers, four light cruisers, nine destroyers – twenty-six in all, more than either the US Navy or the Imperial Navy had lost during the whole of the ferocious Guadalcanal campaign.

Even these figures do not give the full extent of the disaster that had befallen Japan. Admiral Nimitz would later describe Leyte Gulf as 'the Trafalgar of World War II' that had 'wiped out the Japanese fleet as an effective fighting force'. Admiral Mitsumasa Yonai, Japan's Navy Minister at the time of the battle, would state that 'our defeat at Leyte was tantamount to the loss of the Philippines' and when the Philippines were lost, 'that was the end of our resources'.

Notes

1 Third Fleet, for all practical purposes, contained the same ships as Fifth Fleet had done. In June 1944, it had been decided that henceforward they would be commanded alternately by Halsey and Spruance, while the one not in command retired to Pearl Harbour to plan his own next assault with his staff – this greatly reduced the intervals between operations. Halsey had taken over on 26 August, whereupon Fifth Fleet changed its title to Third Fleet; when Spruance resumed control later, it became Fifth Fleet again. Similarly Task Force 58 under Spruance became Task Force 38 under Halsey, though for a time it remained under the command of Vice Admiral Mitscher.

2 It should be stated that the organizers of the Kamikaze attacks did not merely send ardent young men to their deaths. Many of them flew on such missions themselves. Both the first and the last Kamikaze raids were carried out by flag officers: Arima, on 15 October 1944, and Vice Admiral Matome Ugaki, once Yamamoto's Chief of Staff, on 15 August 1945 respectively. The founder of the 'Special Attack Corps', Vice Admiral Onishi, committed 'seppuku' in the early hours of 16 August 1945. This did not kill him outright. Refusing both medical attention and a quick death, he lingered in agony all day before finally expiring – an act of atonement because his men's sacrifice had failed to achieve ultimate victory.

3 There was little excuse for Halsey's error. He had been notified, for instance, that Ozawa had four battleships with him. Yet Intelligence reports had shown that there

were only nine Japanese battleships in existence and seven of these had been located with Kurita or Nishimura. There could thus have been only two in the Northern Force and they had to be *Hyuga* and *Ise* with their limited armament – a fact confirmed by information that at least one had a flight deck aft. Incidentally, Intelligence had also revealed that the Japanese had long considered using this pair as decoys, so their presence should perhaps have raised some doubts in Halsey's mind – as it did in that of Vice Admiral Lee for one.

4 *Akitsuki* and three of the other destroyers then with Ozawa were big vessels of 2,700 tons. The Americans consistently reported them as light cruisers and Ozawa's genuine light cruisers, *Oyodo*, *Tama* and *Isuzu*, as heavy cruisers – a further way in which the strength of the Northern Force was exaggerated.

5 It is impossible to leave these little ships without recording two tributes that were paid to them and their crews. One came from Lieutenant Commander Robert Copeland, skipper of *Samuel B. Roberts*, who declared that 'no higher honour could be conceived than to command such a group of men'. The other was given by the captain of the Japanese destroyer that finally sank *Johnston*, who was seen by her survivors standing rigidly at the salute as she took her final plunge.

Chapter 10

Maximum Range

In any other war the Japanese defeat at Leyte Gulf would have brought as speedy an end to hostilities as had the even more shattering defeat of the Russians at the hands of the Japanese at Tsushima in 1905. It is true that at Tsushima the Russian fleet had been annihilated, whereas after Leyte Gulf the Japanese still had a 'fleet in being' – but it was one that posed no threat to later American operations.

After the war, Vice Admiral Ozawa would state that Japan's warships 'became strictly auxiliary'. Those doughty warriors *Hyuga* and *Ise*, for example, were used to ferry loads of petrol from Singapore to Japan. Destroyers continued to land men and supplies at Ormoc Bay to aid their soldiers on Leyte, but American air supremacy made this a costly business. On 27 October, the airmen from *Essex* sank destroyers *Fujinami* and *Shiranuhi* and on 11 November, Third Fleet's carriers sank destroyers *Hamanami*, *Naganami*, *Shimakaze* and *Wakatsuki*, not to mention a number of troop transports.

Most major Japanese surface warships remained uselessly in harbour, though this would not save them. While Seventh Fleet gave close support to the American forces on Leyte, Third Fleet concentrated on targets such as Manila, the main Japanese naval base in the Philippines. Aircraft from *Lexington* sank heavy cruiser *Nachi* in Manila Bay on 5 November. On the 13th, Third Fleet sank five more Japanese warships there: light cruiser *Kiso* and destroyers *Akebono*, *Akishimo*, *Okinami* and *Hatsuharu*. The harbour facilities at Manila were also damaged and large numbers of Japanese warplanes destroyed on nearby airfields. And on the 25th, heavy cruiser *Kumano* was sunk at Dasol Bay to the north of Manila by aircraft from US carrier *Ticonderoga*.

Japan's own carriers also usually stayed in harbour. On the rare occasions when they ventured out, they did so singly and with baleful consequences. A particular thorn in their flesh was US submarine *Redfish*. On 9 December, she put two torpedoes into *Junyo*, damaging her so badly that she was out of action for the rest of the war. Not content with that, ten days later, *Redfish* attacked one of Japan's latest carriers, *Unryu*. This time she scored only one hit aft, but it brought *Unryu* to a halt, on fire. Evading counter-attacks by escorting destroyers, *Redfish* attacked again and scored another hit. *Unryu* sank 20 minutes later.

At the time of *Unryu*'s loss, two sister-ships, *Amagi* and *Katsuragi*, were still afloat and three others, *Aso*, *Ikoma* and *Kasagi*, were under construction. By then, however, Japan's industrial capacity was also starting to fail as the severance of her supply lines caused a lack of suitable materials. Early in 1945, work on all three uncompleted *Unryu*-class carriers ceased, as it did also on *Ibuki*, a proposed 12,500-ton carrier being converted from a cruiser, and on five smaller vessels being converted from tankers.

Only one of the carriers on which work was proceeding at the time of Leyte Gulf would ever be completed. This was *Shinano*, converted from the hull of a *Yamato*-class battleship. Of 68,000 tons displacement, almost 72,000 tons fully laden, she had a flight deck 840 feet long by some 130 feet wide, made of steel more than three inches thick. The armour of her hull and her hangar deck was eight inches thick, increasing to almost fourteen inches around her magazines. Yet when she left Tokyo Bay on her maiden voyage at 1800 on 28 November 1944, bound for Matsuyama near Hiroshima where she would complete her fitting-out, she had been made ready so hastily that her watertight compartments were not in fact watertight. Moreover, about 60 per cent of her crew had never previously served on a warship.

Late that evening, *Shinano* was sighted by US submarine *Archerfish*. This doggedly pursued her, aided by the fact that she was steering a zig-zag course, until at 0317 on 29 November, a perfect firing position was reached and six torpedoes sped towards their target. At least four, possibly all of them, found their mark but Captain Toshio Abe, certain that *Shinano* was unsinkable, maintained course and speed while flooding continued unabated. At 1055, she rolled over and sank, taking Abe and some 500 of her crew with her. She was the shortest-lived capital ship ever to have gone to sea.

The decline of Japan's industrial capacity, the poor workmanship on *Shinano*, the ability of US submarines to sink a major warship so close to the coast of Japan, the lack not only of experienced aircrew but of experienced seamen, all pointed to the helplessness of the Imperial Navy. Realization of this prompted Admiral Yonai and many of Japan's leading naval commanders (but not Admiral Toyoda) to join their country's civilian ministers and their Emperor's advisers in urging that a continuation of the war was pointless and peace should be secured as soon as possible.

Unfortunately, at the Casablanca Conference in January 1943, President Roosevelt, with the concurrence of Churchill, had demanded the 'unconditional surrender' of the Axis powers. While some historians have argued that this had no adverse effects, few of those military leaders who had to deal with the consequences agree with them. Admiral Nimitz, for one, points out that it meant: 'Terms would neither be offered nor considered. Not even Napoleon at the height of his conquests ever so completely closed the door to negotiation.'

Moreover the demand contradicted the claims of Britain and America that they had no quarrel with the people of the enemy countries, only their leaders. Chilling utterances of senior American officers that after the war the Japanese language would be spoken only in hell or that killing Japanese was no different from killing lice, seemed to indicate that if Japan surrendered unconditionally, no mercy would be shown. In apparent confirmation, on 24 November 1944, Superfortresses from Tinian in the Marianas began a series of attacks on Tokyo and other Japanese cities such as Nagoya, Osaka and Kobe. These culminated on the night of 9/10 March 1945 in a raid on the capital by over 300 bombers, openly acknowledged by the Americans as intended to destroy not just factories but large areas of the city and its inhabitants; it set more than 25,000 buildings ablaze, drove about a million homeless to seek shelter in the countryside and burned to death at least 83,000 civilians.

As a result, even the most moderate Japanese leaders dared not advise surrendering unconditionally and this immensely strengthened the position of the die-hards, of whom the chief was the War Minister, General Korichika Anami, whose desire was to raise a citizens' army of men and women alike to confront any American invasion of Japan. As

Nimitz rather cynically notes: 'To adopt such an inflexible policy was bad enough; to announce it publicly was worse.'

So the war continued and since after Leyte Gulf warships were all but useless, the Imperial Navy's best, almost its only effective weapon was its Kamikaze Corps. The suicide pilots' principal targets would always be carriers and in consequence, from late 1944 onwards, the US 'flat-tops' as well as supporting and guarding landings, had to pay increasing attention to their own protection. As an illustration of this, in December 1944, *Lexington* and *Ticonderoga*, followed later by other fleet carriers, increased the number of their Hellcats by about twenty at the expense of a corresponding reduction in the strength of their strike aircraft.

That this attitude was both wise and necessary had already been demonstrated. On 28 October, an orthodox bombing raid on Third Fleet was broken up by the Combat Air Patrol and thirteen enemy aircraft destroyed for the loss of four Hellcats. Whereas on the 29th, carrier *Intrepid* was hit by a Kamikaze and slightly damaged, and on the 30th, Kamikazes hit *Franklin* and light carrier *Belleau Wood*, the former losing fifty-six men dead, fourteen injured and thirty-three aircraft destroyed; the latter ninety-two dead, fifty-four injured and twelve aircraft destroyed; and both being put out of action. And on 5 November, a Zero rammed *Lexington*; she remained fit for combat but another fifty dead and 132 wounded were added to Third Fleet's casualty list.

A culmination to these assaults came with a whole series of suicide attacks on 25 November. Of the six Zeros that made for carrier *Hancock*, the Combat Air Patrol shot down all but one and this was blown up just in time by AA fire, only a blazing wing falling on the flight deck. Another Kamikaze, however, did hit and slightly injure *Essex*, and a second hit and a third near missed light carrier *Cabot*, the former damaging her flight deck, the latter tearing a six-foot hole in her hull. Two more crashed into the flight deck of the unlucky *Intrepid*, causing so much damage that she could no longer operate her aircraft. The Fast Carrier Force was temporarily withdrawn from Philippine waters.

Fortunately by this time the Americans were slowly but surely gaining the upper hand on Leyte Island. The decisive blow was struck on 7 December when Seventh Fleet landed in Ormoc Bay, taking the

Japanese forces in the rear and preventing any more reinforcements from reaching them. By Christmas Day, MacArthur could declare that organized resistance had ended. Professor Morison wryly points out that 'Japanese unorganized resistance can be very tough' and mopping-up operations would continue until May 1945, but MacArthur was correct in believing that the Japanese now had no chance of recovering Leyte. The larger but strategically less important island of Samar had already been secured on 19 December.

In the Ormoc Bay Landings, aerial support had been provided by Army and Marine aircraft from Tacloban aerodrome on Leyte but American carriers were again present at the next step forward – to Mindoro on 15 December. The invasion was uneventful as there was only a sparse garrison on the island but there were plenty of Japanese airfields in the vicinity from which the landing force could be engaged. It was therefore covered by six of Seventh Fleet's escort carriers, while Third Fleet's fast carriers made preliminary strikes on enemy bases both in daylight and during the hours of darkness. For the loss of twenty-seven aircraft, mainly to AA fire, these destroyed some 170 enemy machines on the ground or in the air. The escort carriers' pilots shot down twenty more.

Mindoro was followed by major landings at Lingayan Gulf on the north-west coast of Luzon, planned for 9 January 1945. General MacArthur was again in command and under him was Lieutenant General Krueger's Sixth Army, carried by Vice Admiral Kinkaid's Seventh Fleet, with five escort carriers among the covering warships. Twelve other escort carriers supported the six battleships of Vice Admiral Oldendorf that were sent ahead to bombard shore positions. Admiral Halsey's Third Fleet provided distant cover.

On 3 January 1945, Third Fleet began preparatory assaults on airfields in Luzon, Formosa and Okinawa. In addition to seven large and five light carriers for daylight work, Halsey had a special Task Group built around carrier *Enterprise* and light carrier *Independence* for night operations. Carrier *Essex* had thirty-seven Corsairs on board as well as fifty-four Hellcats. This was the first time that Corsairs would see combat from an American carrier, though for almost a year they had served with British 'flat-tops'. Sadly, their poor deck landing qualities persisted and during the next month, *Essex* would lose thirteen of them in accidents.

In all during these preliminary raids, Third Fleet lost forty-six aircraft in action, again chiefly from AA fire, and another forty operationally. Its airmen shot down only twenty-two enemy machines in combat but they also accounted for almost 200 on their own airfields. They did not, however, succeed in removing the greatest threat to Seventh Fleet: the Kamikazes.

Chief targets for these were the vessels of Oldendorf's Bombardment Force. On the afternoon of 4 January, one crashed into the flight deck of escort carrier *Ommaney Bay*, starting a huge fire that reached her magazines. As explosions shook her, flames spread throughout her length and enormous clouds of smoke rose high into the air there was no alternative but to order 'Abandon Ship'. She was finished off by an American destroyer.

On the 5th, a formation of fifteen bomb-carrying Zeros, with two more acting as escorts, delivered another suicide attack. It was led by Lieutenant Shinichi Kanaya who had repeatedly volunteered for such a mission but had hitherto been refused because of his value as a tireless trainer of Kamikaze units. Having had his wish granted at last, he directed a very efficient assault that damaged seven US vessels including escort carriers *Manila Bay* and *Savo Island*.

Next day, Oldendorf's command reached Lingayan Gulf and thereby prompted a continuous series of suicide raids.[1] Ten vessels including two battleships were damaged. One minesweeper was sunk, as were two more minesweepers on the 7th. On the 8th, Kinkaid's main strength approached the Gulf and also came under attack, escort carriers *Kadashan Bay* and *Kitkun Bay* being rammed and so damaged that they had to withdraw from the combat-zone. Despite further attacks, however, the landings proceeded as planned next day. MacArthur, Krueger and their staffs went ashore on the 13th – on which date, Seventh Fleet had its last Kamikaze casualty: escort carrier *Salamaua* severely damaged.

While Seventh Fleet supported Sixth Army ashore and guarded its supply lines; Third Fleet, on 10 January, moved into the South China Sea, west of the Philippines. Here its aircraft continued to whittle down Japan's surface warships. They had already sunk destroyer *Momi* near Manila on the 5th, and they now added light cruiser *Kashii* on the 12th, and destroyers *Hatakaze* and *Tsuga* on the 15th. They also sank a dozen tankers and over thirty other merchantmen. Third Fleet escaped any retaliation until it delivered a strike on Formosa on 21 January. This brought out the Kamikazes. First a Zero, then a Judy bomber crashed into carrier *Ticonderoga*, starting widespread fires and causing so much damage that she had to withdraw from the combat-zone. Other Judys rammed and damaged light carrier *Langley* and destroyer *Maddox*.

Soon afterwards, the whole of Third Fleet followed *Ticonderoga* out of the battle area and on 27 January, Admiral Spruance assumed command. Fifth Fleet as it therefore again became known, was somewhat different from Third Fleet because damaged ships had withdrawn, while new or repaired ones had replaced them; Corsairs had joined the Hellcats on *Wasp*, *Bunker Hill* and *Bennington* as well as on *Essex*; and *Saratoga*, like *Enterprise*, had become a night-action specialist. In all, Spruance commanded eleven fleet carriers and five light carriers; moreover Seventh Fleet, which remained in the Philippines to carry out a series of subsidiary landings, transferred its escort carriers, to become Fifth Fleet's Support Force.

Fifth Fleet also controlled two Amphibious Forces that were under orders to secure island bases for a final assault on Japan. Their first objective was Iwo Jima in the Volcano Group. Mention has already been made of the Superfortress raids on Japan. Their long journey to and from Tinian compelled them to reduce their bomb load to less than a third of its maximum weight; in addition, they could not be given a fighter escort and any damaged aircraft would probably run out of fuel before they could reach safety. But the capture of Iwo Jima, midway between the Marianas and Tokyo, would solve all these problems as well as depriving the Japanese of a base from which warning of the approach of the Superfortresses could be given and fighters sent up to attack them as they passed overhead.

Iwo Jima was known to be held by a strong garrison, headed by Lieutenant General Tadamichi Kuribayashi. An officer whose professional ability was rightly admired even by his enemies, he had designed an impressive system of interlocking fortifications, connected by tunnels and with the surface positions splendidly camouflaged. A few basic facts will show how grim a proposition was 'Bloody Iwo'. Though the island is only 4½ miles long by 2½ miles wide, the United States Marines took over a month to capture it. They lost 6,000 dead, 17,000 wounded and over 1,600 'combat fatigue casualties' – and they earned twenty-four Congressional Medals of Honour.

Fifth Fleet did all it could to assist them both prior to and during the fighting on the island. On 16 February, Vice Admiral Mitscher's fast carriers became the first ones to strike at Tokyo since the Doolittle raid in April 1942. Their targets on this and the following day were airfields and aircraft plants; their aim was to distract Japanese attention from and prevent Japanese reinforcements to Iwo Jima. Bad weather and large numbers of enemy fighters handicapped their efforts and although the Hellcats proved their worth as usual, the Corsairs, admittedly flown by less experienced pilots, were again disappointing, claiming eleven 'kills' but losing ten of their own number in action or operationally.

Also on 16 February, the eight battleships and five heavy cruisers of Fifth Fleet's Support Force began a preliminary bombardment of Iwo Jima that lasted for three days but achieved minimal results against Kuribayashi's underground defences. The aircraft of Fifth Fleet's escort carriers were more successful, dropping incendiary bombs that burned away vegetation and camouflage to reveal many hidden positions and then making precision strikes on them with rockets. The little carriers also conducted anti-submarine patrols and two of them, *Anzio* and *Tulagi*, formed the centres of Hunter-Killer groups similar to those that did such good work in the Atlantic.

Finally on 19 February, a tremendous barrage from the heavy gunnery units and constant attacks from all Fifth Fleet's aircraft, including those from Mitscher's carriers, heralded the landings and the start of the Marines' ordeals. Mitscher then moved away to provide distant cover by attacking enemy bases from which help might come. The escort carriers remained to provide close support and fighter protection, and since it was not until March that aircrews experienced in night operations were received by them, specifically by *Sangamon*, Mitscher sent *Saratoga* to join them and attend to any requirements after dark.

Saratoga's service was to be brief. Because of the distance from enemy air bases, there was never the same scale of attacks as at Leyte Gulf or Lingayan Gulf; but on 21 February, a series of raids took place with *Saratoga* inevitably as the prime target. The first, by Zero fighter-bombers in the late afternoon, hit her with three bombs, while one Kamikaze struck her on the flight deck and another on the waterline, opening a huge hole in her side. As the sky darkened, a mixed formation of Zeros and Bettys, led by Lieutenant Hiroshi Murakawa, chosen for his experience in more orthodox forms of attack, selected several targets. Another Kamikaze crashed into *Saratoga*'s flight deck, starting raging fires. These were eventually mastered but *Saratoga* was so damaged that she had to withdraw, ultimately to the United States, her place with the escort carriers being taken by *Enterprise*. Of her crew, 123 were killed and 192 wounded, forty-two of her aircraft were destroyed, and she took no further part in the war.[2]

Her accompanying escort carriers did not escape either. A Betty struck the flight deck of *Lunga Point* a glancing blow, skidded along it and plunged into the sea, causing only minor damage. Two others crashed into *Bismarck Sea* only a few seconds apart. Both exploded, causing fires that spread rapidly. A series of explosions followed as ammunition began to detonate. Finally the flames reached the after magazine that blew up, tearing off her stern. 'Abandon Ship' was ordered and two hours after the attack, she capsized and sank, taking some 350 men down with her.

Even before Iwo Jima was secured, preparations were being made to gain the Americans' last objective prior to the invasion of the Japanese home islands. This was Okinawa, about 350 miles south-east of Japan that would provide a springboard for that final invasion and landing fields from which it could be supported. On the other hand, it was well within range of air bases in Japan, Formosa and neighbouring islands and it was guarded by 100,000 enemy soldiers, led by Lieutenant General Mitsuru Ushijima.

The American carriers detailed to cover the Okinawa invasion, scheduled for 1 April, had come a long way from their original base at Pearl Harbour. Their base now was Ulithi Atoll in the northern Carolines that had been occupied without resistance on 23 September 1944. Even here they were not immune from attack and on the night of 11/12 March 1945, a dozen land-based long-range Yokosuka Frances bombers made a suicide raid on the anchorage, one of them striking the flight deck of fleet carrier *Randolph*, putting her out of action for a fortnight. On 27 March, the Americans secured an advance base by seizing the lightly held Kerama Islands, 15 miles west of southern Okinawa. Yet providing fuel, ammunition and spare parts for the carriers' aircraft was still a colossal task that probably only the United States had the capacity to perform.

British carriers were operating even farther from home. The Indian Ocean was sufficiently distant but in October 1943, escort carrier *Battler* joined the British Eastern Fleet there to assist in operations against German and Japanese submarines. On 12 March 1944, her aircraft sighted the German tanker *Brake* refuelling a pair of U-boats and she was subsequently sunk by destroyer *Roebuck*, thus greatly hampering the enemy's operations. Also in March 1944, escort carriers *Shah* and *Begum* arrived in the Indian Ocean, and gradually the submarine menace was mastered here as it had been in the Atlantic and the Arctic.

At the same time, the British were building up a force of fleet carriers. When Admiral Sir Bruce Fraser, the officer who had commanded the forces that sank the *Scharnhorst*, took command of the Eastern Fleet on 22 August 1944, it already contained *Illustrious*, *Indomitable* and *Victorious* and in December, they were joined by *Indefatigable*. They could have presented a powerful threat to the Japanese position in Malaya and the Dutch East Indies but, understandably if probably mistakenly, Churchill was determined that the Royal Navy should fight alongside the US Navy in the final campaigns against the Japanese.

Accordingly in January 1945, the carriers of the British Pacific Fleet, as it had been renamed, prepared to leave the Indian Ocean. The work of the escort carriers in that ocean and particularly in the Bay of Bengal was far from over, however. Eventually built up to sixteen in number, they carried out anti-submarine patrols, photo–reconnaissance missions over Burma and Malaya, and searches for enemy warships. It was as the result of the sighting reports sent by Avengers from *Emperor* and *Shah* that a destroyer flotilla was able to intercept and sink the Japanese heavy cruiser *Haguro* in the early hours of 16 May.

As in the Mediterranean and the Pacific, escort carriers provided cover for amphibious landings. *Ameer* performed this duty at Akyab and Ramree Islands off the Burmese coast in January, and on 2 May, a landing at the mouth of the Rangoon River was protected by *Emperor*, *Khedive*, *Hunter* and *Stalker*, while *Shah* and *Empress* were included in a covering force that guarded against interference by Japanese surface warships. The Burmese capital was duly occupied next day, but it must be conceded that there was an element of farce in this operation since the Japanese had in fact abandoned Rangoon ten days earlier.

Much more successful were the final missions flown by the British fleet carriers before their departures from the Indian Ocean. These were strikes at Palembang in Sumatra, where the Japanese possessed the two largest oil refineries in South-East Asia, capable of supplying three-quarters of all their aviation fuel; they were attacked separately, one on 24 January, the other on the 29th.

For the first raid, it was intended to use forty-seven Avengers armed with bombs, sixteen Hellcats, thirty-two Corsairs and twelve Fireflies. The last-named were two-seater fighters designed as replacements for the Fulmars. They had a top speed of under 320 mph and a poor rate of climb but were surprisingly manoeuvrable and had a long range, making them very useful bomber-escorts. They also did well as night-fighters and on this and other occasions they carried eight rocket projectiles.

Despite problems that prevented two Avengers and a Firefly from taking off and caused five Avengers and one Corsair to return prematurely, and despite flak, fighters and – much to the annoyance of the airmen who had been assured there would be none such – barrage balloons, the attackers shot down eleven enemy aircraft, destroyed several more on their airfields and, best of all, hit the refinery so badly that its output was halved. The British lost two Avengers, one Hellcat and six Corsairs, with a further Corsair forced to 'ditch'.

The second raid followed a course very similar to that of the first one. Forty-eight Avengers, sixteen Hellcats, thirty-six Corsairs and two Fireflies (for armed reconnaissance) took off. One Avenger had to 'ditch' almost immediately, three Avengers and four Corsairs turned back early; but again numerous enemy aircraft were destroyed on the ground or in combat and the second refinery was damaged so severely that it ceased production for two months. Four Avengers, two Corsairs and a Firefly were shot down; six damaged Avengers had to 'ditch'.

After these undoubted if costly achievements, the British carriers proceeded to Australia. Here Admiral Fraser followed the example of Admiral Nimitz and remained in Sydney to co-ordinate all aspects of his Fleet's administration, of which the most difficult was keeping it supplied with all its requirements by means of a Fleet Train, formed in great haste from the limited number of ships available, regardless of their suitability for the purpose. The Fleet at sea was entrusted to Vice Admiral Sir Bernard Rawlings, who took it first to the appropriately-named Admiralty Islands and then, on 19 March, to Ulithi.

By that time, the Americans had already made their preliminary moves. On 18 March, Vice Admiral Mitscher's sixteen fast carriers attacked the Japanese islands, their warplanes being directed against airfields on which they inflicted considerable damage. The Japanese counter-attacked; *Enterprise* and *Yorktown* being struck by bombs, and *Intrepid* by a Kamikaze. In all cases the damage was slight and Mitscher's men were back on the following day, this time concentrating mainly on the ports of Kure and Kobe, at both of which they wrecked dockyards and at the former of which they also damaged light carrier *Ryuho*.

Later raids had been planned but before any could be delivered, five Judys hurtled down on *Wasp* and *Franklin*. It has been said they were suicide attackers but it seems they were orthodox bombers, though their reckless courage made the mistake easily understandable. One bomb hit *Wasp*'s flight deck and though she was able to continue operations, she suffered 370 casualties, 101 of them fatal. Two bombs landed on *Franklin*'s flight deck just as she was launching her aircraft. Both burst through into the hangar where they set off raging fires and explosions that killed 724 of her crew and wounded 265 more. Yet so high was the standard of American damage control parties and so efficient was their latest fire-fighting equipment that *Franklin*, though listing badly, was able to withdraw – ultimately to the United States for repairs.

The remainder of the Fast Carrier Force retired with her, successfully repulsing other small raids as they did so. On the 21st, Hellcats from *Hornet* and light carrier *Belleau Wood* made a particularly important interception of eighteen Bettys. These were led by Lieutenant Commander Goro Nonaka, a veteran torpedo-bomber pilot, but his aircraft on this occasion were carrying not torpedoes but Okas.

An Oka – the word means 'cherry blossom', a symbol of purity in Japan – was in essence a manned flying bomb with 2,645lb of explosive in the nose, specifically designed for suicide attacks. It was a fraction under 20 feet long with a wingspan of almost 16½ feet. It could neither take off nor land on its own, so was carried under a modified Betty, with which the suicide pilot could communicate by means of a telephone circuit. The Betty would take it to within about 20 miles of its objective before releasing it, after which its pilot would glide towards his chosen

202 Carriers at War

target, increasing speed if required by using five rockets fitted in the tail section. These enabled the Oka to reach the then enormous speed of 650 mph and this, together with its lack of size, made it almost impossible to stop by AA fire.

Theoretically therefore, the Oka presented a terrible threat and if the Americans gave it the mocking name of 'Baka bomb' – 'baka' being Japanese for 'mad' – this was in part at least to disguise the apprehension it inspired. Yet in practice the Oka/Baka never fulfilled anything like its true potential, partly because it was extremely difficult to control after leaving its Betty, but mainly because American radar, fighters and interception techniques were now so good that the lumbering Betty rarely had a chance to launch it in the first place. This was demonstrated dramatically on 21 March 1945, when all the Bettys carrying Okas were shot down at a safe distance. Twenty of their thirty escorting Zeros were destroyed as well. In all during the course of the US carriers' sortie into Japanese home waters, their flak or fighters downed 161 enemy warplanes and though they lost 116 of their own aircraft, they had ensured that it would be some time before their enemies could mount really sizeable raids against the forces closing in on Okinawa.

These included an impressive number of carriers. On 23 March, Mitscher's remaining 'flat-tops' began preliminary strikes on Okinawa. Fifth Fleet's eighteen escort carriers joined in next day, and two days after that, the four British carriers arrived. They and their supporting warships were placed under Spruance's command, designated Task Force 57 and given the responsibility for neutralizing airfields in Formosa and the Sakishima Islands, between it and Okinawa, and for intercepting any aircraft attempting to intervene in the Okinawa fighting.

To perform these important if unglamorous tasks, Rear Admiral Sir Philip Vian, who controlled the carriers under the overall command of Vice Admiral Rawlings, had a total of sixty-five Avengers, twenty-nine Hellcats, seventy-three Corsairs, forty Seafires, nine Fireflies and two Walrus amphibians used for air-sea rescue duties. This was less than the strength of any American Task Group and the variety of aircraft types meant that a disproportionate number of spare parts, and indeed of spare aircraft was needed; these were supplied by escort carriers *Striker* and *Slinger*, for which escort carrier *Speaker*'s sixteen Hellcats provided fighter protection. It is rather humiliating to recall that when Vian's four fleet carriers had to leave the combat zone for a period of about a fortnight to be refuelled and replenished, their duties were undertaken, perfectly capably, by four small American escort carriers.

Nonetheless, the British carriers did have one advantage that was particularly important in the Okinawa campaign. On 1 April, the invasion of the island began; but curiously enough, although this was assisted by American fleet carriers, light carriers and escort carriers, the only 'flat-tops' subjected to air attack were those of the Royal Navy. The Combat Air Patrol broke up several small raids, but at about 0720, three bomb-carrying Zeros were able to attack *Indefatigable*. One of her pilots, Sub-Lieutenant Richard Reynolds, shot down two of them and fatally damaged the third – an achievement that made him the war's highest-scoring Seafire pilot – but the crippled aircraft was still able to dive on *Indefatigable* and struck her flight deck squarely at the base of the island structure.

If this had happened to an American carrier with a wooden deck, it could have caused serious damage; but though *Indefatigable* had eight men killed and twenty-two wounded, six of whom died later, her steel deck only received a three-inch deep dent, a small fire that had been started was quickly extinguished and she remained in formation. The Americans with their unpleasant experiences of Kamikaze attacks were duly impressed.

They were soon to have many more such experiences. By this date, the Japanese, in desperation, were compulsorily allocating whole units to make suicide attacks. Yet this, as Captain Roskill notes, 'brought few signs of any decline in morale and most of the conscript crews seem to have set out with the same selfless dedication as the volunteers'. They made few attacks at first, though escort carrier *Wake Island* was damaged on 3 April, but on the 6th, mass Kamikaze assaults began. They were called 'Kikusui' or 'floating chrysanthemum', like the cherry blossom, a symbol of purity.

The first of these was also the biggest. No fewer than 355 Kamikazes took part, accompanied by almost the same number of orthodox attackers. Though ordered, as usual, to make carriers their prime objectives, they achieved only near misses that caused minor damage to light carriers *San Jacinto* and *Cabot* – but they had other successes. Two of them crashed into ammunition ships, both of which duly exploded, while their main victims were the 'radar pickets', small groups of destroyers posted all around Okinawa at distances of up to 100 miles to give warning of approaching enemy aircraft. They sank two of these destroyers, wrecked two more so completely they had to be scrapped and damaged eight others plus two destroyer-escorts.

That same evening, *Yamato*, escorted by light cruiser *Yahagi* and eight destroyers, set out for Okinawa. The giant battleship had only enough fuel for a one-way journey, but Admiral Toyoda – a convinced supporter of General Anami's determination to fight to the bitter end whatever happened – preferred that she should perish in action after inflicting the maximum damage on her enemies, rather than skulk uselessly in harbour and perhaps be tamely handed over to the victors if the very worst occurred.

In practice, *Yamato* and her accompanying warships would have no opportunity to harm more than the US carrier-aircraft that would attack them. American submarines reported them on the night of the 6th/7th, and Vice Admiral Mitscher was certain that they would be making for Okinawa. However, his responsibilities with regard to supporting the landings meant that he could not move too great a distance from the island. He therefore decided he would steam as far north as was possible while still being able to fulfill this commitment and strike at the Japanese warships from long range. At dawn on the 7th, his scouts took off to search for the enemy. Four luckless Corsairs ran out of fuel and had to 'ditch', one pilot being lost, but at 0822, a Hellcat from *Essex* flown by Lieutenant William Estes sent the sighting report that Mitscher was eagerly awaiting.

It shows clearly how futile was the Japanese sortie when it is noted that, although *Enterprise*, *Randolph* and light carrier *Independence* had retired to refuel; Task Force 58 still contained *Bunker Hill* (Mitscher's flagship), *Essex*, *Hancock*, *Hornet*, *Bennington*, *Intrepid* and *Yorktown*, and light carriers *Bataan*, *Cabot*, *San Jacinto*, *Belleau Wood* and *Langley*, with a total of 986 aircraft on board. At 1000, 439 of these began to take off. On their way to the target, the group from *Hancock*, fifty-three strong, lost touch with the others in bad weather and returned to their carrier, a Corsair from *Bunker Hill* crashed into the sea for no apparent reason, killing the pilot, and an Avenger and a Hellcat from *Bennington* turned back with engine trouble. That still left 383 warplanes in the attacking formations and their striking power was particularly great on this occasion, because to back up the Helldiver bombers and the Avengers, some armed with bombs but most with torpedoes, a majority of the Hellcats and Corsairs were also carrying bombs.

Their attack began at about 1230, and was made in three waves. The officer responsible for co-ordinating the first one, Commander Edmond Konrad of *Hornet*, was determined not to concentrate on just one target as had the pilots who had attacked Kurita's Central Force at Leyte Gulf, but to sink not only *Yamato*, but all her escorts as well. At the very start of the action, destroyer *Asashimo* was hit by two torpedos, blew up and went down in less than three minutes. Ten minutes later, destroyer *Hamakaze*, struck by several bombs and at least one torpedo, probably more, also exploded and sank. Light cruiser *Yahagi*, her engines wrecked by one torpedo and her propellers and rudders smashed by another, slowed to a halt.

Not that Commander Konrad neglected *Yamato* either. Helldivers achieved at least two bomb hits, one of them going through two decks before exploding, as well as several near misses. Avengers put two torpedoes into her port side. These and the damage done by the near misses caused flooding and a consequent list to port that had to be rectified by counter-flooding.

During these assaults, Konrad had remained in constant radio communication with Commander Harmon Utter of *Essex* who was to co-ordinate the second wave of attackers. It seemed clear that *Yamato* was by no means crippled yet, so Utter ensured that most of the heaviest strikes by his wave were made on the battleship. She was hit by four bombs that left smoke pouring from her, and though the number of torpedo hits was grossly exaggerated, it seems that at least seven found their mark. Water poured into the doomed giant and her speed steadily fell away.

While their torpedo-planes struck at *Yamato*, many of the American dive-bombers and fighter-bombers continued to assault the escort vessels. Three destroyers were badly damaged. *Kasumi* was left burning furiously and not fully under control. *Isokaze* was also set on fire and was shaken by explosions. *Suzutsuki*'s bow was shattered by bomb hits and apparently also by a stray torpedo. And a rain of bombs left light cruiser *Yahagi* with her superstructure in ruins, listing and blazing furiously. She was already slowly sinking when the third American wave arrived and again made her a target. It is believed that she took a total of twelve bomb hits and perhaps five torpedoes in this and the earlier attacks. At 1405, this tough little ship finally capsized and sank. As she disappeared, a last explosion lit up the sky with a huge ball of flame.

Meanwhile other American aircraft were seeking out *Yamato*. Two more bomb hits and numerous near misses increased her already serious list, and a torpedo-bomber scored a hit on her stern, jamming the rudder. As all power failed, her great gun turrets jammed as well. 'Abandon Ship' was ordered. A final strike by Avengers hit her twice more – but this was a waste of torpedoes. At 1423, *Yamato* turned over completely; then exploded. A tremendous cloud of smoke, thousands of feet high, visible over a hundred miles away, marked another triumph of naval air-power.

So ended the Battle of the East China Sea. It had cost the lives of the Japanese Fleet Commander, Vice Admiral Seiichi Ito, *Yamato*'s captain Rear Admiral Kosaku Ariga, and more than 4,200 officers and men, over 3,000 of them in *Yamato*. Destroyers *Isokaze* and *Kasumi*, too badly damaged to be saved, were finished off by Japanese torpedoes or gunfire. *Suzutsuki*, with 20 feet of her bow missing, crawled slowly back to port, stern-first. Two other destroyers had been damaged. The Americans lost fifteen aircraft shot down or forced to 'ditch', but only twelve airmen died. Lieutenant William Delaney, an Avenger pilot from *Belleau Wood* who had been forced to bale out and thereafter watch the action unfold while clinging to his life raft in the middle of the enemy fleet, was snatched to safety under the noses of the surviving Japanese destroyers by an American flying-boat.

Unfortunately, the victory did nothing to check the onslaught of the suicide pilots. Between 26 March, when the preliminary attacks on Okinawa commenced, and 22 June, when the island was declared secure, Japanese air raids sank twenty-eight ships of various types and damaged 237 more. Twenty-six of the vessels sunk and 176 of those damaged were victims of the Kamikazes.

Despite the official exhortations of their commanders and the unofficial action of one destroyer that had an arrow painted on its deck pointing over the side, accompanied by the caption 'Carriers That Way', the most common targets of the Kamikazes were still the 'radar pickets'. One particularly dramatic attack on 12 April deserves special mention. A bomb-carrying Zero smashed into the engine room of destroyer *Mannert L. Abele*, leaving her dead in the water. As she lay helpless, another suicide pilot hit her amidships and she broke in half, to sink in five minutes. It was the first, and happily as it transpired, the only 'kill' made by the Oka/Baka.

Inevitably, though, the carriers could not escape the Kamikazes entirely. On 7 April, just as the American airmen were preparing to engage *Yamato* and her screening vessels, a Zero dived on *Hancock*, dropped a bomb that penetrated to her hangar and then crashed into her flight deck, setting nineteen of her aircraft ablaze. Damage control parties mastered the flames after a tense 40 minutes, but seventy-two dead and eighty-two injured was the high price exacted by one enemy fighter-bomber and one determined pilot.

There were plenty of other pilots willing to sacrifice their lives for the chance of hitting a carrier and some of them did just that. *Enterprise* was damaged on 11 April. *Intrepid* was struck on the 18th, and suffered ninety-seven casualties, ten of them fatal. Escort carrier *Sangamon* was hit on 4 May, set ablaze and so damaged that she had to withdraw from the battle area. And worse was yet to come.

On 11 May, Vice Admiral Mitscher's flagship, *Bunker Hill*, was struck twice. First a Zero put a bomb onto her flight deck, itself crashed through the aircraft on her deck, setting them on fire – and fell over the side. Before anyone had had a chance to recover, a Judy bomber came down in a vertical dive to smash right through the flight deck at the base of the island superstructure. Swept by flames and listing badly, the great ship was saved by the heroic efforts of her damage control personnel but she too had to withdraw. Of her crew, 392 were killed and 264 wounded.

Vice Admiral Mitscher now hoisted his flag in *Enterprise* but the Kamikazes still pursued him. Two days later, one crashed into *Enterprise*'s forward elevator, causing an explosion that blew this high into the air, seeming to be balanced on top of a great column of smoke. Mitscher moved on to *Randolph*, while *Enterprise*, like *Sangamon* and *Bunker Hill*, had to leave the area to effect repairs – as did escort carrier *Natoma Bay*, crashed by a Kamikaze on 6 June. Yet the Americans remained firm and, as stated earlier, on 22 June, Okinawa was finally secured, whereupon the carriers retired to rest and refit in preparation for the final assault on Japan.

The British Task Force 57 also had its encounters with Kamikazes.

On 4 May, a large number of raiders were shot down at a safe distance by flak or fighters but a Zero attacking *Formidable* – she had joined Vian's strength in mid-April to replace *Illustrious*, badly in need of a refit – could not be stopped. Its bomb exploded on the flight deck, putting it out of action temporarily, and it then crashed among the aircraft on the deck, setting eleven of them on fire, killing eight men and wounding forty-seven others, many very seriously. A few minutes later, another Zero hit *Indomitable* but bounced over the side into the sea, where its bomb exploded. Damage was slight but *Indomitable*'s radar, an improved American version that was the only one in the force, was knocked out and could not be repaired since there were no spare parts available.

Five days later, the Kamikazes came again. Of the five Zeros that made up the raid, one was destroyed by fighters, one by AA fire and two hit *Victorious* but her armoured deck prevented more than minor damage. *Formidable* was again the unlucky one. As on the previous occasion, the Kamikaze crashed on top of the aircraft on her deck. A fire swept over this but happily it was quickly brought under control. Seven of *Formidable*'s aircraft were destroyed, fourteen more were damaged, but the only fatal casualty was a luckless seaman who was decapitated by a wheel hurled into the air by an exploding aircraft.

Sadly, though, while the Kamikazes could be overcome, the British supply problems could not, and on the evening of 25 May, Task Force 57 retired, ultimately to Sydney. Here it was joined by another carrier, HMS *Implacable* controlling twenty-one Avengers, twelve Fireflies and forty-eight Seafires, for which satisfactory drop-tanks had at last been found, greatly increasing their range and hence their usefulness. She was quickly given a mission of her own and during 14 and 15 June, her aircraft attacked the Japanese base of Truk in the Carolines, both by day and at night with the aid of flares.

Truk had long since been bypassed and isolated and *Implacable* found few worthwhile targets but the operation did provide further examples of the various tasks performed by carriers and the varied experiences of naval airmen. *Implacable* was accompanied by escort carrier *Ruler*, to provide not only increased fighter cover but an additional deck for the large carrier's aircraft to land on in emergency; on 15 June for instance, she received six of *Implacable*'s Seafires that had lost their mothership in a violent rain squall.

To illustrate the pilots' experiences it seems fitting to quote that of Commander Alan Swanton. As a young sub-lieutenant on *Ark Royal* he had, as we saw, taken part in the attack that crippled the *Bismarck* and returned safely in a Swordfish damaged beyond repair. He was now CO of 828 Squadron and on 14 June, had just taken off from *Implacable* when engine trouble forced his Avenger to 'ditch' right in front of the carrier, then travelling at 30 knots. She had no chance of taking evasive action and simply trampled the Avenger under water. Happily, Swanton and his two crewmen were carried down the sides of the carrier and clear of her propellers by her bow wave and all were picked up safely by a destroyer.

By 16 July, *Implacable* had rendezvoused with the American Fast Carrier Force. This was now part of Third Fleet as Halsey had taken over from Spruance at the end of May, and since 10 July it had been striking at targets in the Japanese home islands. *Indomitable* and *Indefatigable* were refitting, but *Victorious* and *Formidable* also formed part of what was now Task Force 37, escort carrier *Ruler* again provided replacement aircraft and four other escort carriers were engaged in ferrying supplies. Once more, alas, the British 'flat-tops' were badly handicapped by having the use of only a few small tankers and in any case they formed only a minor part of the Allied strength compared with the sixteen fast US carriers, now under the control of Vice Admiral John McCain who flew his flag in *Shangri-la*.

This difference in strength was reflected in the duties the British and American carriers were allocated. On 18 July for instance, the former struck at airfields in the Tokyo area, inflicting minor damage; but the American carriers destroyed most of the installations at the Yokosuka naval base and crippled, though they did not sink, battleship *Nagato*. Third Fleet, incidentally, had already sunk destroyer *Tachibana* on the 14th, and now made preparations to complete the destruction of the Imperial Navy by assaults on other naval bases, especially the one at Kure, where most of those few major Japanese warships that still survived had been located.

After a delay caused by bad weather, a series of assaults began on 24 July and was followed by others on the 25th and 28th. The Japanese surface warships, without fighter cover, immobilized by lack of fuel and of value only as floating batteries, were easy prey. The exultant American carrier-pilots sank battleship *Haruna*, the two battleships with flight decks *Hyuga* and *Ise*, heavy cruisers *Aoba* and *Tone*, light cruiser *Oyodo* and destroyer *Nashi*.

Japan's remaining aircraft carriers were still more pathetic, deprived not only of fuel but of aircraft for want of trained pilots to man them. The large carrier *Amagi* was hit repeatedly, capsized and sank. The sole remaining escort carrier, *Kaiyo*, was also sent to the bottom. *Amagi*'s sister ship *Katsuragi* was put out of action for the short remainder of the war. After the war, three badly damaged carriers were scrapped: *Katsuragi*, *Junyo*, already crippled by a submarine's torpedoes, and light carrier *Ryuho*, an earlier victim of air attack. As was *Hosho*, Japan's first-ever carrier, and the only one to survive the war undamaged. Such was the sad fate of the carriers built by the country that had been the first to make them her most important naval vessels; and thereby unwittingly taught her enemies one of the major means by which she could be defeated.

The carriers of the country that had first pioneered their use were not allowed to participate in these raids. Admiral Halsey, as he would admit after the war, did not want British ships to share any of the credit for striking these final blows at the once-mighty Japanese Navy. Since it is difficult to see what harm their participation would have done to American interests, his action would appear as unnecessary as it was selfish and ungracious. The seamen and airmen in the British Pacific Fleet, who had travelled a world away from home to render loyal support to their great ally, had every reason to feel aggrieved. The unkindness of fate had not ended either. Their finest moment lay just ahead, but it would pass almost unnoticed amid the world-shaking events occurring around the same time.

Confronted with the need to decide the final steps necessary to complete their victory, the Americans considered they had only three alternatives. An invasion of Japan must prove terribly costly and would probably initiate the slaughter of all Allied prisoners of war since the Japanese would be unlikely to waste manpower guarding them. An intensified naval blockade and aerial bombardment would undoubtedly succeed but only after a delay, during which American lives would continue to be lost. And in mid-July, a new weapon had become available that should avoid the need for either invasion or delay.

Yet in reality there was a fourth alternative. The war could be brought to a swift end if the Japanese were allowed to surrender on terms, and this they were very willing and eager to do. In April, Tojo's successor as Prime Minister, General Kuniaki Koiso, had resigned. His office and his seat on the six-man Supreme War Council he had created had been taken by Admiral Kantaro Suzuki, who was a convinced believer in the need for a speedy peace, and had resumed with increased determination Koiso's previous attempts to persuade Russia to act as an intermediary between Japan and the western Allies.

This alone indicated that the Japanese expected severe terms. In November 1943, the Cairo Declaration by Britain and the United States had promised Chiang Kai-shek that Japan would be compelled to relinquish all captured territories. That the Russians, who had not forgotten or forgiven their defeat by Japan in 1905, would also insist on this as the price for acting as mediator was accepted even by General Anami's extremists. Moreover, this was known to the Americans because they had broken the Japanese diplomatic code. Thus by the time the Potsdam Conference was held in July 1945 between Churchill, the Russian dictator Josef Stalin and the new American President Harry Truman,[3] the British Prime Minister could declare: 'We knew of course that the Japanese were ready to give up all conquests made in the war.'

On the other hand, as explained earlier, not even Admiral Suzuki's Peace Party dared surrender on no terms at all – and this also was known to the Americans. Their code-breakers deciphered a message sent on 13 July, from Japan's Foreign Ministry to her Ambassador in Moscow, stating that: 'Unconditional surrender is the only obstacle to peace.' Even earlier, in talks with Truman's personal envoy Harry Hopkins at the end of May, Stalin had declared that Japan would accept almost any terms the Allies cared to offer but would fight to the death before surrendering unconditionally. At Potsdam, Stalin offered similar advice to Churchill who thereupon asked Truman if it might not be possible to obtain 'all the essentials for peace and security', while leaving the Japanese 'some show of saving their military honour and some assurance of their national existence'. When Truman retorted that the Pearl Harbour attack had shown the Japanese had no military honour, Churchill observed that 'at any rate they had something for which they were ready to face certain death in very large numbers'.

It seems that this argument had its effect, because steps were now taken to explain what unconditional surrender would entail. The

Potsdam Declaration, based on a memorandum written by Henry
Stimson, the US Secretary of War, repeated that Japanese sovereignty
should be limited to their home islands, and further stated that those
responsible for Japan's militarist policies must be deprived of all
'authority and influence' and 'stern justice will be meted out to all war
criminals'. The Japanese extremists were prepared to accept these
terms, though they wished the war criminals to be tried in Japanese
courts. They were less willing to contemplate an occupation of Japan
until the Allies' objectives had been attained but since the Declaration
also confirmed that this would be temporary and the Japanese would
not be 'enslaved as a race nor destroyed as a nation', it appears probable
that if talks had now commenced, some face-saving formula could have
been agreed.

Unfortunately, the Declaration expressly forbade further talks and
warned that if its terms were not accepted without delay, 'the
alternative for Japan is complete and utter destruction'. Worse still,
though Stimson's memorandum had urged that it would 'substantially
add' to the likelihood of acceptance if the Allies indicated that they
would agree to a constitutional monarchy under the present Japanese
ruling house, the Declaration made no mention of this vital point. Yet
the Emperor was the symbol of the unity of the Japanese people in a
manner far exceeding that of other heads of state, and the longevity of
their Imperial family, 'unbroken through ages eternal', marked for them
their uniqueness as a nation.

Consequently Suzuki announced that the Potsdam Declaration
added nothing to the earlier Cairo Declaration and so was of no great
importance. It appears that this cryptic utterance was intended as a hint
that Japan would accept the conditions laid down provided other
matters were clarified, but in the circumstances no one could possibly
expect the Americans to have realized this, and it was surely
unforgivable of Suzuki not to have 'come clean' and stated frankly the
one matter that really made the Potsdam Declaration unacceptable.

For the Allied threats of destruction had not been idle ones. On 6
August 1945, an atomic bomb obliterated the Japanese city of
Hiroshima. Two days later, Stalin, eager to partake of the spoils of
victory, declared war on Japan and sent his armies into Manchuria. And
on 9 August, a second atomic bomb was dropped on the city of
Nagasaki.

It was also on 9 August that Lieutenant Robert Hampton Gray, a Canadian Corsair pilot of 1841 Squadron serving aboard *Formidable*, attacked an enemy warship in Onagawa harbour. Though usually described as a destroyer, this was in fact an escort vessel, the 870-ton *Amakusa*, armed with three 4.7-inch guns and a useful AA battery. Flying very low, the Corsair quickly became a target for the guns of several warships and shore defences alike. It was hit repeatedly and its port wing set on fire but Gray was able to drop his single 1,000-lb bomb with deadly accuracy. It struck *Amakusa* amidships and she exploded and sank. The Corsair climbed briefly, trailing a long tail of flame, then dived into the harbour.

Lieutenant Gray was later awarded a posthumous Victoria Cross. This received so little publicity that most of the men who served in the British Pacific Fleet were quite unaware of the incident, and it merits only a brief footnote in Captain Roskill's Official History. Nonetheless, it deserves to be emphasized because it was the only time that the supreme decoration was earned by an airman operating from a British aircraft carrier.[4]

It was a particularly sad incident as well. The war was so nearly over. During the night of 9/10 August, when after hours of argument, Japan's Supreme War Council was still divided on whether or not to accept the Potsdam Declaration, Suzuki, 'with the greatest reverence', asked the Emperor for an opinion. General Anami, who was well aware of his sovereign's wishes – and had steadfastly disregarded them – protested, correctly, that this was unconstitutional, but by now his supporters were grateful for any excuse to change their views. The Emperor stated clearly that 'the time has come when we must bear the unbearable' to avoid further futile 'bloodshed and cruelty'.

Next morning, the Japanese government formally accepted the Potsdam Declaration 'on the understanding' that this would not 'compromise any demand which prejudices the prerogatives of His Majesty as sovereign ruler'. On 11 August, the Allies replied: 'From the moment of the surrender the authority of the Emperor and the Japanese government to rule the state shall be subject to the Supreme Commander of the Allied Powers.' The extremists argued that this qualification could not be accepted, but again the Emperor intervened decisively and demanded that it should be. On the 15th, on the conditions laid down in the Potsdam Declaration and the conditions agreed as to the Emperor's authority, Japan surrendered 'unconditionally' – which is perhaps the best summary of that idiotic slogan.

There were a few last-minute convulsions. An attempt was made to prevent the surrender broadcast, but this failed and General Anami who knew of, but did not support the plot, committed 'seppuku'. HMS *Indefatigable* had now rejoined the British carriers and in the last British air combat of the war, her aircraft shot down nine Zeros for the loss of one Seafire and one Avenger. The American airmen from *Yorktown* also had a fierce clash with Zeros, destroying another nine at the cost of four Hellcats. The last encounter came at 1120 on 15 August, when a Judy dropped two bombs very close to *Indefatigable* and was then downed by Corsairs from USS *Shangri-la* – a symbolic illustration of how it was America that now ruled the waves.

The formal ceremony ending the conflict took place on battleship *Missouri* in Tokyo Bay on 2 September, six years and one day since the German attack on Poland had precipitated the Second World War. General MacArthur, who had been appointed Supreme Commander of the Allied Powers, signed on behalf of all the Allied nations; Fleet Admiral Nimitz on behalf of the United States. The British representative, Admiral Sir Bruce Fraser, had arrived in another battleship, HMS *Duke of York*. But as the formalities ended, it was appropriate that a triumphant fly-past of 450 carrier aircraft should have swept over the assembled warships, for it was naval air-power that in the Mediterranean, the Atlantic, the Arctic and finally the Pacific, had played the most important role in achieving victory at sea.

Notes

1 The last of these raids was carried out by five damaged but repaired Zeros that were the only ones their unit had available. The pilots, carefully selected on the basis of ability, were Lieutenants Yuzo Nakano and Kunitane Nakao, and Warrant Officers Kiichi Goto, Yoshiyuki Taniuchi and Masahiko Chihara. Their Operations Officer, Commander Tadashi Nakajima, later stated that as they taxied forward ready for take-off, each one called out his thanks for having been chosen for the mission.

2 *Saratoga* was used thereafter only for training purposes. In 1946, she was sunk by the Americans during their atomic bomb tests at Bikini. Also sunk at Bikini were *Nagato*, the only Japanese battleship to survive the war, and *Prinz Eugen*, the largest surviving German warship. It is worth recording that in April and May 1944, *Saratoga* had

temporarily joined the British Eastern Fleet in the Indian Ocean and, together with HM carrier *Illustrious*, had carried out raids on targets in the Dutch East Indies.

3 President Roosevelt had died suddenly on 12 April 1945. The news had been greeted with loathsome glee in Berlin but it is pleasant to be able to record that the announcement on Radio Tokyo was brief, restrained and dignified.

4 It will be recalled that a posthumous VC had previously been awarded to a Fleet Air Arm pilot, Lieutenant Commander Esmonde, at the time of the escape of *Scharnhorst*, *Gneisenau* and *Prinz Eugen* from Brest. However, it will also be recalled that Esmonde had flown from a land base, not a carrier.

Bibliography

ARNOLD-FOSTER, Mark: *The World at War*. Collins 1973.
BALLENTYNE, Iain: *Killing the Bismarck*. Pen & Sword 2010.
BARKER, Ralph: *The Hurricats*. Pelham Books 1978.
BEKKER, C.D.: *Swastika at Sea*. Kimbers 1953.
BROWN, David: *Carrier Fighters*. Macdonald & Jane's 1975.
BROWN, David: *Carrier Operations in World War II* (2 Volumes). Ian Allan 1968.
CAMERON, Ian: *Red Duster, White Ensign*. Frederick Muller 1959.
CAMERON, Ian: *Wings of the Morning*. Hodder & Stoughton 1962.
CAMPBELL, Vice Admiral Sir Ian & MACINTYRE, Captain Donald: *The Kola Run*. Frederick Muller 1958.
CHESNEAU, Roger: *Aircraft Carriers of the World 1914 to the Present*. Brockhampton Press 1998.
CHURCHILL, Sir Winston: *The Second World War* (6 Volumes). Cassell 1948-1953. In particular: Volume I: *The Gathering Storm* 1948. Volume VI: *Triumph and Tragedy* 1953.
COSTELLO, John: *The Pacific War*. Collins 1981.
CUNNINGHAM, Admiral of the Fleet, Viscount: *A Sailor's Odyssey*. Hutchinson 1951.
D'ALBAS, Captain Andrieu: *Death of a Navy*. Robert Hale 1957.
DULL, Paul S.: *A Battle History of the Imperial Japanese Navy (1941-1945)*. Patrick Stephens 1978.
FUCHIDA, Mitsuo & OKUMIYA, Masatake: *Midway: The Battle that Doomed Japan*. Hutchinson 1957.
FULLER, Major General J.F.C.: *The Decisive Battles of the Western World* (Volume 3). Eyre & Spottiswoode 1957.
FULLER, Major General J.F.C.: *The Second World War 1939-1945*. Eyre & Spottiswoode 1948 (Revised Edition 1954).
GRENFELL, Captain Russell: *The Bismarck Episode*. Faber & Faber 1948.
GRIFFITH, Brigadier General Samuel B., USMC: *The Battle for Guadalcanal*. The Nautical & Aviation Publishing Company of America 1979.
HANSON, Professor Victor Davis: *Why the West has Won*. Faber & Faber 2001.
HOWARTH, Stephen: *Morning Glory: A History of the Imperial Japanese Navy*. Hamish Hamilton 1983.
INOGUCHI, Captain Rikihei & NAKAJIMA, Commander Tadashi with

PINEAU, Roger: *The Divine Wind*. Hutchinson 1959.

JACKSON, Robert: *Strike from the Sea*. Arthur Barker 1970.

JAMESON, Rear Admiral Sir William: *Ark Royal 1939-1941*. Rupert Hart-Davis 1957.

JOHNSON, Brian: *Fly Navy*. David & Charles 1981.

KAHN, David: *The Codebreakers*. Weidenfeld & Nicolson 1973.

KEMP, Lieutenant Commander P.K.: *Victory at Sea 1939-1945*. Frederick Muller 1957.

KENNEDY, Ludovic: *Pursuit: The Chase and Sinking of the Bismarck*. Collins 1954.

KILLEN, John: *A History of Marine Aviation 1911-68*. Frederick Muller 1969.

LEWIN, Ronald: *The Other Ultra: Codes, Ciphers and the Defeat of Japan*. Hutchinson 1982.

LEWIN, Ronald: *Ultra Goes to War: The Sectret Story*. Hutchinson 1978.

LIDDELL HART, Captain B.H.: *History of the Second World War*. Cassell 1970.

LORD, Walter: *Day of Infamy: Pearl Harbour, December 7th 1941*. Longmans, Green & Co 1957.

LORD, Walter: *Incredible Victory: The Battle of Midway*. Hamish Hamilton 1968.

MACARTHUR, General Douglas: *Reminiscences*. William Heinemann 1964.

MACINTYRE, Captain Donald: *Aircraft Carriers, the Majestic Weapon*. Macdonalds 1968.

MACINTYRE, Captain Donald: *The Battle of the Atlantic*. Batsford 1961.

MACINTYRE, Captain Donald: *The Battle for the Mediterranean*. Batsford 1964.

MACINTYRE, Captain Donald: *The Battle for the Pacific*. Batsford 1966.

MACINTYRE, Captain Donald: *Fighting Admiral*. (Somerville). Evans Brothers 1961.

MACINTYRE, Captain Donald: *Narvik*. Evans Brothers 1959.

MACINTYRE, Captain Donald: *The Naval War Against Hitler*. Batsford 1971.

MACINTYRE, Captain Donald: *The Thunder of the Guns*. Frederick Muller 1959.

MACINTYRE, Captain Donald: *Wings of Neptune: The Story of Naval Aviation*. Peter Davies 1963.

MCLACHLAN, Donald: *Room 39: Naval Intelligence in Action 1939-45*. Weidenfeld & Nicolson 1968.

MENZIES, Sir Robert: *Afternoon Light*. Cassell 1967.

MILLOT, Bernard A.: *The Battle of the Coral Sea*. Ian Allan 1974.

MILLOT, Bernard A.: *Divine Thunder*. Macdonalds 1971.

MOFFAT, Lieutenant Commander John with ROSSITER, Mike: *I Sank the Bismarck*. Bantam Press 2009.

MORISON, Professor Samuel Eliot: *History of United States Naval Operations in World War II* (15 Volumes). Little, Brown & Co. 1947-1962. In particular: Volume IV: *Coral Sea, Midway and Submarine Actions May 1942 - August 1942* 1948. Volume V: *The Struggle for Guadalcanal August 1942 - February 1943* 1949. Volume XII: *Leyte June 1944 - January 1945* 1958.

MORISON, Professor Samuel Eliot: *The Two-OGean War: A Short History of the United States Navy in the Second World War*. Little, Brown & Co. 1965 (This is not only a summary but an updating of his earlier history).

MORRIS, Ivan: *The Nobility of Failure*. Holt, Reinhart & Winston 1975.

MÜLLENHEIM-RECHBERG, Baron Burkard von: *Battleship Bismarck*. Bodley Head 1981.

NEWTON, Don & HAMPSHIRE, A. Cecil: *Taranto*. Kimber 1959.

OKUMIYA, Masatake & HIRIKOSHI, Jiro with CAIDIN, Martin: *Zero!: The Story of the Japanese Naval Air Force 1937-1945*. Cassell 1957.

PACK, Captain S.W.C.: *The Battle of Matapan*. Batsford 1961.

POOLMAN, Kenneth: *Ark Royal*. Kimber 1956.

POOLMAN, Kenneth: *Illustrious*. Kimber 1955.

POTTER, E.B. & NIMITZ, Fleet Admiral Chester W.: *The Great Sea War*. George W. Harrap & Co. 1961.

RICHARDS, Denis & SAUNDERS, Hilary St G.: *Royal Air Force 1939-1945* (3 Volumes). HMSO 1953-1954.

ROSKILL, Captain S.W.: *Churchill and the Admirals*. Pen & Sword 2004.

ROSKILL, Captain S.W.: *The Navy at War 1939-1945*. Collins 1960.

ROSKILL, Captain S.W.: *The War at Sea* (3 Volumes). HMSO 1954-1961.

ROSSITER, Mike: *Ark Royal*. Bantam Press 2006.

RUGE, Vice Admiral Friedrich: *Sea Warfare 1939-1945: A German Viewpoint*. Cassell 1957.

SCHOFIELD, Vice Admiral B.B.: *The Russian Convoys*. Batsford 1964.

SETH, Ronald: *Two Fleets Surprised: The Story of the Battle of Cape Matapan*. Geoffrey Bles 1960.

SHANKLAND, Peter & HUNTER, Anthony: *Malta Convoy*. Collins 1961.

SHORES, Christopher: *Air Aces*. Bison Books 1983.

SHORES, Christopher, RING, Hans & HESS, William N.: *Fighters over Tunisia*. Neville Spearman 1975.

SHORES, Christopher & CULL, Brian with MALIZIA, Nicola: *Malta: The Hurricane Years 1940-41*. Grub Street 1987.

SHORES, Christopher & CULL, Brian with MALIZA, Nicola: *Malta: The Spitfire Year 1942*. Grub Street 1991.

SMITH, Michael: *The Emperor's Codes*. Bantam Press 2000.

SMITH, Peter C.: *Arctic Victory: The Story of Convoy PQ 18*. Kimber 1975.
SMITH, Peter C.: *Pedestal: The Malta Convoy of August 1942*. Kimber 1970.
SMITH, Stan: *The Battle of Leyte Gulf*. Belmont Books 1961.
SPURR, Russell: *A Glorious Way to Die*. Sidgwick & Jackson 1982.
STEWART, Adrian: *The Battle of Leyte Gulf*. Robert Hale 1979.
STEWART, Adrian: *Guadalcanal: World War II's Fiercest Naval Campaign*. Kimber 1985.
STORRY, Professor Richard: *A History of Modern Japan*. Penguin Books 1960.
TAYLOR, A.J.P.: *The War Lords*. Hamish Hamilton 1978.
THOMAS, David A.: *Japan's War at Sea: Pearl Harbor to the Coral Sea*. Andre Deutsch 1978.
TOMLINSON, Michael: *The Most Dangerous Moment*. Kimber 1976.
TULEJA, Professor Thaddeus: *Climax at Midway*. Norton 1960.
VAN DER RHOER, Edward: *Deadly Magic*. Charles Scribner's Sons 1978.
WATTS, A.J.: *Japanese Warships of World War II*. Ian Allan 1966.
WILLMOTT, H.P.: *The Barrier and the Javelin: Japanese and Allied Pacific Strategies February to June 1942*. Naval Institute Press, Annapolis 1983.
WILLMOTT, H.P.: *Empires in the Balance: Japanese and Allied Pacific Strategies to April 1942*. Naval Institute Press, Annapolis 1982.
WINTON, John: *The Forgotten Fleet*. Michael Joseph 1969.
WOODMAN, Richard: *Arctic Convoys 1941-1945*. John Murray 1994.
WOODMAN, Richard: *Malta Convoys 1940-1943*. John Murray 2000.
WOODWARD, C. Vann: *The Battle for Leyte Gulf*. Macmillan 1947.
WOODWARD, David: *The Tirpitz*. Kimber 1953.
WRAGG, David: *Swordfish: The Story of the Taranto Raid*. Cassell 2003.
WRAGG, David: *Wings over the Sea: A History of Naval Aviation*. David & Charles 1979.

And the following Booklets prepared by the Ministry of Information for the Admiralty:

East of Malta, West of Suez. HMSO 1943.
Fleet Air Arm. HMSO 1943.
The Mediterranean Fleet: Greece to Tripoli. HMSO 1944.

Index

226   Carriers at War

SHIPS
Australian:
  Heavy Cruisers:
    Australia, 165; *Canberra*, 103, 120–1, 164;
    Shropshire, 121, 175
  Light Cruiser:
    Perth, 26
  Destroyers:
    Arunta, 175; *Vampire*, 50–2

British:
  Aircraft Carriers:
    Ark Royal, 5, 7–11, 13, 15, 18, 35–9, 50,
    53, 80, 82–5, 98, 209; *Courageous*, 4–5,
    8, 84; *Eagle*, 3, 5, 15–16, 18, 25, 86,
    88–93, 95; *Formidable*, 25–30, 34, 49,
    96, 142–4, 146, 208–209, 213; *Furious*,
    2–5, 10–11, 82–3, 88, 99, 142–4, 148;
    Glorious, 4–5, 10–14; *Illustrious*, 16–25,
    30, 34, 96, 146, 199, 208, 215;
    Implacable, 208–209; *Indefatigable*, 199,
    203, 209, 214; *Indomitable*, 49, 91–6,
    146, 199, 208–209; *Victorious*, 34, 82,
    91–5, 116, 126, 128–30, 141–4, 148,
    199, 208–209
  Light Carriers:
    Argus, 3, 5, 41, 80–3, 86, 89–90, 142–3,
    146; *Hermes*, 3, 5, 8, 49–52; *Unicorn*, 146
  Escort Carriers:
    Activity, 137, 139; *Ameer*, 199; *Archer*,
    126, 135–6, 146; *Attacker*, 146; *Audacity*,
    124–6; *Avenger*, 126, 130–6, 139, 142,
    146; *Battler*, 146, 199; *Begum*, 199; *Biter*,
    126, 136, 142, 144; *Campania*, 137;
    Chaser, 139; *Dasher*, 126, 142, 144, 162;
    Emperor, 148, 199; *Empress*, 199; *Fencer*,
    138–9, 148; *Hunter*, 146, 199; *Khedive*,
    199; *Nabob*, 148; *Nairana*, 137, 139;
    Pursuer, 139, 148; *Queen*, 149; *Ruler*,
    208–209; *Searcher*, 148–9; *Shah*, 199;
    Slinger, 202; *Speaker*, 202; *Stalker*, 146,
    199; *Striker*, 202; *Tracker*, 139; *Trumpeter*,
    149
  Merchant Aircraft Carriers:
    Empire MacAlpine, 137; *Empire MacKay*,
    137
  Fighter Catapult Ship:
    Maplin, 123
  CAM–Ship:
    Empire Morn, 134
  Battleships:
    Barham, 25–6, 31; *Duke of York*, 147,
    214; *King George V*, 35, 39; *Nelson*, 83;
    Prince of Wales, 33, 39, 48; *Queen
    Elizabeth*, 31; *Rodney*, 35, 39; *Valiant*,
    25–6, 31; *Warspite*, 16, 23, 25–6, 28, 30
  Battle–Cruisers:
    Hood, 33, 35; *Renown*, 9, 35; *Repulse*, 48
  Heavy Cruisers:
    Cornwall, 50–1; *Dorsetshire*, 39, 50;

Hibernia, 2; *Norfolk*, 33, 39; *Suffolk*, 33
  Light Cruisers:
    Ajax, 26; *Gloucester*, 26; *Liverpool*, 90;
    Manchester, 83, 96; *Orion*, 26–7; *Sheffield*,
    35–8, 52–3
  AA Cruisers:
    Cairo, 96; *Scylla*, 130
  Destroyers:
    Acasta, 12–13; *Ardent*, 12–13; *Beagle*, 139;
    Bramham, 93, 96; *Bulldog*, 141; *Cossack*,
    98; *Fearless*, 83; *Foresight*, 94; *Ledbury*, 96;
    Onslow, 132; *Penn*, 96; *Roebuck*, 199;
    Stanley, 125
  Minesweeper:
    Rye, 96
  Hospital Ship:
    Vita, 52
  Submarines:
    Graph, 141; *Oxley*, 14; *Seawolf*, 128;
    Triton, 14
  Tanker:
    Ohio, 91, 96–7
  Merchantmen:
    Brisbane Star, 96; *Denbighshire*, 98;
    Deucalion, 93, 96; *Empire Stevenson*, 132;
    Mary Luckenbach, 133; *Melbourne Star*,
    96; *Orari*, 90; *Port Chalmers*, 96; *Rochester
    Castle*, 96; *Troilus*, 90

Dutch:
  Merchantman:
    Bantam, 98

French:
  Battleship:
    Jean Bart, 146
  Light Cruiser:
    Primaguet, 145

German:
  Aircraft Carriers:
    Graf Zeppelin, 7, 129; *Peter Strasser*, 7
  Battleships:
    Bismarck, 33–40, 50, 52–3, 98, 127, 141,
    209; *Tirpitz*, 127–9, 147–9
  Battle–Cruisers:
    Gneisenau, 5, 12–13, 34, 127, 215;
    Scharnhorst, 5, 12–13, 34, 127, 147, 199,
    215
  Pocket Battleship:
    Admiral Graf Spee, 9
  Heavy Cruisers:
    Prinz Eugen, 33–4, 52–3, 127, 214–15;
    Seydlitz, 129
  Light Cruiser, *Königsberg*, 6
  Submarine:
    U-29, 8; *U-39*, 8; *U-66*, 140; *U-73*, 91;
    U-81, 83; *U-88*, 131; *U-89*, 136; *U-110*,
    141; *U-131*, 125; *U-155*, 146; *U-203*, 136;
    U-288, 139; *U-331*, 31; *U-354*, 148; *U-*